GCSE
Business Studies

Complete Revision and Practice

Contents

Contents

Published by Coordination Group Publications Ltd

Editors:
Ali Palin, Sam Norman.

Contributors:
Colin Harber Stuart, Jeff Harris, David Kittson, Tim Major, David Morris, Adrian Murray, Andy Park, Ami Snelling, Katherine Stewart, Claire Thompson, Lynda Turner, Julie Wakeling, Sharon Watson, Keith Williamson, Andrew Wright.

With thanks to Victoria Skelton for the proofreading.

AQA material is reproduced by kind permission of the Assessment and Qualifications Alliance.
Edexcel examination questions are reproduced by permission of Edexcel Ltd.
OCR examination questions are reproduced by kind permission of OCR.

ISBN: 978 1 84146 382 7
Website: www.cgpbooks.co.uk
Printed by Elanders Hindson Ltd, Newcastle upon Tyne.
Clipart source: CorelDRAW® and VECTOR

Exam Style Questions

Before getting stuck into the book, we'll start off with some handy advice on how to answer the different types of questions you'll meet in your Business Studies exam. To gain top marks you need to understand exactly what the questions are asking and what kind of answers the examiners are looking for.

This book is full of practice questions and there's an exam made up of actual past paper questions. Read through these tips carefully and you'll be able to give sparkling answers which'll stand you in good stead for the real exam.

Multiple Choice Questions *Aren't as Easy* as You Think

These are only used by Edexcel on their Foundation Tier Paper. You'll be given a statement with a number of possible responses. Only one is correct — you have to select the right one.

> **EXAMPLE 1**
> The balance sheet is a measure of:
> **A** how much profit a firm made last year;
> **B** the amount of cash in the firm's bank account at the end of the month;
> **C** how much the business is worth on a particular date;
> **D** how many employees have joined and left the firm over the past year.   *Answer* **C**

If you don't know the right answer — guess. You'll have a 25% chance of getting the right answer. And if you're fairly sure you can eliminate two possible answers, you increase the odds of getting it right to 50%.

Just remember — if you don't answer a question you have a 0% chance of getting a mark.

Short Answer Questions Test Your *Detailed Knowledge*

These questions are used by all the exam boards. They test whether you have detailed knowledge and understanding of particular bits of the Business Studies syllabus.

As with all questions, use the marks available as a guide to how much you should write.

EXAMPLE 2
a) Identify and explain two reasons why McTavish's Kilt-Makers PLC would wish to merge with McGregor's Woollen Mills PLC. (*4 marks*)

b) Describe how McTavish's Kilt-Makers PLC can use destroyer pricing to increase its monopoly power. (*3 marks*)

> *Answer...*
> a) *The new firm would be vertically integrated and so the kilt-maker would be able to obtain secure supplies of wool from its wool mills. The two firms would also gain economies of scale because there would be only one head office.*
>
> b) *McTavish's could charge very low prices for its kilts — so low that other kilt-makers would go out of business. With fewer competitors in the market McTavish's would then be able to increase prices and earn high profits.*

Tip: Don't just write a list of facts — make sure you apply your knowledge to the context you're given.

Tip: Here you get 1 mark for identifying each reason and 1 mark for explaining what it means.

Tip: You don't need to write pages for these questions — they're only worth 3 or 4 marks.

Count the marks, get set, go...
Always make sure you check how many marks are available for each part of the question.
The number of marks is a very good guide to how much detail you should put into your answer.

Exam Style Questions

Two more kinds of question to prepare you for now — and they're a bit <u>tougher</u> I'm afraid...

Open-ended Questions are a Real **Pain in the Neck**

These are the questions that most people <u>dread</u> — you'll know you've got one when suddenly the answer booklet gives you <u>half a side</u> of lines after the question. Use them <u>wisely</u>.

These questions are designed to test your ability to explain a <u>difficult idea</u> in <u>detail</u>. The question usually invites you to <u>describe</u> something <u>in depth</u> or to give your <u>own opinion</u>.

EXAMPLE 3
In recent years there has been an increase in the number of part-time workers in Cumbria. Are these changes good or bad for the inhabitants of Cumbria? Give reasons for your answer. (*8 marks*)

Answer...
Increased part-time working is good for people such as parents who do not want a full-time job, and it also gives people more leisure time. A problem is that part-time workers earn less money than full-time workers so they can't afford to buy as much — as a result their material living standards are lower. I think that most people who work part-time would prefer a full-time job, so in my opinion an increase in the number of part-time workers is bad for the people of Cumbria.

Tip: Explain the good points and the bad points, then round off with your opinion at the end.

Data Response Questions want you to **Apply** Knowledge

These are <u>very common</u>. Questions are based upon a <u>piece of data</u>. The data is usually figures in a table or a chart, but sometimes it is a piece of text. Questions test whether you can <u>apply</u> your knowledge and understanding in <u>unfamiliar situations</u>.

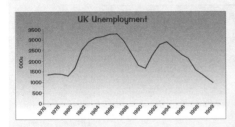

EXAMPLE 4
a) Explain what is meant by 'unemployment'. (*2 marks*)
b) Describe the main trends in UK unemployment since 1990. (*2 marks*)
c) Identify and explain two possible ways that a UK retailer might be affected by a reduction in unemployment. (*4 marks*)

Tip: Parts a) and c) require you to use your knowledge of unemployment.

Tip: You answer part b) by interpreting the graph — not by using your own knowledge.

Answer...
a) *Unemployment is when someone wants paid employment but is unable to find a job.*
b) *Between 1990 and 1994 unemployment nearly doubled, but since 1994 it has steadily fallen so that at the end of the period unemployment was lower than at the start.*
c) *Retailers make money by selling goods to customers — so a fall in unemployment should be good news because more people in work means that consumers have more money to spend. This should result in higher profits. However, a fall in unemployment may make it harder for retailers to recruit new staff — so they might have to pay higher wages and this could reduce their profits.*

Open-ended questions — it helps to plan your answer...

Open-ended questions are tricky, but you'll find them easier with <u>practice</u>. It's a good idea to do a <u>brief plan</u> of your answer. Jot down in the margin a <u>list</u> of points you want to make — give each one a number so the list is in the right order. Then remember <u>how much time</u> you should spend writing. Then write away.

Exam Style Questions

Okay, here's the last type of question — <u>case studies</u>. Finally there's some <u>words</u> you should know the meaning of.

Case Studies are like Big *Data Response* Questions

1) Case studies are a bit like <u>big data response questions</u> — they can be anywhere between a single page and a small booklet. A case study contains information about a business, along with charts and figures. The <u>good</u> thing is that you often get to <u>see</u> the case study weeks before the exam.

2) The <u>advantage</u> of seeing the case study before the exam is that you get a chance to study it <u>in depth</u> and carry out <u>additional research</u>. The <u>disadvantage</u> is that all the questions are <u>compulsory</u> and you only get to see them in the exam.

3) You get asked a <u>mixture</u> of short answer, open-ended and data response questions. You need to <u>base your answers</u> on the <u>information</u> in the case study and your <u>knowledge</u> of Business Studies.

Command Words Tell You What the *Examiner Wants*

A command word is the <u>word in the question</u> that tells you <u>how to answer</u> the question. The command words in example 2 on page 1 were "identify", "explain" and "describe". Together with the <u>marks available</u> they are the <u>best clue</u> about what the examiner <u>wants to see</u> in your answer.

Define — Describe — List — State   What (is meant by...) **Explain** (what is meant by...) — **Identify**.

- These command words test your <u>knowledge</u> and <u>understanding</u> of Business Studies.
- Questions beginning with these words usually only have a <u>few marks</u> available. Keep your answer <u>short</u> and <u>to the point</u>.
- If you <u>know the facts</u> it is <u>easy</u> to get <u>full marks</u>.

Give (reasons for...) — **Calculate** — **Explain** (why something has happened) — **Why** — **What** (are the advantages of...).

- These command words ask you to <u>apply</u> your knowledge and understanding to a <u>particular issue</u>.
- When you answer these questions you need to <u>stick to the context</u> of the question.
- These are <u>harder</u> than "knowledge" questions.

Compare — Which (pieces of information...) **— How** (can the information help...) — any question containing the words **"use the information"** or telling you to **"use pages"** of the case study.

- These command words ask you to <u>select</u>, <u>make sense of</u> and <u>use information</u> from different sources.
- When you answer these questions you should <u>justify</u> why you have used the information you have chosen.
- These are <u>harder</u> than "apply" questions.

Assess — Evaluate — Compare — Which (option should be taken...) — **Recommend — Should** (something happen...).

- These command words ask you to make <u>judgements</u> about business issues by considering the <u>evidence</u> and coming to a <u>conclusion</u>.
- Sometimes these questions put you in the role of a <u>business consultant</u>.
- When you answer these questions it is sometimes a good idea to <u>begin</u> with "<u>in my opinion</u>" and <u>explain</u>, saying "<u>this is because</u>".
- These are the <u>hardest</u> questions of all.

Command Words tell you how to answer the question..

Don't get <u>too bothered</u> about learning everything on this page now — it'll be here for you to <u>refer</u> to if you get stuck with any questions later on. In the exam, make sure you read through each question <u>carefully</u> and have a <u>quick think</u> about how to approach it before writing your answer.

Why Businesses Exist

A business gets <u>started</u> when somebody decides that they can earn a <u>profit</u> by <u>making goods</u> or <u>providing a service</u> and <u>selling</u> it to people who are willing to <u>pay</u> for it.

Most Businesses have the **Same** Main **Objective**

An <u>objective</u> is anything that the business wants to <u>achieve</u>.
Your objective in using this book is to get a better GCSE grade.

1 The <u>most important</u> objective is to make a <u>profit</u> in order to <u>survive</u>. If a business does not make a profit it will go <u>bankrupt</u> and have to <u>close down</u>.

Businesses will have other objectives which they might pursue too:

2 Some will try to be the <u>biggest</u> in their <u>market</u>.

3 Others will try to provide the highest <u>quality</u> product possible.

4 Some might aim to maximise <u>profit</u>, <u>sales</u> or <u>wealth creation</u>.

5 Others might be more concerned with <u>stability</u> — maintaining their <u>market share</u> or a <u>reasonable income</u>.

6 Some will focus on <u>expanding</u> the business.

7 Other possible objectives include being <u>independent</u>, <u>satisfying customers</u>, or trying to limit the <u>environmental damage</u> caused.

> <u>Two</u> more facts about objectives:
> - Objectives can be influenced by the <u>type</u> and <u>size</u> of the business.
> - Businesses may have to <u>change</u> their objectives depending on the <u>economic situation</u> or <u>conflicts of interest</u> within the business.

> Usually firms will only pursue these other objectives if it will <u>help make a profit</u> in the longer term. Firms might give up some profit for other objectives, but only if they have public-spirited owners. <u>Most</u> company owners are ultimately <u>only interested</u> in <u>profit</u>.

Some will not try to make a profit at all. This is either because they are a <u>charity</u> or they are in the <u>public sector</u>.

Charities and public sector businesses need to earn <u>enough</u> income to <u>cover their costs</u>. In this case their objective is to achieve a <u>surplus</u>. This is put back into the business.

The Economy has Two **Sectors** — **Public** and **Private**

These are <u>important</u> terms to remember — it's crucial that you don't get confused about what it means for a business to be in the <u>public sector</u> or the <u>private sector</u>.

The Public Sector

1) The <u>public sector</u> includes everything that is <u>owned</u> by the <u>government</u>.
2) This is things like the <u>army</u>, the <u>police force</u>, and most <u>schools</u> and <u>hospitals</u>.
3) <u>Public</u> means that they are owned by the government for the <u>benefit</u> of <u>everyone</u>.

The Private Sector

1) The <u>private sector</u> contains all the businesses <u>owned</u> by <u>private individuals</u>.
2) Almost all the businesses you can think of are in the private sector.
3) <u>Private</u> means that these businesses are run for the <u>benefit</u> of the people who <u>own</u> them.

Most businesses need to make a profit to survive...

Well that's an easy enough page to start with — but it's <u>really important</u> you learn those key terms. It's why you bought this book. Make sure you know the <u>different objectives</u> a firm can pursue. Try <u>covering everything up</u> — then scribble down what you remember. <u>Repeat</u> until you've got it all. It's the only way — and it <u>works</u>.

Economic Systems

There are <u>three</u> different types of economic system — but most countries have some form of <u>mixed economy</u>. Make sure you know the <u>main features</u> of each system.

Free-Market Economies have No Public Sector

1) All <u>economic systems</u> have to decide the <u>answers</u> to <u>three questions</u>: <u>What</u> is to be produced? <u>How</u> is it to be produced? <u>Who</u> gets to consume what is produced?

2) A <u>free-market economy</u> leaves it all up to <u>private sector businesses</u>. Basically the only things that get produced are what private sector firms can make a <u>profit</u> from. <u>For example</u> the only pupils who will be <u>educated</u> are those who can afford to pay the fees charged by <u>profit-seeking schools</u>.

3) A <u>benefit</u> of a free market is that products should be made <u>efficiently</u>. Also products should be of a <u>high quality</u>. This is because firms will <u>only make products</u> that they know they can <u>sell</u>.

4) A <u>problem</u> is that <u>unprofitable</u> things <u>won't get produced</u>. Also some people may not be able to <u>afford</u> to pay the fees charged by private schools and hospitals — so their <u>education and health will suffer</u>.

5) An <u>example</u> of a <u>country</u> closest to the free-market model today is the <u>USA</u>.

Planned Economies have No Private Sector

1) <u>Planned economies</u> are also called <u>centrally</u> planned economies or <u>command economies</u>. Basically they're the <u>opposite</u> of free-market economies. All economic <u>decisions</u> are taken by the <u>government</u>. All <u>firms</u> and important <u>resources</u> are <u>owned</u> by the <u>government</u>.

2) This means that the government can take decisions that it believes are in the <u>interest of the people</u>. <u>For example</u> they might want to give everyone a <u>job</u>, somewhere to <u>live</u> and <u>free education</u> and <u>healthcare</u>.

3) A <u>problem</u> with planned economies is that the economy is really <u>too complex</u> for the government to <u>manage it properly</u>. Also, <u>firms</u> are normally <u>not required</u> to make a <u>profit</u> and so have <u>no incentive</u> to provide the right high quality products that people want.

4) The best <u>example</u> of a planned economy was the <u>Soviet Union</u> before 1989.

Mixed Economies have a Public and Private Sector

<u>Most countries</u> in the world today are <u>mixed economies</u> — that is they have both a <u>public sector</u> and a <u>private sector</u>. This means that in theory they should get the <u>best of both worlds</u> — efficient, competitive <u>firms</u> providing the goods and services people want and a public sector providing for their <u>welfare</u> needs.

Mixed economies strike a balance...

A free-market economy means the <u>poor lose out</u>, but a planned economy is <u>hard to manage</u>. So most countries have a mixed economy. I know this isn't exactly exciting stuff, but make sure you know the <u>differences</u> between the three types of economic system and can give some <u>benefits</u> and <u>problems</u> of each.

Business Ownership Structures

There are <u>four</u> types of business structure you need to learn. We'll start with <u>sole traders</u> and <u>partnerships</u>.

1 *Sole Traders* — *the Easiest Business to Start*

Most <u>small businesses</u> are sole traders. You don't need to do anything except <u>start trading</u>.
Examples include plumbers, hairdressers, newsagents and fishmongers.

ADVANTAGES

1) They are <u>dead easy</u> to set up. Get an idea and you're in business.
2) You get to be your <u>own boss</u>.
3) You alone decide what happens to any <u>profit</u>.

DISADVANTAGES

1) You have to work <u>long hours</u>. You don't get many holidays either.
2) You have <u>unlimited liability</u>. If the business goes bust owing £10 million, you may have to sell <u>everything you own</u> to pay your debts.
3) Sole traders are <u>unincorporated</u> — the business is not legally separate from its owner. So if someone dies from eating a dodgy dover sole, they sue the fishmonger <u>personally</u> — not the business. Or the fish.

2 *Partnerships* *are like Two or More Sole Traders*

Partnerships are <u>not that common</u> — but you get them a lot in jobs like accountancy, solicitors and doctors. By law a business can have between <u>2 and 20</u> partners.

Partners have an <u>equal say</u> in making <u>decisions</u> and an <u>equal share</u> of the <u>profits</u> — unless that is they have an agreement called a <u>deed of partnership</u> that says different.

ADVANTAGES

1) More owners means <u>more ideas</u>, and more people to <u>share the work</u>.
2) More owners means <u>more capital</u> (money) can be put into the business.

DISADVANTAGES

1) Each partner is <u>legally responsible</u> for what all the <u>other</u> partners do.
2) Like sole traders, partnerships are <u>unincorporated</u> and have <u>unlimited liability</u>.
3) More owners means more <u>disagreements</u>. You're not the only boss. If the partners disagree about <u>which direction</u> the business should go in and <u>how much</u> time to put in, it can get unpleasant.

Howdy partner, this unlimited liability has sure gotten us a raw deal...
It's gonna be a <u>rough deal</u> for this lot if they go <u>bankrupt</u> — and do you know why? It's all down to this important idea of <u>unlimited liability</u>. Examiners <u>love</u> testing you on it so you should know what it means.

Business Ownership Structures

The final two types of structure are <u>more expensive</u> to set up but carry <u>less financial risk</u> for the owners.

Limited Companies have **Five Differences**

There are <u>two types</u> of limited company — private and public. But <u>both kinds</u> have these five important differences compared to <u>sole traders</u> and <u>partnerships</u>.

1) The business is <u>incorporated</u> — has a <u>separate legal identity</u> from the owner.
2) It has <u>limited liability</u> so the owners only risk losing the money they invest in the business — no matter how big its debts are.
3) It must have a <u>Memorandum of Association</u>. This tells the world <u>who</u> the business is and <u>where</u> it is based.
4) It must also have an <u>Article of Association</u>. This sets out <u>how</u> the business will be run.
5) It is owned by <u>shareholders</u>. The <u>more shares</u> you own, the <u>more control</u> you get.

③ **Private** Limited Companies — Ownership is **Restricted**

Private means that shares can only be sold if <u>all the shareholders</u> agree. The shareholders are often all members of the same family. Private limited companies have <u>Ltd.</u> after their name.

PRIVATE LIMITED COMPANIES — ADVANTAGES

1) The <u>big advantage</u> over sole traders and partnerships is <u>limited liability</u> — you can't lose more than you invest.
2) Being <u>incorporated</u>, the company can continue trading after a shareholder dies — unlike partnerships.

PRIVATE LIMITED COMPANIES — DISADVANTAGES

1) They're <u>more expensive</u> to set up than partnerships because of all the <u>legal paperwork</u> you have to do.
2) Unlike sole traders or partnerships, the company is <u>legally obliged</u> to <u>publish its accounts</u> every year.

④ **Public** Limited Companies — **Anyone** Can Buy Shares

<u>Public</u> means that <u>anyone</u> can buy shares in the company — if they can find someone who wants to sell them. Public Limited Companies have <u>PLC</u> after their name.

Firms generally become PLCs when they wish to <u>expand</u>.

PUBLIC LIMITED COMPANIES — ADVANTAGES

1) Much more <u>capital</u> can be raised by a PLC than by any other kind of business.
2) That helps the company to <u>expand</u> and <u>diversify</u>.

PUBLIC LIMITED COMPANIES — DISADVANTAGES

1) Each shareholder has <u>very little say</u> in how the company is run — unless they own an <u>awful lot</u> of shares.
2) It's easy for someone to buy enough shares to <u>take over</u> the company — if they can convince shareholders to sell.
3) A PLC can have a large number of shareholders — and there needs to be a general agreement <u>on company objectives</u>. This makes it <u>difficult</u> for a PLC to sacrifice profit to other objectives, like helping the environment.

Limited liability takes a weight off your mind...

The <u>key</u> thing to remember here is that limited companies have <u>limited liability</u>. Make sure you know what this means. You should also know how buying and selling shares is different in <u>Ltds</u> and <u>PLCs</u>.

Franchises, Co-operatives and Public Corporations

These three ownership structures are <u>less common</u> — but <u>franchising</u> is becoming <u>more popular</u> and so examiners are beginning to ask questions about it.

A *Franchise* is the Right to Sell Another Firm's Products

1) For years some manufacturers have given other companies the right to sell their products. <u>For example</u> most <u>car manufacturers</u> sell their cars through <u>dealer franchises</u>. These franchises trade under their <u>own name</u> but advertise that they sell a particular manufacturer's products.

2) <u>Branded Franchises</u> take this one stage further. The <u>franchisee</u> buys the right to trade under the name of the other firm (the <u>franchisor</u>). As far as the <u>public</u> are concerned it appears that they are buying from the franchisor, not a different firm.

3) Most of the big firms in the <u>fast-food</u> industry sell their products through <u>branded-franchise</u> outlets. The <u>franchisee</u> usually <u>buys everything</u> needed to run the business from the <u>franchisor</u> — including the <u>ingredients</u> needed to make the finished product.

Franchises have Benefits and Problems

For the franchisee...

The main <u>benefit</u> to the <u>franchisee</u> is that they are buying the rights to sell an <u>established product</u> — this makes setting up a franchise <u>less of a business risk</u> than selling something brand new. The main <u>problem</u> is that the business can <u>only sell</u> the products of the franchise — so the owner's <u>freedom</u> is <u>limited</u>.

For the franchisor...

The main <u>benefit</u> to the <u>franchisor</u> is that they are able to <u>increase</u> their <u>market share</u> without increasing the size of their own firm — this can make franchising a very <u>profitable</u> way to <u>expand</u>. A <u>problem</u> is that they may have <u>little control</u> over how the franchisee sells their products.

Co-operatives are Owned by their Workers

1) Co-operatives work a bit like <u>limited-liability partnerships</u>. <u>Producer co-operatives</u> are <u>owned and controlled</u> by their <u>workforce</u>, and <u>retail</u> co-operatives are owned and controlled by their <u>customers</u>.

2) The main <u>benefit</u> is that there should be <u>no conflict</u> between the main <u>stakeholders</u> — they are the same people. A <u>problem</u> is that the only main <u>sources of finance</u> are the owners' capital and <u>retained profits</u> — this makes it <u>harder</u> for the co-operative to <u>expand</u>.

See p14 for more about stakeholders.

Public Corporations are Owned and Funded by the Government

1) A good example is the <u>BBC</u>. Unlike a PLC it does not have a board of directors chosen by shareholders — it has a board of <u>governors</u> who are <u>appointed</u> by its owner — the <u>government</u>.

2) The main source of <u>funds</u> is a government grant, paid for by the <u>licence fee</u>. However, the BBC is also encouraged to generate its <u>own funds</u> by selling goods and services for a <u>profit</u>.

3) Public corporations do <u>not</u> have to make a <u>profit</u> — instead they follow <u>objectives</u> set by the government. This can make it <u>easier</u> to satisfy all its <u>stakeholders</u>.

Co-operative firms are nice to their customers...

These business structures are never-ending. Make sure you know <u>how a franchise works</u> — scribble down the <u>benefits</u> and <u>problems</u>. Then do the same for <u>co-operatives</u> and <u>public corporations</u>. There'll be more on business structures after the break.

Warm-Up and Worked Exam Questions

Warm-up Questions

1) Name the two sectors of the economy.
2) List the three different types of economic system.
3) How many partners can there be in a partnership?
4) Name the two types of limited company.
5) What is a franchisee?
6) What is the most important objective for most businesses?

Worked Exam Questions

It's really important to get the key business terms clear in your mind before going on to the rest of the section. Have a look at these worked exam questions, then have a go at the questions on the next page.

1 Briefly explain the meaning of the term "unlimited liability".
   Name a type of business which has unlimited liability.

   Unlimited liability means the owners of the business are personally [1 mark]
   liable for the debts of the business. The owners may have to sell their [1 mark]
   possessions to pay off the debt. Sole traders and partnerships have [1 mark for either example]
   unlimited liability.

   There are 3 marks available for this question. You'll get 1 mark for naming a type of business with unlimited liability, so the definition of the term is worth 2 marks. That means you need to give at least two pieces of information in the definition.   *(3 marks)*

2 Anyfirm Ltd is changing from a private limited company to a public limited company (PLC). Explain the advantages for Anyfirm Ltd of this decision.

   Anyfirm Ltd will be able to trade its shares openly on the stock [1 mark] [1 mark]
   exchange. This means they can raise capital more easily. The extra
   capital can be used to reduce debt, or to expand or diversify the
   business. [1 mark for stating any use of the extra capital]
   (3 marks)

3 Is a sole trader incorporated or unincorporated? How does this affect the legal status of the owner of the business? [1 mark]

   A sole trader is unincorporated. This means that the owner and the
   business are treated as being the same in law. [1 mark]
   (2 marks)

Exam Questions

1 Anna Conda runs a branded franchise selling industrial cleaning products.

   a) What is a branded franchise?

....

....

(2 marks)

   b) Explain the advantages and disadvantages for Anna of having a branded franchise.

....

....

....

(4 marks)

   c) Anna's business sells mainly to public sector organisations.
      List two public sector organisations.

....

(2 marks)

2 David and John work in television. David works for the BBC, and John works for a public limited company.

   a) What type of organisation is the BBC?

....

(1 mark)

   b) David and John discuss the differences between their organisations. John says that PLCs are better broadcasters because their service is free at the point of delivery. How might David defend the BBC in response to this claim?

....

....

....

....

....

(4 marks)

   c) Why do you think David and John might be keen to criticise one another's employer?

....

(1 mark)

Organisational Structure: Hierarchies

A <u>hierarchy</u> — the posh term for a <u>pecking order</u>. That basically means the boss at the top and the workers at the bottom. You'll need to know where <u>directors</u> and <u>managers</u> fit in and what <u>responsibilities</u> they have.

*The **Larger** the Firm the **Bigger** the Hierarchy*

1) Sole traders usually have <u>no employees</u> — there is <u>no hierarchy</u>. A <u>large PLC</u> may have <u>several layers</u> in its hierarchy.

2) At the <u>top</u> of the hierarchy are the owners — <u>shareholders</u> in a limited company. The shareholders appoint the <u>directors</u>, who are in overall <u>day-to-day control</u> of the company.

3) The directors appoint the <u>managers</u> — they <u>carry out the policies</u> set by the directors. The managers appoint the <u>operatives</u> — they do the <u>everyday work</u> of the business.

Shareholders
Directors
Managers
Operatives

*Shareholders Have **Ownership** but Not Control*

1) In most PLCs the shareholders also own shares in many <u>other</u> companies. So shareholders <u>delegate responsibility</u> for the general direction — the <u>strategy</u> — of the business to the <u>directors</u>. The directors decide on strategy at regular <u>board meetings</u>. The directors can be <u>removed</u> from their job by the shareholders.

2) The top director is called the <u>Chair of the Board</u>. He/she runs the board meetings. The next most important director is the <u>Managing Director</u>. He/she runs the business between the main board meetings.

3) The directors delegate responsibility for <u>implementing</u> their strategy on a <u>day-to-day basis</u> to the <u>managers</u>. A large business will have senior, middle and junior managers. Managers are <u>responsible</u> for the <u>operatives</u> carrying out their tasks properly. They will each have responsibility for a specific group of operatives.

4) <u>Operatives</u> are given <u>specific tasks</u> to perform by managers. If they do not perform these tasks properly they can be <u>dismissed</u>.

5) Everyone has <u>some</u> control over how the company is run. But the directors have the <u>most</u> — as long as they keep the shareholders happy.

DIRECTORS — MAIN RESPONSIBILITIES	MANAGERS — MAIN RESPONSIBILITIES
1) <u>Strategic direction</u> — like deciding to build a new factory in France.	1) <u>Planning</u> — like deciding how the new factory should be built.
2) <u>Setting targets</u> for the company — say, 10% sales growth in the next year.	2) <u>Controlling</u> — checking the progress to make sure it will be built on time.
3) <u>Legal responsibility</u> for what the business does — so if an injured worker sues the company, the directors have to represent the company in court.	3) <u>Co-ordinating</u> — making sure the machinery for the factory will arrive when the factory is ready.
	4) <u>Motivating</u> — trying to keep the workers happy in their nice new factory.

Delegation means giving work to others...

There you are — a nice easy page about <u>levels of command</u>. The <u>number</u> of levels depends on the type of business, and each level <u>delegates responsibilities</u> to the next. Make sure you understand what the <u>main responsibilities</u> of each level are. You know what to do by now — learn, cover the page and scribble the facts down.

Organisational Structure: Organisation Charts

There are <u>three main ways</u> a business can structure its organisation. There is <u>no right or wrong</u> way — it's up to each individual business to decide which structure <u>works best for them</u>.

1 You can Organise by *Function*...

1) You get this a lot in <u>limited</u> companies.

2) Each <u>department</u> does one part of the work of the business.

3) The main advantage is that <u>specialists</u> can concentrate on their particular job.

4) The main disadvantage is that the different departments may not <u>work well together</u>.

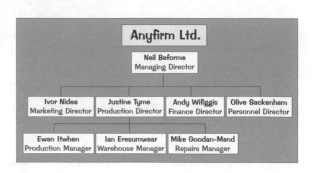

2 ...Or you can Organise by *Product*...

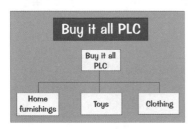

1) This is common with <u>large manufacturers</u> who make lots of different products.

2) A product-based structure splits the organisation into different <u>sectors</u>. In the example, there are <u>three</u> sectors — home furnishings, toys and clothing.

3) The <u>main advantage</u> is that managers can make decisions that are <u>relevant</u> to each product division.

4) A <u>disadvantage</u> is that there can be a <u>wasteful duplication</u> of resources between divisions.

3 ...Or Organise by *Region*

1) This is normal for a <u>multinational</u> business.

2) The divisions may be <u>regional</u> or <u>national</u>.

3) Firms called <u>holding companies</u> also have this structure.

4) The <u>main advantage</u> is that spreading management between regions makes <u>day-to-day control</u> easier.

5) A <u>disadvantage</u> is that there can be a <u>wasteful duplication</u> of resources between regions.

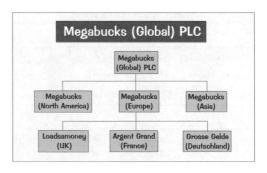

Organisations can be *Centralised* or *Decentralised*

Centralised organisations

1) <u>All major decisions</u> are made by one person or a few senior managers at the <u>top</u> of the business.

2) <u>Advantages</u> are that these senior managers tend to have plenty of <u>experience</u>, and can get an <u>overview</u> of the whole business. Policies will be <u>uniform</u> throughout the business.

3) On the <u>downside</u>, decisions can take a <u>long time</u> to filter through to employees. This means that the organisation reacts <u>slowly</u> to change. Also central managers may <u>lack specialist knowledge</u>.

Decentralised organisations

1) The authority to make most decisions is <u>shared out</u> — for example, power might be delegated to <u>regional managers</u> or to more <u>junior employees</u>.

2) <u>Advantages</u> are that employees can use <u>expert knowledge</u> of their sector to make decisions, and these decisions can be made more <u>quickly</u>.

3) The <u>disadvantages</u> are that <u>inconsistencies</u> may develop between departments or regions. Also the decision makers might not be able to see the <u>overall</u> needs of the business.

Businesses choose a structure to suit their needs...

<u>Three</u> diagrams for you to learn here. Make sure you know <u>which</u> types of organisations each structure is most suitable for. Remember — firms often start out with a centralised structure, but are forced to <u>decentralise</u> as they become <u>too big</u> to make all the decisions at the top.

Measuring Business Success

Business Studies examiners want you to tell them that there's <u>more</u> to being a <u>successful business</u> than just making a <u>big profit</u>. This page tells you how else business success can be <u>measured</u>.

The *Firm* and its *Stakeholders* may have Different *Views* About *Success*

1) Different stakeholders (see p14) will have different opinions about what the business needs to do in order to be successful. Some of these might be in <u>conflict</u> with the objectives the <u>firm</u> sets itself.

2) For the <u>business</u> to be successful it has to meet the objectives which it has set for itself. The way that the business <u>co-ordinates</u> the activities of its various <u>departments</u> in order to try and achieve these objectives is called a <u>strategy</u>. The business will set itself <u>success criteria</u> — these are the <u>targets</u> it will use to <u>measure</u> whether or not it has met its objectives.

There are *Four Main Ways* of *Measuring Success*

1) <u>SIZE</u> — The size of a business can be measured in the following different ways:
   - <u>Job creation</u> is the extent to which the firm creates <u>employment</u> for people — this helps to raise their <u>standard of living</u>. It is usually measured by counting the <u>number of employees</u>.
   - <u>Turnover</u> is the <u>sales revenue</u> that a business earns. For example, a business with an annual turnover of <u>£3000</u> million would be considered <u>larger</u> than one with a <u>£30</u> million turnover.
   - <u>Profit</u> — For example, a business with a pretax profit of <u>£200</u> million would be considered <u>larger</u> than one with a pretax profit of <u>£50</u> million.
   - <u>Market share</u> is measured by <u>dividing</u> the <u>sales</u> of the <u>firm's products</u> into the <u>total sales</u> of the <u>market</u>. Basically the <u>bigger</u> the market share, the <u>greater</u> is the firm's <u>market power</u>.

2) <u>PROFITABILITY</u> is measured by indicators such as <u>Profit Margin</u> and <u>Return on Capital Employed</u>. These are explained in <u>Section Five</u> but basically the <u>bigger</u> they are the <u>more profitable</u> the firm is. Profitable firms are an important source of <u>wealth creation</u> for the <u>economy</u>.

3) <u>CONSUMER SATISFACTION</u> measures how <u>happy</u> consumers are with the <u>products</u> made by the firm. The firm can <u>measure</u> this by carrying out <u>customer opinion surveys</u>, a type of <u>market research</u>.

4) <u>ETHICAL CONSIDERATIONS</u> include things like the <u>impact</u> of the firm's activities on the <u>environment</u>. Basically something is ethical if <u>society</u> believes that it is the <u>right way to do things</u>. For example, many consumers now think that it is <u>wrong</u> to test cosmetics on animals.

You need to know how the <u>different stakeholders</u> will have <u>different ideas of success</u> based on their <u>interests</u>. Here are four examples — learn them.

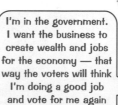

I am an activist in a pressure group. I think most firms are too big and powerful. They pollute the environment and treat animals badly. I know they create lots of jobs but I think we'd be better off with a lower income and a healthier planet.

I'm a consumer. I want the firm to make good quality products at a low price — but I worry that some firms are too powerful and charge too much. I am also concerned about the environment but I can't always afford to buy environmentally friendly products.

I'm a shareholder. I want the firm to be as profitable as possible so I can earn a large dividend when the profit gets divided up. I don't care too much how the business achieves this, but I don't want the firm upsetting the other stakeholders too much — otherwise profitability might suffer.

I'm in the government. I want the business to create wealth and jobs for the economy — that way the voters will think I'm doing a good job and vote for me again at the election.

Edna the activist has different priorities from Colin the cabinet minister...

The basic idea is that success can be <u>measured</u> — but <u>different</u> people will measure <u>different</u> things. What they measure depends on what they want from the business. Learn the methods, cover and scribble them all down. Then make a <u>list</u> of the different <u>success criteria</u> that each <u>stakeholder</u> on Page 14 would use. (Page 14 follows shortly.)

Stakeholders

Everyone who is affected by a business is called a stakeholder. There are two types — <u>internal stakeholders</u> and <u>external stakeholders</u>. They're both <u>vitally important</u> for businesses to function and for you to <u>learn</u>.

Internal Stakeholders are Inside the Firm

1) The <u>owners</u> are the most important stakeholders. They make a <u>profit</u> if the business is successful and decide what happens to the business. In a limited company they are the <u>shareholders</u>.

2) <u>Employees</u> are interested in their <u>job security</u> and <u>promotion prospects</u> — they also want to earn a <u>decent wage</u> and have <u>pleasant working conditions</u>. If the company does badly they may become <u>unemployed</u>.

External Stakeholders are Outside the Firm

1) <u>Customers</u> want <u>high quality</u> products at <u>low prices</u>.

2) <u>Suppliers</u> are who the firm <u>buys raw materials</u> from. The firm provides them with their income. They may face <u>cash flow problems</u> if they do not get paid quickly enough. They will also <u>lose work</u> if the firm is forced to close.

3) The <u>local community</u> where the business is based will suffer if the firm causes <u>noise and pollution</u>. They may gain if the firm provides <u>good jobs</u> and <u>sponsors</u> local activities. Firms may also provide <u>facilities</u> which the local community can use.

4) The <u>government</u> will receive <u>taxes</u> when the firm makes a profit.

Most Important are the Shareholders

1) No business can ignore its <u>customers</u>. If it can't sell its products it will go bankrupt.

2) And if a business doesn't keep its <u>workers</u> happy it may become <u>unproductive</u>.

3) But a company may not mind being <u>unpopular</u> in the <u>local community</u> — if it sells most of its products somewhere else.

4) The one group no business can ignore for long is its <u>shareholders</u>. If they are unhappy they can <u>sack</u> the directors or <u>sell</u> the business to someone else.

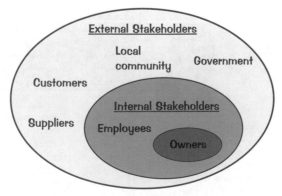

Memorise that lovely diagram...

This is <u>really simple</u>. Basically, business activities affect loads of groups of people — both <u>positively</u> and <u>negatively</u>. A business will usually try to keep as many of these groups as happy as possible. But when it comes to the <u>crunch</u> — it's more worried about <u>what its shareholders think</u> than anyone else. Make sure you <u>memorise</u> all the different stakeholders and whether they're <u>internal</u> or <u>external</u>.

Business Basics — Important Ideas

All of the ideas on this page are <u>really important</u> — without them <u>businesses</u> and the <u>tough decisions</u> that they need to make would <u>not exist</u>. And there'd be <u>no need</u> for you to learn Business Studies — there's a thought.

We have *Limited Needs* but *Unlimited Wants*

1) We all have the same <u>five basic needs</u> that are <u>essential</u> for human <u>survival</u>.
2) These are — water, food, clothing, shelter and warmth.
3) These are <u>limited</u>. Once we have these then we can start to worry about satisfying our <u>wants</u>.
4) We all have <u>different wants</u> — or desires.
5) Once we start buying <u>luxuries</u> we start to want bigger and better things.
6) If people didn't have <u>unlimited wants</u> businesses would soon run out of things that they could sell.

There is *Scarcity* so we have to Make a *Choice*

1) The world only has a <u>limited</u> amount of <u>resources</u> at any one time. For example, deposits of fossil fuels are non-renewable. And people only have a limited amount of money.
2) But the existence of unlimited wants means that there <u>aren't enough</u> resources to fulfil <u>all</u> of them.
3) In other words, resources are <u>scarce</u> — there are not enough to go around.
4) So individuals, businesses and governments have to make a <u>choice</u> as to which wants they will fulfil.

> **Economists divide resources into four factors of production:**
> - <u>Land</u>: Natural resources
> - <u>Labour</u>: People
> - <u>Capital</u>: Money and equipment
> - <u>Enterprise</u>: Business owners
>
> The <u>relationship</u> between these factors of production is constantly changing. Over the last half-century there has been a change from <u>labour-intensive</u> industry to <u>capital-intensive</u> industry in the UK.

Choice results in *Opportunity Cost*

1) Every time we make a choice we <u>give up</u> the <u>opportunity</u> to have <u>another</u> of our unlimited wants.
2) For example, I could either go to Scunthorpe or Skegness for my summer holiday. If I go to Scunthorpe I give up the <u>opportunity</u> to go to Skegness.
3) The <u>opportunity cost</u> of going to Scunthorpe is going to Skegness.
4) Opportunity cost is the <u>next best option</u> we would have chosen instead.

Profit is the Owner's *Reward* for Risking Capital

1) <u>Every</u> business decision has an <u>opportunity cost</u>.
2) There is a <u>risk</u> that the decision will be <u>wrong</u> and the business will make a <u>loss</u>.
3) <u>Profit</u> is the <u>owner's reward</u> for taking risks with their capital.

Watching TV — the opportunity cost of reading this page...

Phew — not the easiest of pages this one. That's mainly because it's about <u>ideas</u> and not <u>facts</u>. Still, you've got to learn it just the same. Cover the page, and scribble it down. Then read it all through <u>once more</u> — just for <u>luck</u>.

Warm-Up and Worked Exam Questions

Warm-up Questions

1) Which of the following businesses is unlikely to have a hierarchy — a PLC, the army, a sole trader, a multinational company?

2) What is the name of the top director in a company?

3) What are the three ways in which a business can structure its organisation?

4) List two internal and two external stakeholders.

5) What are humans' five basic needs?

6) Name the four factors of production.

Worked Exam Question

Here's a typical exam question. Try covering up the answers and working through the question on your own. Then you can compare your answers with the answers in blue.

1   Affirm plc, a company that manufactures furniture, has the objective of increasing market share. In order to achieve this, it has decided to organise its UK business by region instead of by function.

Try to avoid woolly definitions. You need to state exactly how market share is calculated for both marks.

a)   What is meant by the term "market share"?

Market share is the firm's total annual sales divided by the ✓ [1 mark] *total annual sales for the whole market, expressed as a* ✓ [1 mark] *percentage.*

(2 marks)

b)   Explain how a company increasing its market share might affect the customer.

The market may become more competitive, which may lower prices ✓ [1 mark] *for consumers. If the company's market share increases too much, however, the market may become a monopoly. This would mean the company could charge customers more because they would have* ✓ [1 mark] *little competition.*

A monopoly is when one supplier's market share is 25% or above.

(2 marks)

c)   Describe how Affirm plc's decision to reorganise might affect its suppliers.

The decision by Affirm plc to organise itself by region may mean that suppliers have to distribute to the different regions, which ✓ [1 mark] *may increase costs. The suppliers may have to negotiate locally* ✓ [1 mark] *rather than centrally, and might have to meet slightly different* ✓ [1 mark] *needs in the different regions.*

(3 marks)

Exam Questions

1   Clothes Seller plc is a clothes retailer with 450 stores nationwide, selling a wide
    range of fashionable clothing, footwear and jewellery aimed at teenage girls.

a)   Would you say that Clothes Seller plc satisfies its customers' **wants** or their **needs**?

    ....

    ....
    (2 marks)

b)   Clothes Seller plc has just increased production of its range of denim skirts.
     Give one opportunity cost to the business of this decision.

    ....
    (1 mark)

c)   Give one example of each of the factors of production used in Clothes Seller plc.

    ....

    ....

    ....

    ....
    (2 marks)

d)   Describe how Clothes Seller plc might be organised.

    ....

    ....
    (2 marks)

e)   The directors of Clothes Seller plc issue a statement stating that they wish to
     increase profits by improving productivity by 15 percent. Imagine that you are an
     employee of Clothes Seller plc worried by what this may mean for you and the rest
     of the workforce, and ultimately for the company. Write down your concerns.

    ....

    ....

    ....

    ....

    ....
    (4 marks)

f)   Explain one way in which employees might benefit from increased productivity.

    ....
    (1 mark)

Revision Summary for Section One

Okay, so that's the first section over with — now it's time to find out how much you remember. Have a bash at these questions. If you can do them all, pat yourself on the back and feel smug. If you can't, then go back and look at the section again and keep plugging away until you can answer them all. Yes, I know it's a pain but life's like that — and after all, it's the only way you're going to get ready for the exam.

1) Do charities aim to make a profit?

2) What are some of the objectives other than just profit that businesses might pursue?

3) What is the difference between the public sector and the private sector?

4) Which two of these are problems if you're a sole trader?

   a) long hours;   b) unlimited liability;   c) you're legally responsible for what other partners do.

5) What does a sole trader gain and lose if it becomes a partnership?

6) What information might be contained in a deed of partnership?

7) If you own part of a business and the business goes bankrupt, would you rather have limited or unlimited liability? Why?

8) What does a partnership gain and lose if it becomes a private limited company?

9) What big advantages does a PLC have over a private limited company?

10) What is a franchise?

11) Explain two benefits and two problems of franchising for both the franchisor and the franchisee.

12) Describe four differences between a director and a manager.

13) Who is at the bottom of the hierarchy:

    a) shareholders;   b) operatives;   c) plankton.

14) What are the three main ways that businesses can be structured?

15) Say which type of structure would be most suitable for these companies:

    a) a transnational oil company with offices all over the world;

    b) a limited company that manufactures washing machine parts.

16) Extend Anyfirm Ltd's organisation chart (on page 12) to show the production operatives.

17) Describe the differences between a centralised and a decentralised organisation.

18) Give four ways of measuring the size of a business.

19) Name six stakeholders and say which are internal.

20) Which is the most important stakeholder and why?

21) Explain the difference between a need and a want and give an example of each.

22) Why are resources scarce?

23) A business that manufactures fluffy toy crocodiles and fluffy toy hippos gets a large new order for fluffy toy hippos. Explain one opportunity cost to the business of increasing its production of fluffy toy hippos.

Marketing — What It Is

Marketing is a <u>surprisingly tricky</u> concept. Most people think they know what it means — and they're usually <u>wrong</u>. Marketing is <u>more</u> than just <u>selling</u> or <u>advertising</u>. It is the art of making it as <u>easy as possible</u> to get the potential customer to buy your product.

There are **Four Ps** in Marketing

The four Ps are the <u>key</u> to understanding what marketing is all about.
If a firm gets them <u>right</u> it will be <u>easy</u> to sell its product. If it gets <u>even one</u> of them <u>wrong</u> it is in <u>trouble</u>.

Together the four Ps are called the <u>marketing mix</u>.

1. PRODUCT — the firm must come up with a product that people will <u>want</u> to buy. It must fulfil some of the customer's <u>needs or wants</u>.

2. PRICE — the price must be one that the customer thinks is good <u>value for money</u>. This is not the same as being cheap.

3. PROMOTION — the product must be promoted so that potential customers are <u>aware</u> that it exists.

4. PLACE — the product must be available for sale in a place that the customer will find <u>convenient</u>.

Markets are Where **Sales Happen**

The term "market" means the <u>meeting place</u> between customers and suppliers — i.e. where goods are traded. It's also used to describe the <u>type of product</u> being bought and sold, for example, the leisure market, or global oil market.

1) <u>MASS MARKETS</u> sell ordinary things to <u>very large</u> numbers of people at quite <u>cheap</u> prices. Businesses can get high volume sales but at a fairly <u>low profit margin</u> — i.e. there is little difference between what it costs to make the product and what the business can sell it for.   *Profit margins are explained on page 78.*

2) <u>NICHE MARKETS</u> serve <u>specialist consumers</u> and can give <u>high profit margins</u>. <u>Small</u> businesses are especially suited to niche markets because they can afford to devote <u>lots of time</u> to production which would be unprofitable for a big firm.

Markets are **Segmented** into **Different Groups** of People

It's <u>obvious</u> when you think about it — we are all different. Some people even like to wear flares.
There are <u>seven main ways</u> of dividing people into different market segments.

AGE ⟶ for example, the teenage market, or "grey power" (the over-55s).

GENDER ⟶ for example, chocolate manufacturers target some items at women (e.g. Flake) and some at men (e.g. Yorkie).

SOCIAL CLASS ⟶ class A (professionals) down to class E (the unemployed).

LOCATION ⟶ try selling stottie cakes outside the Northeast, or jellied eels outside London.

CULTURE OR RELIGION ⟶ different groups have their own unique products (e.g. bagels, lassi).

INCOME ⟶ the size of consumer income will affect decisions about the product, e.g. the quality.

SIZE OF HOUSEHOLD AND PEOPLE IN IT ⟶ for example, the types and quantity of products bought by someone who lives alone will be very different from those bought by a family with three kids.

The marketing mix — a recipe for success...

So now you know — marketing is quite <u>simple</u> really. Just give the <u>customer</u> what they want. The only trick is to make a <u>profit</u> as well. Make sure you know <u>all four Ps</u> — there'll be lots more on these in the next few pages. Cover the page and scribble them down. Then do the same with market segments.

Market Research

Since marketing is all about giving the <u>customer</u> what they <u>want</u>, it makes sense to try to <u>find out</u> what that is. So if you ignore this page not only will your marketing suffer — but so will your exam marks.

There are <u>two types</u> of research — <u>field research</u> and <u>desk research</u>.

Field *Research is Doing Your* Own *Donkey Work*

1) Field research is also called <u>primary</u> research or <u>original</u> research.

2) It's useful for finding out <u>new information</u>, and getting <u>customers' views</u> of your products.

3) It involves things like <u>questionnaires</u>, <u>telephone surveys</u>, <u>product testing</u> and working with <u>consumer groups</u>.

4) Advantages are that it provides data that's <u>up to date</u>, <u>relevant</u> and <u>specific</u> to your products.

5) Disadvantages are that it's <u>expensive</u> to collect, it's <u>time consuming</u>, and it needs a <u>large sample size</u> to be accurate.

Desk *Research is Looking at* Other People's *Work*

1) Desk research is also called <u>secondary</u> research or sometimes <u>published</u> research.

2) It's useful for looking at the <u>whole market</u>, and analysing <u>past trends</u> to predict the future.

3) It involves looking at things like <u>market research reports</u> (such as MINTEL), <u>government publications</u> (such as the Family Expenditure Survey or Social Trends), and <u>newspaper</u> and <u>magazine</u> articles.

4) Advantages are that it's <u>cheaper</u> than field research, the data is <u>easily found</u> and <u>instantly available</u>.

5) Disadvantages are that it's <u>not always relevant</u> to your needs, it's <u>not specifically</u> about your products, and it's often <u>out of date</u>.

Data can be Quantitative *or* Qualitative

1) Suppose you want to sell chocolate pizza. You can find out <u>two kinds</u> of information.

2) QUANTITATIVE information is anything you can measure or <u>reduce to a number</u>. Asking "How many chocolate pizzas will you buy each week?" will give a quantitative answer.

3) QUALITATIVE information is all about people's <u>feelings and opinions</u>. Asking "What do you think of chocolate pizzas?" will give a qualitative answer.

4) Qualitative data is <u>tricky</u> to analyse because it is <u>hard to compare</u> two people's opinions. Good market research will use <u>both types</u> of information.

Looking at other people's work — not a good idea in the exam...

... but a <u>great</u> idea if you're doing a spot of market research. Nothing to get too excited about — but it's <u>really</u> <u>important</u> stuff. The trick is to know what you want to find out first and then select the <u>best method</u> to collect the data. Learn this page well and then scribble off a mini-essay on 'methods of market research'.

Primary Research Methods

Some specifications require you to know about this for the exam. But you'll definitely need to do some field research for your <u>coursework</u> — so it's worth learning how to do it <u>properly</u>.

Seven Rules to Writing a Good Questionnaire

The basic rules are the same whatever method of field research is used. The only difference is that with <u>questionnaires</u> it's likely that the <u>respondent</u> will fill in the information <u>themselves</u> — this means it's important to <u>communicate</u> exactly what you want them to do.

1 Decide what <u>information</u> you want to <u>find out</u>.

(This is <u>not the same</u> as deciding what responses you want people to give.)

2 Decide what <u>questions</u> you can ask to find out each piece of information.

(Choose the <u>best one</u>.)

3 Use a balance of <u>open and closed questions</u>.

<u>Open</u> questions allow the respondent to give a <u>detailed answer</u> — e.g. "How do you feel after drinking organic rhubarb juice?"

<u>Closed</u> questions only allow a <u>specific answer</u> — e.g. "How many bottles of organic rhubarb juice do you drink each week?"

4 Write the questions using language that is <u>unambiguous</u>.

If the respondent doesn't understand the question then they can't give an honest answer. <u>E.g.</u> you might want to find out <u>how much</u> of the product will be consumed so you ask "How many times a week do you drink organic rhubarb juice?" The respondent says once — because they drink it at the same time every day at breakfast.

5 Allow the respondent to give an <u>answer</u> that reflects their <u>opinion</u>.

For example make sure they're given the option to say no to a question.

6 Avoid <u>leading questions</u>.

<u>Don't ask</u> "How much do you prefer drinking organic rhubarb juice to petrol?" <u>Instead</u> ask them which they prefer.

7 <u>Test</u> the questionnaire — you may need to <u>rewrite</u> the questions. This is called a <u>pilot</u> study.

Three Main Ways to Choose Your Sample

Giving <u>everyone</u> the questionnaire is <u>time-consuming</u> and <u>expensive</u>, so it's better to question a <u>subset</u> of the <u>population</u> called a <u>sample</u>. To get <u>unbiased results</u> that <u>represent</u> the population, the sample must share its <u>characteristics</u>. The <u>bigger the sample</u> the <u>less chance</u> it will be biased.

1) <u>RANDOM SAMPLES</u> are ones where the <u>total population is known</u> and people are <u>selected from a list</u> at random. <u>Random</u> means that <u>everyone</u> in the population has an <u>equal chance</u> of being selected. Just using a telephone directory isn't good enough — not everyone has a telephone.

2) <u>QUOTA SAMPLING</u> is used when the <u>names</u> of the total population <u>aren't known</u> but their <u>characteristics</u> are. <u>For example</u> 4% of the population might have purple eyes — so 4% of the sample need to have them.

3) <u>TARGET SAMPLING</u> is used if the firm just wants to sample a <u>particular group</u> in the population. This might be because its products are only bought by a particular <u>market segment</u>.

How many days until the Business Studies exam? — A closed question...

Lots of lovely facts to learn on this page. Learn the <u>seven steps</u> to good questionnaire writing, then <u>cover</u> up the page and <u>scribble</u> them down. Choosing <u>how</u> to sample can be tricky — make sure you know the <u>three</u> main methods. Remember, the <u>more</u> people you sample, the more <u>reliable</u> your results should be.

Presentation and Analysis of Market Research Results

Now you know how to conduct your research, you'll be wanting to know how to <u>analyse and present your findings</u>. This is another page which'll come in very handy for your <u>coursework</u>, even if you don't need it for the exam.

Summarise Questionnaire Results using a *Data Logging Sheet*

So you've conducted your survey — the tricky part is <u>making sense</u> of the results. A <u>data logging sheet</u> like the one below can help turn your rain-soaked scraps of paper into <u>meaningful information</u>. A data logging sheet <u>tallies</u> how many people chose each option in a multiple choice question.

> **EXAMPLE**
>
> '<u>Crazy Juice Ltd</u>' want to launch a new flavour of juice. They have used a questionnaire to research public opinion.
>
> You need to be able to <u>interpret</u> what the data means. For this example you might say...
> *'The results suggest that Crazy Juice should choose blueberry as their new flavour of juice because it has by far the highest number of responses.'*

Question Which of the following flavours would you be most likely to buy?	Number of respondents	% of total repondents
Blueberry juice	580	58%
Rhubarb juice	130	13%
Apricot juice	100	10%
Damson juice	190	19%
Total respondents	**1000**	**100%**

Pie Charts are used to show *Proportions*

1) Pie charts are used for showing <u>market share</u>. They are also used to show the <u>proportion</u> of <u>respondents</u> giving each answer. Each 1% share is represented by a <u>3.6°</u> section of the pie (because there are 360° in a circle and 360 ÷ 100 = 3.6).

2) Advantages of pie charts are that they are <u>simple</u> to use and <u>easy to understand</u>.

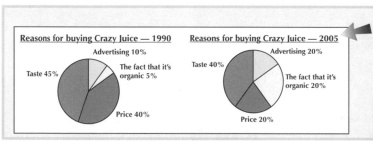

> **EXAMPLE**
>
> These pie charts show the results of Crazy Juice Ltd's <u>recent</u> research into <u>why</u> people buy their juice, as well as the results from similar research carried out in <u>1990</u>.
>
> An analysis of <u>what</u> the charts <u>show</u> would include points like...
> *'Taste is still the most important factor,'* or *'The biggest increase is the fact that it's organic.'*

Bar Charts are good for Showing *Trends*

1) Bar charts show different values for a <u>single</u> variable. They are especially useful for showing <u>trends</u> in data — for example, the monthly sales of a product over one year.

2) Advantages of bar charts are that they're <u>easy</u> to <u>construct</u>, easy to <u>interpret</u> and have <u>high visual impact</u>.

3) On the downside they can be <u>confusing</u> if the <u>vertical scale</u> doesn't start at <u>zero</u> — it can look like there is a really big difference between two bars when there isn't really.

> **EXAMPLE**
>
> This bar chart shows Crazy Juice Ltd's <u>sales</u> in apple juice during 2004.
>
> An analysis of <u>what</u> the bar chart <u>shows</u> would say something like...
> *'Sales are fairly constant between January and April, and October to December, but increase sharply in the summer months.'*

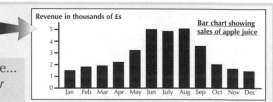

Data analysis makes sense of market research results...

I know this page looks like it's escaped from a Maths book, but statistics are <u>really useful</u> in Business Studies. In the exam, you'll not only have to <u>say what the data shows</u>, but be able to relate it to the firm's <u>marketing strategies</u>.

The Product — Five Golden Rules

This is the first P. Getting the product right is the basis of all good marketing.

1 Be *Market-Driven* — *not Product-Driven*

1) MARKET-DRIVEN firms will use market research to find out what people want, then make it.
   This usually means the product is useful — like an MP3 player with a built-in radio.
2) PRODUCT-DRIVEN firms will design or invent a new product and then try to sell it. This often means
   they make something nobody really wants — like an MP3 player with a built-in toaster.
   With very few exceptions market-driven firms do best.

2 Know *Yourself* and Your *Market*

SWOT stands for Strengths, Weaknesses, Opportunities and Threats. SWOT analysis helps managers to take a look
at how the business is doing and to see possible opportunities for future products and development.

1) Managers look at internal factors — factors within the business. Strengths are things like a good product range,
   a well motivated workforce or a well known brand name. Weaknesses include things like not having enough
   products, an inexperienced workforce or having lots of debts.
2) External factors are also looked at — factors outside the business. Opportunities are factors that create possibilities
   for a business to develop — like improving economic conditions or the opening up of new markets. Threats are
   things that make it harder for a business — like increased competition or a worsening economic climate.

3 Get the *Detail* of the Product Right

1) The DESIGN must be fit for its purpose. It's no good making a car that doesn't start.
2) The PRODUCT NAME must be catchy. Call your car the Thunderball, not the X3MS5. A brand name is a unique
   name for a product, or range of products, which can't be used by any other firm. Firms often like to build up a
   brand image. This is a good way of making products distinctive and can help to create customer loyalty.
3) There must be a suitably broad PRODUCT RANGE to give options to all your potential customers. So make your
   car in saloon and hatchback, manual and automatic.
4) PACKAGING can help to distinguish a product. Packaging is also used to protect a product — so it reaches the
   consumer in perfect condition. E.g. new cars are covered in a thin layer of wax to protect them in transit.

4 Know your Product's *Life Cycle*

All products go through the same life cycle — but the sales life of some products is longer than others. For
example, the sales life of most cars is about ten years, but the sales life of a computer game is only a few months.

1) Products start life in the development stage. Research and Development (R&D) and
   market research combine to develop an idea and turn it into a product fit for the market.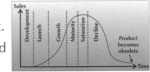
2) Next it's the launch — the product is put on sale for the first time. This is usually backed
   up with lots of advertising and sales promotions.
3) During the growth phase, sales and profitability gradually increase, until the product becomes well established in
   the market. This is known as maturity. Firms will continue to advertise, but less frequently than at the launch.
4) Towards the end of the maturity phase, the market becomes saturated. There is no more room to expand — sales
   are at their peak. Firms might try to extend the life of a product by using an extension strategy. This might include
   making changes to the design or offering discounts.
5) Eventually sales start to decline as rival products take over, and the product becomes obsolete.

5 Make your Product *Different* from the Competition

1) Product differentiation is what all firms are after. It has been achieved if the firm knows the answer to this
   question: "What is different about our product compared to the competition that makes people want to buy it?"
2) It might be that your product has a unique design feature, or a reputation for reliability, or a cool brand image.
   Whatever. If you don't have product differentiation, people think your product is identical to others, and they will
   only buy it if it's cheaper — which means less profit for you.

Warm-Up and Worked Exam Questions

Warm-up Questions

1) What is the marketing mix?
2) What is niche marketing?
3) Name the two types of market research.
4) What is qualitative information?
5) List the three main ways to choose a sample.
6) Describe how pie charts are used to display results of market research.
7) What does 'SWOT' stand for in 'SWOT analysis'?

Worked Exam Questions

Marketing is an important part of any business. It's also an important part of lots of Business Studies exams. Have a look at these worked exam questions, and think whether you would have given the same answers.

1 Explain briefly the meaning of the following terms used in marketing, and give an example of each.

a) Mass market product

A standard product sold to large numbers of people at fairly cheap ✓ [1 mark] *prices. Mass market products usually have low profit margins. An* ✓ [1 mark] *example is televisions.* ✓ [1 mark] *There are lots of examples you could give — washing machines, teabags, chocolate bars, etc.*

(3 marks)

b) Field research

Collecting and analysing information that does not already exist using ✓ [1 mark] *techniques such as questionnaires and phone surveys. An example is* ✓ [1 mark] *a customer satisfaction questionnaire for a supermarket.* ✓ [1 mark]

(3 marks)

2 A car manufacturer wishes to prolong the sales life of one of its models.

a) What is the name of a strategy designed to extend the sales life of a product?

An extension strategy. ✓ [1 mark]

(1 mark)

b) Give details of a strategy that the car manufacturer could use.

The car manufacturer could provide additional extras at no *additional price, e.g. alloy wheels, to give improved value for money* ✓ [1 mark] ✓ [1 mark] ✓ [1 mark] *and to improve product differentiation.* ✓ [1 mark]

(4 marks)

Exam Questions

1 Bob is thinking of starting a business. He is considering opening a 'sports bar' aimed at young people aged 18-30 years.

   a) How might Bob use primary and secondary research before setting up the business?

   ....

   ....

   ....

   ....

   ....

   ....

   (8 marks)

   b) Bob decides to carry out a questionnaire. He stands outside his local supermarket and asks people between the ages of 18 and 30 if they would go to his sports bar at least once a week. Draw a pie chart of his results.

Question: Would you go to the sports bar at least once a week?		
Answer	Number of respondents	% of total respondents
Yes, definitely	40	22%
Yes, probably	18	10%
Maybe	16	9%
No	106	59%
Total respondents	180	100%

   (5 marks)

   c) Based on the results above, would you say it was a good idea for Bob to open a sports bar?

   ....

   ....

   ....

   ....

   ....

   ....

   (6 marks)

   d) Describe three ways in which Bob might differentiate his business from other bars.

   ....

   ....

   ....

   (3 marks)

Exam Questions

2   'Joose', a high-energy fruit drink, was launched at the end of 1994. It has sales revenues as shown in the table below.

Year	1993	1994	1995	1996	1997	1998	1999	2000	2001	2002	2003	2004
Sales (£000s)	0	0	5	12	22	36	49	52	52	49	45	38

a)   Plot a graph of the sales revenues for the period 1993 to 2004.

(6 marks)

b)   Label the graph with the following terms:
i) decline   ii) development   iii) growth   iv) launch   v) maturity   vi) saturation.

(6 marks)

c)   State two advantages and two disadvantages of withdrawing 'Joose' from the market at the start of 2005.

....

....

....

(4 marks)

d)   "The falling sales revenues of 'Joose' are an indication that the manufacturer has failed to respond to a changing business environment." Discuss.

....

....

....

....

....

....

....

....

....

....

(10 marks)

e)   Would you say that soft drinks are a niche market or a mass market?
Explain your answer.

....

....

....

(3 marks)

Price — Demand and Supply

Here we move on to the second P — price. These graphs look tricky, but I reckon the ideas behind them are quite simple. The golden rule is that firms will usually charge the highest price that consumers are prepared to pay.

Demand — what Consumers are Prepared to Buy

1) Demand means the quantity of a product that consumers are willing and able to buy. The law of demand is that as the price increases the quantity demanded will fall — and vice versa.

2) There are two reasons. At a lower price more people can afford the product. And it becomes cheaper compared to its substitutes — that is, similar goods that people might buy instead.

3) Basically it's simple common sense — you'll buy more of something when it's cheaper.

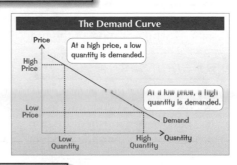

Supply — what Producers are Prepared to Sell

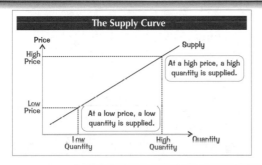

1) Supply is the quantity of a product producers are willing and able to make for sale. The law of supply is that as the price increases, the quantity supplied increases — and vice versa.

2) When the price is low, very few producers will be able to make a profit — so the supply is small. At high prices even inefficient producers can make a profit — so the supply is large.

3) Again it's common sense. Firms will make more of a thing if they can get a good price.

Equilibrium — where Producers and Consumers Agree

1) Producers want to sell at a high price. Consumers want to buy at a low price. Luckily the marketplace forces them to reach a compromise. It's dead clever — this is how it works.

2) If the price is too low there'll be a shortage. Some consumers will be willing to pay more, so producers will be able to increase prices.

3) If the price is too high, there'll be a surplus. Producers will have to reduce prices to persuade more people to buy their unsold goods.

4) Eventually producers and consumers agree on the price and quantity to be exchanged. The point where they agree is called the equilibrium.

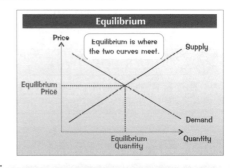

Price Elasticity of Demand — how Demand Changes with Price

1) Price elasticity of demand shows how much demand changes in response to changes in price.

2) Price elastic products have a large % change in demand for a small % change in price. Price inelastic products are the opposite — there's a small % change in demand for a big % change in price.

$$\text{Price elasticity of demand} = \frac{\%\,\text{change in quantity demanded}}{\%\,\text{change in price}}$$

3) Price elasticity of demand is always negative. This is because a positive change in price causes a negative change in demand, and a negative change in price causes a positive change in demand. So there's always a minus sign in there somewhere.

4) If price elasticity of demand is greater than 1 (ignoring the minus sign), the product is price elastic. If it's less than 1, it's price inelastic. So –5 means price elastic and –0.25 means price inelastic.

Equilibrium — the compromise between producers and consumers...

A few key ideas to remember here. Learn the laws of demand and supply and the importance of equilibrium, and make sure you can draw the diagrams. Price elasticity of demand is just a way of showing how much price affects demand for a product. Try practising a few sums to get the hang of it.

Pricing Strategies

This is an easier page than the last one — even though there's some maths at the bottom. Examiners like to test if you can <u>match</u> each <u>pricing strategy</u> to a <u>particular type</u> of product. So make sure you <u>learn how to</u>.

Market-Led Pricing

A firm will use a <u>market-led</u> pricing strategy if the <u>price</u> of the product helps decide whether consumers will buy it — which is <u>most of the time</u>. There are <u>five</u> different pricing methods.

1 *Penetration Pricing*

This is where a firm charges a very <u>low</u> price when the product is <u>new</u> to get lots of people <u>interested</u> in it. When this low price is <u>below cost</u> it is called <u>loss leading</u>. Once the product has become <u>established</u> the firm will <u>increase</u> the price. This happens with new consumer products where existing products have <u>brand loyalty</u> — magazines are a good example.

2 *Skimming*

This is the <u>opposite</u> of penetration pricing. Firms charge a <u>high price</u> to begin with — this helps make the product <u>desirable</u> to people with large incomes. When the product has become established the firm will <u>lower the price</u> to help it become a <u>mass-market</u> product. This happens a lot with consumer goods based on <u>new technology</u>, such as digital TVs.

3 *Destroyer Pricing*

This is also known as <u>predatory pricing</u>. This is where firms charge <u>low prices</u> that they know are <u>unprofitable</u> for their competitors. Once they have driven competitors <u>out of the market</u> they will <u>raise prices</u>. Firms who use this <u>anti-competitive</u> method of pricing can find themselves in trouble with the <u>Office of Fair Trading</u> (OFT) (see page 104).

4 *Price Discrimination*

This is where firms charge <u>different prices</u> to <u>different consumers</u> for the <u>same product</u>. A good example is cheaper <u>rail travel</u> for students and OAPs.

5 *Competition Pricing*

This is where the firm has to charge <u>similar</u> prices to <u>other firms</u>. It happens when there is lots of choice and not much product differentiation — like petrol.

Cost-Plus Pricing

Firms will use this method if they are <u>not</u> in <u>price competition</u> with other producers — though of course they can still only charge what people are prepared to pay. There are <u>two main ways</u> it can be done. You may need to revise profit margins (Section Five) first.

1) Work out how much the product costs and then add a <u>percentage mark-up</u>. So if the product <u>costs £2</u> to make, and you want a <u>25% mark-up</u>, you'd sell it for £2 + 25% = <u>£2.50</u>.

2) Work out how much the product costs and increase the price to get the required <u>profit margin</u>. If the product <u>costs £2</u> to make, and you want a <u>20% profit margin</u>, this means that £2 is 80% of your required selling price.
So 80% = 200p
1% = 200 ÷ 80 = 2.5p
100% = 2.5p × 100 = 250p
So you'd sell it for <u>£2.50</u>.

Careful here — notice that a <u>25% mark-up</u> is the <u>same</u> as a <u>20% profit margin</u>. That's because the <u>mark-up</u> is expressed as a percentage of the <u>cost of making</u> the product — 50p is 25% of £2. But the <u>profit margin</u> is expressed as a percentage of the <u>selling price</u> — 50p is 20% of £2.50.

Who'd have thought pricing was so complicated...

There's lots to learn on this page. Try to think up some <u>more examples</u> for each of the different <u>market-led</u> strategies. And make sure you understand the difference between <u>mark-ups</u> and <u>profit margins</u>.

Promotion — Advertising

Next up it's the third P — promotion. We'll start with good old advertising, although there's more to promotion than just adverts (as you'll soon see). Advertising is any message about itself or its products that the firm has paid for. You need to know why, how and where firms advertise — and what the effects are on the consumer.

Firms **Advertise** to **Sell More** Products

There are four reasons why firms advertise:

> 1) To make consumers aware of new products.
> 2) To remind consumers about existing products.
> 3) To persuade consumers to switch from rival products.
> 4) To improve the image of the business.

The ultimate aim of all four, of course, is to sell more products.

Where They Advertise Depends on **Three Things**

1) Your target audience. If you want to sell lace doilies to women over 55, do not place your advert in 'Which Skateboard' magazine.

2) The size of your market. If you are launching 'Death Cola' nationwide, do not just advertise in the 'Bognor Regis Morning Gazette'.

3) The size of your advertising budget. Megabucks PLC will be able to advertise in many different media — Cheapskate Enterprises Ltd. may only be able to afford one.

Advertising can be **Informative** or **Persuasive**

- Informative adverts simply describe the product and its features — in an impressive-sounding way of course.
- They leave the consumer free to make up their own minds about the product.

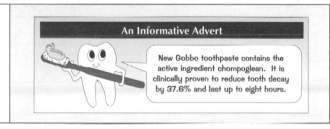

An Informative Advert

New Gobbo toothpaste contains the active ingredient chompoglean. It is clinically proven to reduce tooth decay by 37.6% and last up to eight hours.

A Persuasive Advert

You've got much nicer teeth than the guy I just dumped.

Yes, thanks to Gobbo toothpaste.

If only I'd used Gobbo.

Don't be a loser. Use Gobbo.

- Persuasive adverts try to convince the consumer that they cannot survive without the product. They play on people's fears and vulnerabilities, and create desires where none existed before.
- Some persuasive adverts openly try to convince you that if you do not use the product something nasty might happen to you.
- Others try to persuade you that if you do use the product something nice will happen to you — but the implication is often the same.

Persuasive advertising — I'm not convinced about it...
The best way to learn this page is to make up a table showing why and how firms advertise, then watch some adverts and fill in examples. Decide if the adverts are informative or persuasive too.

Promotion — Advertising Media

You need to know all about the different <u>advertising media</u>. Examiners love to test whether you can pick the <u>best places</u> to advertise particular products.

Each Medium has *Good* and *Bad* Points

1 **TELEVISION** ads can reach <u>millions</u> and you can <u>target</u> people who watch particular programmes. But it's very <u>expensive</u>.

2 **RADIO** is cheaper and you can still target listeners of particular programmes, but it's <u>sound only</u> and audiences are usually <u>smaller</u>.

3 **NEWSPAPERS** and **MAGAZINES** know a lot about their readership so it's <u>easy to target</u> effectively. They'll often be read <u>more than once</u>. But they're static, silent and often not in colour.

4 **POSTERS** and **BILLBOARDS** have a high <u>visual impact</u>, stay in place for a <u>long time</u> and can be seen <u>daily</u> by lots of people. But often they're near roads and drivers only see them for a few seconds, so they <u>can't contain much information</u>. And they're vulnerable to wind, rain and graffiti.

5 **CINEMAS** have a high visual and sound <u>impact</u> and you can target particular films. Unlike all the other media, you have a <u>captive audience</u>. But they're <u>expensive</u> considering the audience size.

6 **LEAFLETS** and **JUNK MAIL** are <u>cheap</u> to produce and distribute, and junk mail's good for targeting. But they're <u>easy to ignore</u>.

7 **INTERNET SITES** can have a high visual impact, be interactive, and <u>link directly</u> to buying the product. But your advert is <u>competing</u> with a lot of other stuff on the net so it has to really grab people.

WHERE TO ADVERTISE

- <u>MASS-MARKET</u> products can be advertised <u>anywhere</u> — television is a particular favourite.
- <u>LOCAL PRODUCTS</u> are best advertised on <u>local radio</u>, in <u>local papers</u>, and on <u>posters and billboards</u>.
- <u>SPECIALIST PRODUCTS</u> are best advertised in <u>specialist magazines</u> and targeted <u>junk mail</u>.

Advantages and *Disadvantages* of *Advertising*

The advantage <u>to a firm</u> in advertising is that it may <u>increase sales</u>. The disadvantage is the <u>opportunity cost</u> — they could be spending the money making more things, or cutting prices.

Advertising has costs and benefits for <u>society</u> as well — here are the main ones.

ADVANTAGES OF ADVERTISING	DISADVANTAGES OF ADVERTISING
1) Advertising gives people <u>information</u> and helps them make a choice.	1) Advertising makes people <u>think they want things</u> they used to be perfectly happy without.
2) Advertising <u>subsidises</u> newspapers and magazines, so they cost less. And it subsidises television programmes and websites, so they're better quality.	2) Advertising costs money, so firms have to <u>charge more</u> for their products to pay for it.
3) Advertising is a big industry — think of all the people it <u>employs</u>.	3) The opportunity cost of employing people in advertising is they could be <u>making things</u>.
	4) Because advertising is expensive, small firms find it <u>difficult to compete</u>.

Advertising — learn the pros and cons...

Lots to learn on this page. I haven't told you whether advertising is good or bad — <u>you decide that</u>. Write a mini-essay explaining the arguments for and against and then <u>say what you think</u>. And remember, the <u>advertising medium</u> you choose depends on <u>what</u> you're selling.

Promotion — Other Methods

Don't make the mistake of thinking promotion is just about advertising. Here are three other ways the firm can get its message across. You need to learn the details.

Sales Promotion — There are Seven Main Methods

These are also called point of sale promotions — because that's where they happen. They're also called below the line promotions because they don't depend on the media.

1) BUY ONE GET ONE FREE (BOGOF). Or buy one get something else free.
2) DISCOUNTS. A good way to get people to notice the product is to stamp '10% off' on the label.
3) COMPETITIONS. Say why new Smello Baked Beans are good for you in less than twenty words — and win a year's supply free.
4) FREE GIFTS. Buy a new skateboard and get a free CD Player with built-in toaster.
5) PRODUCT TRIALS. Set up a stall and invite people to taste new Smello Baked Beans for free.
6) POINT-OF-SALE ADVERTISING. Put tins of new Smello Baked Beans in a special display case at the front of the supermarket.
7) USE OF CREDIT. A good way to get someone to buy a product is to let them buy now but pay later — through hire purchase or a store charge card.

Personal Selling Helps to Promote New Products

This involves talking directly to consumers and getting them to buy the product. It can give the company valuable information about what the public thinks about the product. However, it is very expensive — because it is highly labour intensive.

Some people think this is selling, not marketing — don't believe them.

Public Relations — Any Publicity is Good Publicity

1) Public Relations (PR) is free publicity. It can be either good or bad. There is a saying that "any publicity is good publicity" — this is not completely true, but it makes the important point that sometimes even "bad" publicity can end up helping a firm if it gets their name well known.

2) Most PLCs have a PR department. Its job is to make sure any news stories about the company show it in a good light. Some news events about the company will have been made up by the firm. These are called PR stunts.

3) Another way is to pay film companies to use your products in their films. This is called product placement and it's big business for filmmakers.

Now for some shameless promotion — buy CGP, buy CGP, buy CGP...

So you see there's lots more to promotion than plain and simple advertising. The method of promotion depends on the type of product, size of budget etc. Learn this page using the memorise, cover, and write a mini-essay method.

Place — Where the Product is Sold

Hurrah, we're on to the fourth and final P — place. There are two main decisions to be made here — how the product will reach the customer, and where the product will be sold. These questions are related, but not the same.

Distribution Channels can be **Direct** or **Indirect**

Wholesalers buy products from a wide range of manufacturers and sell them to retailers. Retailers specialise in selling to the consumer. The diagram here shows four distribution channels — 1, 2 and 3 are indirect channels, 4 is a direct channel.

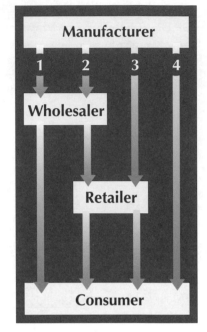

1 MANUFACTURER — WHOLESALER — CONSUMER

This happens when consumers buy the product from a cash and carry warehouse. It's good for the manufacturer because they get bulk orders and the wholesaler takes on the cost of storing the products and the risk of not selling them. The consumer often benefits from lower prices than if they bought from a retailer — but levels of customer service may be lower.

2 MANUFACTURER — WHOLESALER — RETAILER — CONSUMER

This is the traditional route — it's still used mainly in the food and drink industry. The advantages to the manufacturer are the same as for channel 1. The retailer also benefits from dealing with a wholesaler — they reduce the risk by allowing retailers to buy in smaller amounts, and giving them a wide choice of goods. Problems are that goods can take a long time to get from manufacturer to consumer. And manufacturers may be too distant from hearing the needs of consumers.

3 MANUFACTURER — RETAILER — CONSUMER

This route is becoming more common — it's used in the clothing industry. It's faster than dealing with retailers through wholesalers, and the manufacturer gets better consumer feedback about the products. But it's harder for small retailers to avoid having to hold lots of stock.

4 MANUFACTURER — CONSUMER

This is now very popular — examples include factory shops, mail order and internet selling. It's the fastest channel, and often cheapest for the consumer. But it can be more difficult for consumers to shop around, and customer service levels may not be as good.

The **Point of Sale** Says a Lot About the Product

Some producers like to be careful where their product is sold — the point of sale.

For example, some perfume manufacturers market their products as expensive luxury items. They would not be happy if it was sold next to fresh fish on a supermarket shelf.

Direct distribution is becoming more and more popular...

Make sure you learn the four distribution channels — cover the diagram and see if you can draw it. Given any product you should be able to suggest a suitable channel of distribution.

Warm-Up and Worked Exam Questions

Warm-up Questions

1) What does the law of supply say?
2) Explain the difference between skimming and penetration pricing.
3) What is advertising?
4) List five different advertising media.
5) Give five different sales promotion methods.
6) Which distribution channel is the traditional route for most goods, and is still used in the food and drink industry?

Worked Exam Question

There's lots to get to grips with here. Have a look at the questions and answers below.

1   Toward the end of the day, Really Big Supermarket plc reduces the price of its flowers.

a) Use the "law of demand" to explain why the supermarket does this.

The law of demand states that as the price decreases, the quantity ✓ [1 mark]
demanded increases. This predicts that at the lower price, more ✓ [1 mark]
people will want to buy the flowers, so the supermarket will not have ✓ [1 mark]
to throw them away.

Remember to relate the general law to the particular example of the flowers in the supermarket. *(3 marks)*

b) Bunches of carnations normally cost £1.99 at Really Big Supermarket, but are reduced to £1.49 at 6 p.m. The demand for bunches of carnations increases by 30% as a result of the price reduction.
Is demand for bunches of carnations elastic or inelastic? Explain your answer.

Price elasticity of demand $= \dfrac{\% \text{ change in quantity demanded}}{\% \text{ change in price}}$ ✓ [1 mark]

Percentage change in price $= \dfrac{-£0.50}{£1.99} \approx -25\%$, *so p.e.d.* $= \dfrac{30\%}{-25\%} = -1.2$ ✓ [1 mark]

Ignoring minus signs, 1.2 > 1, so the demand for carnations is elastic. ✓ [1 mark]

If you just write "elastic", you'll only get 1 mark. You need to show your working. *(3 marks)*

c) If a can of soup costs 35p from the manufacturer, and the supermarket wants a mark-up of 15%, what will be the selling price of the product?
✓ [1 mark for any correct method]

Mark-up of 15% on 35p = 1.15 x 35p = 40.25p = 40p ✓ [1 mark]

(2 marks)

d) Give two reasons why customers purchase their groceries from Really Big Supermarket plc, rather than direct from the manufacturer.

It is convenient for customers to buy groceries from the
supermarket because they can buy other products at the same ✓ [1 mark]
time. Customers are also able to buy products singly rather than
in large quantities. ✓ [1 mark]

(2 marks)

Exam Questions

1 Yummy Choc plc, an established chocolate manufacturer, is launching a new chocolate bar called "Bloater". "Bloater" will be the same price as similar competitor products.

a) Why do you think chocolate manufacturers often use competition pricing?

....

....

....

(3 marks)

b) Yummy Choc intends to use a persuasive advertising campaign to promote the new chocolate bar. What is persuasive advertising?

....

....

(2 marks)

2 A newly established engineering business is considering using cost-plus pricing to work out the sales price of its products. The business intends to sell precision-engineered steel components to other businesses.

a) Explain the term "cost-plus" pricing.

....

....

(2 marks)

b) Discuss which media you think the engineering business should use for its advertising campaign.

....

....

....

....

(8 marks)

c) Instead of using cost-plus pricing, it has been suggested that the business should use penetration pricing. To what extent would this be a sensible strategy?

....

....

....

....

(10 marks)

Revision Summary for Section Two

Well, we've run out of facts about marketing so you know what that means — time to make sure you've learned the ones I've told you about. You'll need your calculator for some of them. Answers to all number questions are at the bottom of the page — so you can cheat if you want to, but it won't do you any good because you won't learn a thing that way.

1) What are the 4 Ps in the marketing mix?

2) List the seven main ways that markets are segmented.

3) Give three advantages and three disadvantages for field research and desk research.

4) What is the difference between quantitative and qualitative data?

5) Is this an open question or a closed question?

6) What's the difference between a random sample and a targeted sample?

7) What type of chart would you use to show market share proportions?

8) Draw a sketch of the product life cycle.

9) When are a product's sales highest?

   a) maturity;   b) saturation;   c) January.

10) What is an extension strategy?

11) What happens if you don't achieve product differentiation?

12) Why does the demand curve slope downwards?

13) Why does the supply curve slope upwards?

14) Sketch a demand and supply diagram using the data on the right.

   a) What is the equilibrium price and quantity?

   b) What is happening at a price of £6?

      i) consumers are desperate to buy and there's a shortage.

      ii) producers are making too much and there's a surplus.

   c) How about at a price of £21?

Price	Demand	Supply
3	18	2
6	16	4
9	14	6
12	12	8
15	10	10
18	8	12
21	6	14
24	4	16
27	2	18

15) Name the five different market-led pricing strategies.

16) A firm works out it costs £4.50 to make each basketball. What price should it charge if it uses the following cost-plus methods:

   a) a 15% mark-up;   b) a 20% profit-margin;   c) a 30% mark-up;   d) 40% profit-margin.

17) What are the four reasons why firms advertise?

18) What three things influence where a firm will advertise?

19) How is persuasive advertising different from informative advertising?

20) Give three examples of point-of-sale promotions.

21) What is product placement?

22) Why might manufacturers like dealing with a wholesaler?

23) Which parts of the distribution chain are NOT used in a direct channel?

24) What are the advantages and disadvantages of a direct distribution channel?

14) a) £15, 10; b) (i);
c) (ii)
16 a) £5.18; b) £5.63;
c) £5.85; d) £7.50.

Primary, Secondary and Tertiary Industry

Production is all about <u>where and how</u> goods and services are produced. There are <u>three sectors</u> of industry — you need to know what they are.

1 The **Primary** Sector Produces **Raw Materials**

Raw materials are any <u>natural resources</u> which are used to produce goods or services.

1) They can be <u>extracted</u> from the ground — the <u>mining</u> industry provides coal, oil, gas and metals like iron and gold, and the <u>quarrying</u> industry provides stone.

2) They can be <u>grown</u>. The <u>forestry</u> industry chops down rainforests and grows timber on plantations. The <u>farming</u> industry grows food. Animals are also classed as a natural resource — so farmers who breed and slaughter animals are in the primary sector.

3) They can be <u>collected</u> — like <u>deep sea fishing</u> "collects" fish from the sea.

2 The **Secondary** Sector Manufactures **Goods**

<u>Manufacturing</u> is the process of turning raw materials into <u>finished goods</u>. Manufactured goods can be either <u>capital</u> goods or <u>consumer</u> goods.

1) CAPITAL GOODS are used to help <u>make other goods</u> or provide services — examples are welding equipment and delivery vans.

2) CONSUMER GOODS go straight to the <u>final consumer</u>. There are two types: <u>consumables</u> get used up when consumed, like pencils and cans of beans; and <u>consumer durables</u> last a longer time, like TVs and freezers.

3) The <u>building</u> and <u>construction</u> industries are also in the secondary sector. And so are the <u>utilities</u> — companies that supply water, gas and electricity.

3 The **Tertiary** Sector Provides **Services**

<u>Services</u> are provided for the benefit of others. They are <u>intangible</u> — and they often <u>get used up</u> at the time they're consumed.

1) Some services are provided for <u>businesses</u> — like distribution of goods, warehousing and advertising.

2) Some services are provided for <u>consumers</u> — like hairdressing or restaurant meals.

3) <u>Financial</u> services are used by <u>both</u> businesses and consumers — like banking and insurance.

Learn about sectors — and get in the zone...

This is a <u>nice straightforward</u> start to production. Make sure you know <u>all three sectors</u> and understand the <u>flow of activity</u> between them. Just think about the humble fork — starts off life as metal extracted in the primary sector, undergoes its fork-like transformation in the secondary sector, and could easily end up in a restaurant in the tertiary sector. Clever stuff.

Specialisation and Interdependence

It's a simple idea — if I'm good at cooking but can't count, and you're good at accounting but your cooking stinks, then our catering business will do much better if I do all the cooking and you do all the accounting. This is called specialisation. You need to know what it means, the problems it can cause and how it leads to interdependence.

Specialisation leads to Division of Labour

Firms use specialisation to make their production more efficient. It's called division of labour — that means they divide up their workers and get each one of them to do a specific job.

1) Workers can play to their strengths — you might be a naturally gifted brain surgeon, say, or a drummer.

2) Skills are improved. If you spend all your time doing brain surgery or drumming, you get better.

3) Firms always try to break up complex production techniques into a series of simple tasks, and get workers to specialise in those tasks.

4) Workers may do the same task hundreds of times a day — so they get very efficient at it. And this improves the firm's productivity.

Division of Labour has its Problems

It's not all good news, though. Often you have to specialise in something more boring than brain surgery, like screwing the same little bolt onto an endless production line of mopeds.

1) Workers may get bored doing the same thing every day — resulting in low job satisfaction.

2) This can lead to poor quality products, more absenteeism and frequent industrial action.

3) A problem with one group of workers may halt production in the whole business.

4) Workers can become over-specialised — they have difficulty finding another job if their skills are no longer in demand. Unemployment due to occupational immobility may result.

Specialisation Makes Firms Interdependent

- It's not just workers in firms who specialise — firms themselves specialise too. One firm will grow cocoa, another will process it, another will ship it. One firm will make chocolate bars, another will sell them. You generally don't get one firm trying to do all these things — it's not very efficient.

- Firms specialise in what they're best at. This means they don't just supply goods and services to consumers — they also supply each other.

- Firms are interdependent with businesses in the same production chain. If there's a crisis in the cocoa growing industry, Chocs-R-Us are in trouble too.

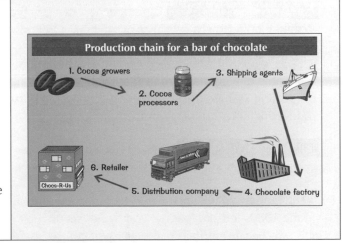

Production chain for a bar of chocolate

1. Cocoa growers
2. Cocoa processors
3. Shipping agents
4. Chocolate factory
5. Distribution company
6. Retailer — Chocs-R-Us

The work done at each stage in a production chain makes the product more valuable than it was before. This is called adding value. It allows businesses to make a profit, since they can sell the product on to the next stage for more than it cost them to buy it.

Specialisation leads to interdependence...

Specialisation is all about concentrating on what you're good at. Sounds sensible, but make sure you know the problems as well as the benefits. Learn, cover, then scribble them down. You'll need to understand how specialisation leads to interdependence — have a go at drawing your own production chain too.

38

Location of Production

All firms, whether they produce goods or services, have to decide <u>where to locate</u>. This often comes down to a choice between being <u>close to their customers</u> or producing where it's <u>cheapest</u> — but there are lots of other possible considerations too. For example, membership of the European Union is persuading more firms to locate production on mainland Europe.

Location is Influenced by Eleven Main Factors

1) **LOCATION OF RAW MATERIALS.** Some firms, such as iron and steel manufacturers, use up a lot of raw materials in making their goods. These <u>bulk-reducing firms</u> locate near to the <u>source</u> of their <u>raw materials</u>, or near to a port — to lower the cost of <u>transporting</u> the raw materials.

2) **LOCATION OF THE MARKET.** Other firms, like breweries, pay more to transport their finished products. These <u>bulk-increasing firms</u> find it cheapest to locate near to their <u>customers</u>. Some <u>services</u>, such as dentists and florists, locate where people can easily get to them.

3) **LABOUR SUPPLY.** Firms who need <u>skilled labour</u> need to locate where they can find these people — often this means industries <u>cluster together</u>, like computer firms in Silicon Valley. Firms who want to <u>keep wages low</u> may have to locate in areas of <u>high unemployment</u>.

4) **TRANSPORT AND COMMUNICATION LINKS.** Firms need to be close to <u>sea ports</u> or <u>airports</u> if they are <u>importers</u> or <u>exporters</u>. Good <u>road</u> and <u>rail links</u> are needed to transport goods and people quickly around the country. Firms need good <u>telephone</u> and <u>postal</u> services as well.

5) **LAND AND PREMISES.** Firms have to find <u>available land or premises</u> which suit their needs — e.g. which are the right size and have the required facilities. The <u>cost of land or premises</u> is an important factor in influencing location. Costs <u>vary between regions</u>, and tend to be higher in town or city centres than in outlying areas. On top of all that, firms who wish to build new premises or develop existing ones will require <u>planning permission</u> from the local authority.

6) **ECONOMIES OF CONCENTRATION.** Sometimes being <u>near your competitors</u> is a good idea. There'll be lots of local skilled labour. Your customers will know where to come. And your <u>suppliers</u> will also want to locate near you — this will <u>reduce</u> transport costs and delays.

7) **GOVERNMENT POLICY.** Governments often pay <u>big multinationals</u> to locate in their country. <u>Regional policy</u> gives subsidies or tax breaks to firms locating in areas of <u>high unemployment</u>.

8) **HISTORY AND TRADITION.** <u>Certain areas</u> have <u>historically</u> been linked with <u>certain industries</u> — for example, Newcastle upon Tyne with ship building. This is because there were advantages to businesses of locating in these areas. <u>If these advantages still exist today</u>, then it makes sense for similar businesses to follow tradition and locate in the same place.

9) **INDUSTRIAL INERTIA.** Firms who have been in one place for a long time might find that high <u>costs of relocation</u> put them off moving, even though it might be cheaper in the long run.

10) **PERSONAL REASONS.** Owners and managers are human. They want somewhere <u>nice to live</u>. In the 1980s lots of Japanese companies set up their new European divisions in Britain. Some said this was because Britain had better <u>golf courses</u> than anywhere else.

11) **CLIMATE.** It's obvious but important — especially in <u>agriculture</u>.

A combination of all or some of the above factors usually influences location decisions. Each factor will be important in <u>some</u> industries and not so important in others. Try to think of some <u>examples</u> for each factor — then think of some <u>industries</u> and decide what the most important location factors will be for them.

Location, location, location...
<u>Only eleven</u> to learn — it could be worse. When you get a question on location, the <u>key thing</u> is to discuss only the factors that are <u>relevant</u> to the situation you're given. Don't go wittering on about all eleven if they don't apply.

SECTION THREE — PRODUCTION

Warm-Up and Worked Exam Questions

Warm-up Questions

1) In which sector of industry is farming?
2) Which sector provides services for the benefit of others?
3) The process of turning raw materials into finished goods describes which sector?
4) Why do firms use specialisation?
5) What word describes the way in which firms rely on each other?
6) Being near your competitors is sometimes a good idea. What term is used to describe this?

Worked Exam Questions

Unlike firms specialising in what they are best at, you have to know all the information for your exam.
Look through and understand these worked exam questions, then try the practice questions on the next page.

1   Andrew Barnes runs a firm that makes furniture for people. He is thinking of introducing specialisation to make his production more efficient.

a)   Which sector of industry is Andrew in?

Secondary ✓ [1 mark]

(1 mark)

b)   He provides consumer goods. Describe what is meant by this term and give an example.

Consumer goods are goods that go straight to the final
✓ [1 mark] ✓ [1 mark]   *Here you get one mark for the definition*
consumer, for example, TVs.   *and one mark for an example.*

(2 marks)

c)   Describe the possible drawbacks for Andrew of introducing specialisation.

Workers may get bored doing the same job all the time, which
may result in low job satisfaction. ✓ [1 mark] *This could lead to poor*
quality products or greater absenteeism. ✓ [1 mark] ✓ [1 mark]

(3 marks)

2   Choosing the right location for a business can be vital to its success.

a)   Suggest three factors that might be taken into account when relocating a business.
✓ [1 mark]   ✓ [1 mark]   ✓ [1 mark]
Location of raw materials, location of the market, labour supply.
Other possible answers: transport and communication links, land and premises, economies
of concentration, government policy, history and tradition, personal reasons, climate.

(3 marks)

b)   Some firms are said to suffer from "industrial inertia". Explain what this term means.

Firms who have been in one place for a long time might find that
the high costs of relocation put them off moving, ✓ [1 mark] *even if it might*
be cheaper to relocate in the long term. ✓ [1 mark]

(2 marks)

Exam Questions

1   Peter Jones is a manufacturer and retailer of pine furniture. His business is currently based in a small village where he has lived all his life, and Peter uses local wood in his products. He is planning on expanding the business and is considering relocating to the nearest city, which is seventy miles away.

Do you think Peter should relocate to the city? Give reasons for your answer.

....

....

....

....

....

....

....

(8 marks)

2   James Right owns a clothes shop. He gets products from a local clothing manufacturer who in turn buys his fabric from a wool mill in Scotland.

a)   James Right is said to be interdependent with other firms. What is meant by the term interdependent?

....

....

(1 mark)

b)   James Right is part of a production chain for clothing. Give two reasons why production chains exist.

....

....

(2 marks)

c)   Unfortunately, the wool mill in Scotland didn't produce as much fabric as normal last year. What effect might this have had upon James Right's business?

....

....

....

....

(3 marks)

Methods of Production

This page covers three methods of production. You need to learn what each one is and which types of products it is best suited for. This is a favourite topic with the examiners so make sure you know it.

❶ Job Production is Making One Thing at a Time

1) Job production is used when a firm manufactures individual, unique products. Each product has a unique design based upon the customer's specification. If they're made in a factory, the firm will need to retool its factory each time it makes a new product.

2) These products often require highly skilled labour and have a high labour-to-capital ratio — they can be very labour intensive.

3) They're usually expensive and take a long time to make. But they're also high quality.

4) Examples include building ships, bridges and handmade crafts such as furniture and made-to-measure clothes.

❷ Mass (or Flow) Production is Making Lots of Things Continuously

1) This is the opposite of job production. All products are identical and the aim is to produce as many as possible. To be efficient, production has to be continuous with no stoppages — many mass production factories operate 24 hours a day with workers rotating in shifts.

2) The aim is to gain from economies of scale and so produce at minimum unit cost. Mass production is highly capital intensive — it costs a lot to buy the equipment but it's cheap to run it afterwards. Modern mass production techniques use robots, not people, to do most of the work.

3) It is used for mass-market products. Most modern consumer goods are produced this way — examples include chocolate bars, personal stereos and toasters.

> The first modern mass producer of identical products was Henry Ford with his Model T car.
> He joked that his customers could have any colour Model T they liked — as long as it was black.

4) Mass production is also sometimes called continuous flow production.

❸ Batch Production is a Mixture of the Two

1) This is a combination of job and mass production. Firms use mass production techniques to make a batch of one thing then stop, reorganise, and make a batch of something else.

2) It is suited to products that are identical to each other, but are only produced in limited quantities — or for a limited amount of time.

3) Examples include furniture, where producers make a limited number of many different designs, and building a batch of identical houses on a new housing estate.

Job production — not a solution to unemployment...

The type of production you should choose depends on what you're making. Learn these three methods and the types of products they're best suited for. Cover the page, write down the headings, then scribble about each.

Organising Production

Organising production is about organising your workforce in the most <u>efficient</u> way. Managers have to choose between giving workers <u>rigid, repetitive tasks</u>, and giving them <u>some freedom</u> to work as they want. Sounds confusing but don't panic — it's all explained below.

1 *Process* Layout — Groups *Tasks* Together

1) This is often used in <u>job and batch</u> production. You <u>divide up</u> the production process into lots of parts, and each is carried out separately on a different part of the <u>production floor</u>.

2) When work at each stage is completed the <u>semi-finished</u> product is <u>moved</u> to the part of the factory where the next stage is carried out. So you might have one group of workers <u>welding</u> bits of metal together on one part of the floor — then they move the welded bits to another part of the floor, where another group of workers <u>paints</u> them.

2 Production **Assembly Lines** are Quick but Dull

1) Assembly lines are the <u>classic way</u> to organise <u>mass</u> production.

2) The production process is first <u>divided up</u> in exactly the same way as process layout. The difference is that then the whole factory is built around a <u>conveyor belt</u> which carries the product along the <u>production line</u>. The firm can speed up or slow down production by <u>changing the speed</u> of the production line.

3) At each stage a worker will perform <u>set tasks</u> as the product travels past. Both the tasks and the tools needed are <u>identical</u> for every product. All each worker needs to do is learn how to <u>do their own task</u> — then repeat it possibly <u>thousands</u> of times a day.

4) This method has all the <u>advantages</u> and <u>disadvantages</u> of division of labour — it's <u>efficient</u> but <u>boring</u>.

5) Good examples are <u>car</u> and <u>chocolate bar</u> production.

There's more about methods of motivation in Section 4.

3 *Team* Production Tries to **Keep Workers Interested**

There are two main methods of team production — <u>group production</u> and <u>cell production</u>. Both aim to reduce the problems of division of labour and the production line by giving workers more <u>variety and responsibility</u>.

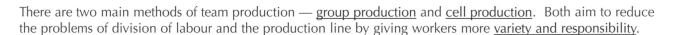

1) <u>GROUP PRODUCTION</u> — a team of workers are responsible for making the <u>whole product</u>. They are given their own place and tools to do the job. They need to be <u>multi-skilled</u>.

2) <u>CELL PRODUCTION</u> — a team of workers are responsible for a number of tasks at a <u>single stage</u> of the process. It is up to the team to decide how to organise itself.

These are also methods of "lean production" — see p43.

More <u>capital equipment</u> may be needed for each team, and the workers may need more training. But the aim is to finance this out of <u>higher labour productivity</u> — if workers are less bored, they might get more done.

Organising revision — the key to exam success...

This page <u>follows on nicely</u> from the last one — that's because how you <u>organise</u> your production depends on which <u>method</u> of production you use. Make sure you learn <u>how</u> each one works and <u>when</u> it's used.

Productivity and Quality Management

Businesses need to be <u>competitive</u> — <u>lean production</u> and <u>quality management</u> are two important strategies that can help achieve this. The next two pages cover the <u>main methods</u> firms use to carry out these strategies. You need to <u>learn</u> them.

Lean Production *Uses as* Few Resources *as Possible*

<u>Lean production</u> is a Japanese approach to making products which aims to use as <u>few resources</u> as possible. <u>Waste</u> and <u>stocks</u> of <u>raw materials</u> are kept to a <u>minimum</u> and workers are encouraged to <u>think about ways</u> to improve their productivity.

Four Stock Control *Methods...*

Stock Control Graphs

A <u>traditional</u> method is to use <u>stock control graphs</u>. In this example, the firm has set the <u>re-order level</u> at 1000 widgets. When stocks fall to 1000 widgets they will re-order 500 widgets. The hope is that by the time the <u>new stock</u> arrives the firm's stock level won't have fallen below the <u>minimum level</u>. A <u>computerised</u> stock control system can calculate stock levels and place orders <u>automatically</u>.

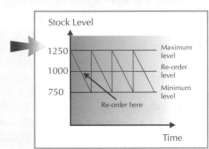

Just-in-time (JIT)

This is a Japanese method that aims to keep stock levels to the <u>bare minimum</u> — ideally zero. The aim is that stock arrives in the factory <u>immediately</u> before it is used. The main <u>benefit</u> is that it reduces the <u>cost</u> of having to keep stocks. The main <u>problem</u> is that it requires a lot of <u>co-ordination</u> between the firm and its suppliers — otherwise the firm could run out of stock.

Just-in-case (JIC)

This is a method of operating a production and distribution system with <u>buffer stocks</u> of items at every stage of the process — from raw materials to finished products, <u>just in case</u> there is a supply shortage or customer demand increases unexpectedly. The idea is that even if there is a problem at one stage of the production process, the buffer stocks will mean there can still be <u>continuous production</u>. The <u>main problem</u> is that firms can be left with big stockpiles of items. JIC has tended to be <u>replaced</u> by JIT and other stock control methods.

Kanban

Here's another Japanese idea. Kanban means <u>signboard</u>. Cards are used at each stage in the production process so that employees can <u>signal</u> to each other when raw materials are needed. The <u>theory</u> is that this helps keep stock levels to a minimum.

Kaizen *means* Continuous Improvement

1) Another fairly new idea — surprisingly it was invented in Japan. It means <u>continuous improvement</u>. Basically the idea is that <u>workers</u> are encouraged to <u>think continually</u> about ways to <u>improve the product</u> and make the production process <u>more efficient</u>.

2) The kaizen approach requires that workers operate in <u>teams</u> such as cells (see page 42) with each team meeting regularly to discuss problems and solutions.

3) This system is a <u>much cheaper</u> way of increasing efficiency than investing in new resources, and leads to <u>increased motivation</u> as workers feel more involved with the production process.

Rationalisation *— Reorganising to* Increase Efficiency

1) This is another method that firms can use to <u>increase efficiency</u>. Firms use rationalisation when they need to <u>reduce overhead costs</u> in order to reduce their <u>break-even point</u>. *There's lots more on break-even on p66.*

2) <u>Methods</u> include
   - closing an administrative department and delegating their work elsewhere
   - closing a factory and moving the production to another site
   - reducing the number of managers

3) Rationalisation can be <u>bad news</u> for some workers as it often results in redundancies.

Productivity and Quality Management

You might have the most productive business in the world, but if your products aren't up to scratch you won't get very far. This is why quality management is so important. Learn the methods below.

Quality Assurance is all about Satisfying Customers

For businesses to be competitive, they have to satisfy the needs of their customers. If faulty goods reach the market, customers will become dissatisfied and stop buying the product.

> Quality Assurance is the attempt to satisfy customers by making sure that quality standards are agreed and met throughout the organisation.

> Quality awards are evidence of high standards. These show customers that certain standards have been met. An example is BS 5750, which the British Standards Institution gives to firms with good quality assurance systems.

Three of the methods that firms use to carry out quality assurance are described below.

1 Quality Control — Spotting Problems Before it's Too Late

1) Quality control involves checking products to make sure quality standards are being met. This used to be done by quality inspectors, but some firms now encourage workers to check their own quality.

2) Products are checked for things like design, appearance, defects and safety, usually at three different stages of the production process. The aim is to stop faulty goods from reaching the customer.

STAGE 1	STAGE 2	STAGE 3
Check the raw materials and components from suppliers. In mass production, it's impossible to check all items, so a random sample is checked instead.	Check the work in progress. Random samples of products are checked for quality. Machinery may also be checked at this stage.	Check the finished product. A random sample of products is tested to see if they meet the required quality. Any faulty items are removed.

3) Defects can be detected as they happen rather than waiting until products are finished. This helps businesses to reduce waste.

4) Quality control can be expensive if a whole batch of goods has to be scrapped. But the cost to the business would be much greater if dissatisfied customers stopped buying their products.

2 Total Quality Management — Establishing a Culture of Quality

1) Total Quality Management (TQM) is a strategy which aims to make quality the responsibility of every employee in an organisation. Employees are encouraged to think about the needs of the customers at all times. The emphasis is on getting things right first time — this helps to reduce costs by cutting down on waste.

2) Quality Circles are an important feature of TQM — the idea is closely linked to the kaizen philosophy (p43). Groups of workers from various departments meet regularly to identify quality problems and suggest solutions. Quality circles can be very effective at raising quality because they utilise the knowledge and expertise of the factory floor staff — as long as they can be persuaded to share their ideas.

3) Another feature of TQM is the emphasis on the quality of after-sales service as well as on the quality of production.

4) The downside is that it takes a long time to introduce TQM. Employees can be demotivated — TQM can seem like a lot of extra work. Workers need training so that they see quality as their responsibility.

3 Statistical Process Control — Another Method of Quality Assurance

The idea here is that firms collect data about how each process that takes place is performing. The data is then compared against a benchmark which might be the best performance that can be expected. The aim is to identify why problems occur so that solutions can be found.

You'd better learn all these methods — just-in-case...

So basically businesses want to make high quality products using as few resources as possible. It's a lot to ask — and so is learning these two pages. But it has to be done. Remember, quality and lean production are closely linked — high quality products means less wastage, which means fewer resources are used.

Warm-Up and Worked Exam Questions

Warm-up Questions

1) What is the name given to the production method which is used to make one thing at a time?
2) During which two production methods is the 'process layout' system of organisation used?
3) What is the main aim of using team production?
4) Describe the main purpose of the just-in-time (JIT) stock control system.
5) What is BS 5750 an example of?
6) What do the initials TQM stand for?

Worked Exam Questions

Revision's a bit like a production line — read, understand and learn the information, then go through these worked exam questions, then try some questions on your own.

1 British Sweets and Chocolates plc produce confectionery that is sold to retail outlets throughout the UK and Europe. The company mainly uses mass production methods to produce its products.

a) Give two reasons why chocolate bars are produced using mass production methods.

The products are identical and can be mass produced very quickly. [1 mark] [1 mark]

Make sure you know which types of products the different methods of production are best suited to. (2 marks)

b) Give two reasons why making products using mass production is cheaper than making products to a customer's specification.

Labour required for mass production is generally cheaper because it is unskilled. [1 mark] *The cost of any machinery and labour is spread over a high number of units.* [1 mark] *You could also say "It takes less time to mass produce each unit."*

(2 marks)

2 a) Just-in-case is a method of stock control which involves keeping 'buffer stocks'.
i) Give two advantages to a manufacturing firm of using the just-in-case method.

The manufacturing firm will be able to satisfy a sudden rise [1 mark] *in demand. If there is a delay in the supply of raw materials,* *the firm will still be able to meet its orders.* [1 mark]

(2 marks)

ii) What is the main disadvantage of this method of stock control?

The firm could be left with a lot of unused stock. [1 mark]

(1 mark)

b) Explain why the just-in-time stock control method is difficult for a firm to manage?

There needs to be a lot of co-ordination between the firm and its [1 mark] *supplier to make sure that it doesn't run out of stock.* [1 mark]

There are 2 marks available here — you have to explain your reason to get the second mark. (2 marks)

46

Exam Questions

1   The managing director of John's Manufacturing and Retail Limited has told his departmental managers that he is very worried about the increasing number of customers complaining about the quality of the firm's products. The managing director thinks that they should adopt a Total Quality Management (TQM) approach to quality assurance.

   a)   What is quality assurance?

   ....

   ....
   (1 mark)

   b)   At what three stages of production does quality control usually take place?

   ....

   ....
   (3 marks)

   c)   The purpose of TQM is to establish a culture of quality within the firm. Quality circles are an important feature of TQM.

      i)   What are quality circles? Briefly explain their main purpose.

   ....

   ....
   (2 marks)

      ii)   Why is the use of quality circles thought to be very effective in improving quality control?

   ....
   (1 mark)

      iii)   Why do you think the managing director might prefer TQM to more traditional methods of quality control?

   ....

   ....

   ....
   (3 marks)

2   a)   Explain how workers might benefit from team production.

   ....
   (1 mark)

   b)   Describe the difference between group and cell production methods.

   ....

   ....
   (2 marks)

Revision Summary for Section Three

This is quite a short section, but don't let that fool you into thinking you can ignore it. There's lots of important stuff to learn here. Remember that examiners love to test you on whether you know about the various ways that production takes place — and which methods are suitable for particular goods. Examiners often complain that students don't know the difference between the three methods — so make sure that you know them. Now go over these questions until you can answer them in your sleep.

1) Write down a definition of the primary, secondary and tertiary sectors. Give two examples of each.
2) What is the difference between a capital good and a consumer good?
3) Why does division of labour lead to more efficiency?
4) Name three problems with division of labour.
5) Why are firms interdependent?
6) What is meant by 'adding value'?
7) Draw a production chain for chocolate and say whether each stage is an example of primary, secondary or tertiary activity.
8) Where do bulk-reducing firms need to locate?
9) Where do bulk-increasing firms need to locate?
10) Why might a firm locate in an area of high unemployment?
11) Explain two benefits of economies of concentration.
12) What does industrial inertia mean?
13) What is the difference between job production and mass production?
14) What is the production method that combines elements of them both?
15) Which method of production should be used in the following examples?
    a) making tee-shirts of varying colours and styles.
    b) making tins of baked beans.
    c) building luxury cruise ships to order, so each ship is a different design.
16) Building the factory around a conveyor belt turns process layout production into what kind of production?
17) Name one advantage and one disadvantage of team production.
18) What does lean production aim to eliminate?
19) Draw a stock control chart for baked beans to show a maximum stock level of 300 cans, a minimum stock level of 100 cans and a re-order level of 200 cans.
20) Explain one benefit and one problem of JIT.
21) What is the main disadvantage of JIC?
22) What is Kanban?
23) What does Kaizen mean?
24) Give two things a firm might do to reduce their overhead costs?
25) What might happen to a business if they allow faulty goods to reach their customers?
26) What does the British Standards Institution do?
27) Give three methods that a firm could use to carry out quality assurance.
28) Describe what is checked at each stage of quality control.
29) What does TQM stand for?
30) Give one advantage and one disadvantage of TQM.

Workers

This section is all about the <u>people</u> involved in businesses. How they're recruited, trained, managed, motivated — even how their disputes are dealt with. Much of this is the work of the <u>Personnel department</u>. We'll start off with a page about the <u>workers</u> themselves.

People Work for *Different Reasons*

Most people go to work to earn an <u>income</u>. This is partly to give a <u>secure standard of living</u> — but also to give money for <u>luxuries</u>. Some people choose to do whatever job earns them the <u>most money</u>. Others may take some of the following <u>non-financial reasons</u> into account.

1) <u>Job satisfaction</u> is important to a lot of people. Many will take <u>less money</u> if it means they have <u>interesting</u> work, <u>good working conditions</u> (clean, quiet, air-conditioned), <u>convenient working hours</u>, useful <u>perks</u> (such as employee discounts in stores, or free childcare for working mothers) and <u>good holidays</u>.

2) Some people are drawn to work which does <u>good for others</u> — it's more important to them to have a <u>fulfilling</u> job than a well-paid one. Examples include social workers, nurses and teachers.

3) Going to work is a good way to <u>meet people</u>, make friends and socialise. The unemployed often have fewer opportunities to meet people.

4) Working is good for your <u>self-confidence</u> — it makes people think that they are <u>valued by society</u>. Being unemployed carries a low status. Some people choose jobs which carry especially <u>high status</u>, like being a doctor. Or which give them a <u>status symbol</u>, like a company car.

5) Jobs give people an <u>identity</u>. You can feel like you <u>belong to a group</u> of people — be it lawyers, bricklayers, whatever. If you ask people "what do you do", they will often think first of their <u>job</u> instead of their hobbies.

People Have Different *Skills* and *Attributes*

SKILLS

These are the <u>requirements</u> needed to do a job — for example, the ability to <u>type</u> 100 words per minute, or to make salads. They are learned through <u>training</u>.

ATTRIBUTES

These are the <u>personal qualities</u> that make someone suitable for a particular type of job. For example, <u>typists</u> have to be quick-fingered, sales staff need to be <u>patient and polite</u>, accountants have to enjoy working with figures and have a good <u>eye for detail</u>.

Some People Want *Promotion* — But *Not Everyone*

Some people are <u>career-minded</u> — keen to get promoted. These people like to be in control and take responsibility.

Others are just happy to turn up, <u>do their job</u> — and then go home. They are happy to let others tell them what to do.

Repeat after me — we are all individuals...

There's <u>nothing too difficult</u> on this page. If you can remember the reasons why people work, that's a <u>good start</u>, but you'll also need to learn the <u>explanations</u> that go with them. They're mostly <u>common sense</u> when you think about them. Make sure you know how a skill is <u>different</u> from an attribute.

Employment and the Law

This page is crammed <u>full of facts</u>, I'm afraid. Any employer who gets anything on this page wrong is in <u>deep trouble</u>. There are <u>four areas</u> of employment law you need to learn.

1 *Recruitment* and *Contracts* of *Employment*

1) Recruitment procedures must not <u>discriminate</u> against women, ethnic minorities or the disabled. This is covered by the <u>Sex Discrimination Act 1975</u>, the <u>Race Relations Act 1976</u> and the <u>Disability Discrimination Act 1975</u>.

2) All employees must receive a <u>written contract of employment</u> within <u>one month</u> of starting work. This is covered by the <u>Employment Rights Act 1996</u>.

3) All employers must provide a <u>discipline procedure</u> for all employees. Minor problems may receive a <u>verbal or written warning</u>. More serious offences that are grounds for instant dismissal will be listed. This is covered by the <u>Employment Protection Act of 1975</u>.

4) The 1998 European Union <u>Working Time Directive</u> limits the working week to <u>48 hours</u>.

5) The Government sets a <u>National Minimum Wage</u> for all workers. In October 2004 it was increased to <u>£4.10/hour</u> for 18-21 year-olds and <u>£4.85/hour</u> if you're 22 or over. The amount is regularly increased, rising in <u>October 2005</u> to <u>£4.25/hour</u> for 18-21 year-olds, <u>£5.05/hour</u> if you're over 22.

2 *Anti-Discrimination* Laws

1) Apart from recruitment the other main <u>equal opportunities</u> issue is <u>pay</u>. The <u>1970 Equal Pay Act</u> says that an employee must be paid the same as another employee doing the <u>same job</u>. The act was intended to give men and women equal pay.

2) Men and women often do <u>different jobs</u> — so exact comparisons are difficult. The <u>1983 Equal Pay Act</u> made it compulsory to give the <u>same pay</u> for <u>work of equal value</u>. So a midwife supervisor should be paid the same as other equivalent managerial jobs.

3) It is also illegal to discriminate against employees with <u>disabilities</u>.

3 *Health and Safety* Legislation

1) The <u>1961 Factories Act</u> set minimum requirements including toilets, washing facilities, lighting and fire escapes.

2) The <u>Health and Safety at Work Act of 1974</u> required all <u>employers</u> and their <u>employees</u> to take <u>responsibility</u> for health and safety.

3) The <u>1992 Workplace Regulations</u> introduced European Union rules including the safe use of <u>computers</u>.

4 *Leaving* Employment

1) The <u>Employment Protection Act 1978</u> protects employees against <u>unfair dismissal</u>. They can only be dismissed if they are incapable of doing their job — like if they're <u>incompetent</u> or have shown <u>gross misconduct</u>.

2) Employees can only be made <u>redundant</u> if the job they are employed to do <u>no longer exists</u> — for example if there is a drop in demand, or <u>automation</u>. The firm <u>cannot re-advertise</u> a redundant job.

3) Employees who think they have been <u>unfairly</u> dismissed or made redundant can appeal to an <u>industrial tribunal</u>. The tribunal can award <u>compensation</u> or <u>reinstate</u> the employee.

Learn all the acts that protect us against discrimination...

Employers can't <u>pretend</u> they <u>don't know</u> these laws exist — and <u>neither can you</u>. You're gonna just have to learn, cover and scribble — and keep on doing it until you've <u>learned them all</u>.

Motivation Theory

Motivation is very important in business — motivated workers will get a lot more done than unmotivated workers. There are three main theories to learn here. Each one tries to explain what managers need to do if they want to motivate their workers to perform their best.

1 Maslow's *Hierarchy of Needs*

Maslow believed that all people are motivated by the same things. The three lower needs at the bottom of the pyramid have to be achieved before the two higher needs can be met.

SELF-ACTUALISATION — people want to feel they are achieving something. Managers should help staff set and reach their own personal targets.

SELF-ESTEEM — people want to feel valued by others. Managers should praise and encourage, and give financial rewards for good performance.

LOVE AND BELONGING — people enjoy the company of others. Managers should encourage teamwork and social contact.

SAFETY — people want to feel safe and secure from harm. Managers should give their workers job security.

PHYSICAL SURVIVAL — people need food, water, shelter, clothing and warmth. These should be met by a basic wage.

Pyramid levels (top to bottom): Self-actualisation, Self-esteem, Love and belonging, Safety, Physical survival

2 Herzberg's *Hygiene Factors*

Herzberg's ideas are much more straightforward than Maslow's. Herzberg believed all the needs of workers can be put into two groups.

1) Hygiene factors are the things a business has to provide to keep workers contented. These include clean, quiet and safe working conditions — as well as adequate rest breaks.

2) Motivating factors are the things that will encourage workers to do their best — like praise from managers, career advancement for good workers and more responsibility.

If the hygiene factors are poor then the motivating factors won't work.

3 McGregor's *Theory X* and *Theory Y*

McGregor believed that there are two types of manager. They motivate workers in different ways.

THEORY X MANAGERS BELIEVE...
Workers are only motivated by money. Workers are lazy, selfish, dislike work and lack ambition. Workers need to be controlled and coerced by managers.

THEORY Y MANAGERS BELIEVE...
Workers are motivated by many needs. Workers can take pride and responsibility in doing a good job. Management should trust workers and help them do their best.

Where's the theory on motivating me to revise...

Examiners are unlikely to ask you to waffle about all three theories, so you're going to have to remember exactly who thought what. McGregor's theory is basically about whether you motivate someone by yelling at them or encouraging them. Maslow's is more tricky — you'll have to learn the triangle and the explanations that go with it.

Two More Motivation Theories

Another two motivation theories to learn — how sneaky of me. And to top it all off, some criticisms of motivation theory for you to learn and impress the neighbours with.

Taylor's Scientific Management

1) Taylor's ideas were formed at the beginning of the twentieth century. At that time workers were usually controlled by supervisors — these were often fellow workers who were good at their job. Taylor thought that this was inefficient.

2) Taylor believed that workers were lazy and were only interested in earning money. His big idea was that the bosses should carry out a time and motion study to work out the most efficient way to perform the tasks that make up a job. Managers would then be appointed to make sure that workers carry out the tasks exactly as planned.

3) The theory was that because workers are controlled by managers their productivity will improve. In practice it wasn't very successful — mainly because of the boredom that results from doing the same tasks all day and every day.

Mayo's Human Relations School

When Taylor's ideas were introduced in the 1920s and 1930s they sometimes worked and sometimes failed — people thought there must be more to motivation than just money.

Mayo thought:

1) that workers are motivated whenever managers take a personal interest in them as people — for example by involving them in decision making;

2) firms need to meet the personal satisfactions of their workers. Firms also need to make sure that the goals of the employees are the same as their goals;

3) that firms should encourage teams of employees to socialise with each other — for example on days out and at office parties.

Problems With Motivation Theory

1) Some of the theories contradict each other — so no single theory is likely to be correct.

2) Many theories were developed a long time ago — when working conditions and the relations between bosses and workers were very different from what they are now. So they may not be very relevant to the motivation needs of workers in the 21st Century.

3) Everyone is different — so no single theory is likely to explain what motivates every employee in a business. For example, people are often motivated by different things at different times in their lives — typically the older you get the more you worry about the future and want security.

Motivation theories have their limitations...

Well, I didn't tell you it would be exciting stuff — so don't blame me. If you add them up there's five motivation theories to learn. But save yourself some time and check out which ones are needed for your exam. There's no point learning the ones you won't be tested on. Unless you're just interested of course. In which case, go ahead.

Financial Rewards

There are <u>lots of facts</u> on this page but it all boils down to <u>two</u> things — what the different ways of <u>paying people</u> are and what work <u>incentives</u> each method gives them.

If People Do **More Work** Their **Wages** Increase...

Wages are paid <u>weekly or monthly</u> — usually to <u>manual</u> workers. Wages are calculated in one of two ways.

1) A TIME RATE pays workers by the hour. If a painter is paid £6 per hour and works 50 hours in a week, their week's wage is £300. Time rate encourages people to work <u>long hours</u> — the problem is they also have an incentive to <u>work slowly</u>. Time rate is best for jobs where <u>measuring output</u> is <u>difficult</u> — like driving a bus.

2) A PIECE RATE is used if the <u>output</u> of each worker <u>can be easily measured</u>. If a worker who sews sleeves onto shirts is paid a piece rate of 10p per sleeve and they sew 2000 sleeves in a week then their weekly wage will be £200. Piece rate encourages people to <u>work quickly</u> — the problem is they work so fast that <u>quality may suffer</u>.

...But a **Salary** Stays the **Same**

1) A <u>salary</u> is a fixed amount paid every <u>month</u>. It is usually paid to <u>office staff</u> who do not directly help to make the product. A salary of £24,000 means you are paid £2000 per month.

2) The <u>advantage</u> of a salary is that the firm and workers both <u>know exactly</u> how much the pay will be. A <u>problem</u> is that it does <u>not</u> link pay to <u>performance</u> in any way.

Employers have to Make **Deductions** from **Gross** Pay

1) <u>Gross pay</u> is the amount of money an employee is <u>paid</u> — their wage or salary. However, the amount that an employee actually gets to <u>keep</u> is called <u>net pay</u>.

2) Net pay is gross pay minus some <u>deductions</u>. Deductions can be <u>compulsory</u> — everyone has to pay <u>income tax</u> and <u>National Insurance contributions</u>. But you can also choose to pay <u>voluntary</u> deductions — like contributions to a <u>pension</u>.

3) <u>Pay slips</u>, like the one opposite, show an employee <u>how much</u> their net pay is and <u>how it's been worked out</u>.

This is just a number that helps your firm calculate how much tax you should pay.

DATE	NAME	TAX CODE	N.I. NUMBER
20/10/04	B. SMART	374L	JB236597A

PAY		DEDUCTIONS		CUMULATIVES TO DATE	
SALARY	1600	INCOME TAX	280	TOTAL GROSS PAY TD	8000
		NAT. INS.	115	GROSS FOR TAX TD	7890
		PENSION	50	TAX PAID TD	1350
				N.I. TD	575
				PENSION TD	250
TOTAL	1600	TOTAL	445	NET PAY 1155	

Performance-Related Pay Matches Rewards to Quality

Performance-related pay (<u>PRP</u>) is becoming more popular — how much people <u>earn</u> depends on how well they <u>work</u>. There are <u>three main types</u> of PRP.

1) <u>Commission</u> is paid to sales staff. They earn a <u>small basic salary</u> and then earn more money for every item they <u>sell</u>.

2) A <u>bonus</u> is a <u>lump sum</u> added to pay, usually once a year. It's paid if the worker has met their <u>performance targets</u>.

3) <u>Profit-sharing</u> gives each worker an <u>agreed share</u> of company <u>profits</u>. If the company does well, the payment will be bigger. A company might also give some of its <u>shares</u> to workers. The <u>better</u> the company does, the more <u>beneficial</u> this will be to the workers.

Fringe Benefits are Extra Incentives for Employees

<u>Fringe</u> benefits are <u>benefits</u> given to employees <u>on top of</u> their salary or wages — like a company car, or discounts on the firm's products.

Different types of payment give workers different incentives...

<u>Three</u> different ways of paying people — although you can <u>top up</u> wages and salaries with <u>PRP</u>. Make sure you know <u>what</u> each method is, <u>who</u> should be paid it and <u>how</u> it might motivate them.

Non-Financial Motivation

If you believe Maslow and Herzberg, these <u>four non-financial</u> means are the <u>best way</u> to motivate people to work better. If you don't, tough — you've still got to learn them.

1 Job **Rotation** — a **Change** is as Good as a Rest

1) Thanks to the wonders of division of labour, most production jobs are <u>boring and repetitive</u>. Job rotation reduces this by occasionally <u>moving</u> workers from <u>one job to another</u>.

2) The <u>benefits</u> are that workers <u>don't get so bored</u>, and <u>learn more jobs</u> — so if someone is ill, someone else will be able to <u>cover</u>.

3) The problem is that <u>one</u> boring job is replaced by <u>another</u> — it doesn't help <u>job satisfaction</u>.

2 Job **Enlargement** — Give Them **More** Things to Do

1) When a worker becomes good at their job, <u>productivity</u> increases — they can do the same work in <u>less time</u>. Job enlargement is when the person is given <u>more tasks</u> to do. This will increase the size of their <u>job description</u>.

2) The <u>advantage</u> is that extra tasks should give the job <u>greater variety</u> — and most people are happy to know that their good performance is being recognised.

3) The <u>problem</u> is that if the person thinks they are just being given <u>more work</u> it can be <u>demotivating</u>.

3 Job **Enrichment** — Give Them **Better** Things to Do

1) The idea of job enrichment is to <u>stop</u> the worker from feeling that their <u>productivity</u> is being <u>punished</u> with <u>more work</u>. The worker is given <u>greater responsibility</u> — for example <u>supervising</u> the work of new staff. This may require more <u>training</u>.

2) A <u>benefit</u> is that the worker may become more <u>motivated</u> and <u>work harder</u>.

3) A <u>problem</u> is that they may expect a <u>pay rise</u> as well.

4 **Kaizen** — Let Them Take **Decisions**

This stuff will look familiar if you've read p43 on lean production.

1) Kaizen is a <u>Japanese</u> word that has become fashionable in some UK businesses. It means <u>continuous improvement</u>. Workers are <u>organised</u> into <u>teams</u> and each team has the <u>responsibility</u> of finding ways to increase its <u>productivity</u> and <u>quality</u> of work.

2) Teams are <u>empowered</u> to take their own decisions — the idea is that motivation and performance will increase. It has been introduced into the UK mainly in the <u>motor industry</u>. Japanese car firms that use it have some of the <u>highest productivity levels</u> in Europe.

Some people say non-financial motivation helps workers achieve their <u>higher needs</u>.

<u>Cynics</u> say it's the bosses' way to get you to <u>work harder</u> for the <u>same money</u>.

Learn these four easy steps to job satisfaction...

A similar page to the last one — more ways to <u>motivate people</u>. I'm sure you can work out why some firms prefer the ones on this page though... Now you know loads about motivation, excellent, but you've got to remember it. If you're still confusing <u>Maslow with Mayo</u>, or <u>job enlargement with job enrichment</u>, read the last 4 pages again.

Management Styles

Managers are the people who have to put all this motivation theory into action. They have the difficult task of setting objectives and organising resources so that these objectives are achieved. Obviously, a well motivated workforce makes their task a lot easier. The style of management they use can have a big effect on the motivation of their workers.

There are Different Types of Management Styles

There are four main management styles. The style a manager uses will depend on the type of organisation, and might need to be adapted to suit different situations — for example, urgent tasks need a different kind of management from routine tasks.

1 AUTHORITARIAN OR AUTOCRATIC STYLE — the manager makes decisions on his or her own. This style can be effective when managing lots of unskilled workers, or when dealing with a crisis. Disadvantages are that it needs lots of supervision and monitoring — workers can't make their own decisions. Also, an authoritarian style can demotivate able and intelligent workers.

2 PATERNALISTIC (FATHERLY) STYLE — the manager still makes decisions, but only after consultation with others. Paternalistic managers explain their decisions to workers to try and persuade them that they are in everyone's interest. They hope that if the workers feel like they're being involved in some way, they'll be more motivated to work harder.

3 DEMOCRATIC STYLE — the manager encourages the workforce to join in the decision making process. They discuss issues with workers, delegate responsibility and listen to advice. Democratic managers have to be good communicators. This style of management shows that the manager has a lot of confidence in the workforce, which can lead to increased motivation. It also takes some of the weight of decision making off the manager.

4 LAISSEZ-FAIRE STYLE — a weak form of leadership. Management rarely interferes in the running of the business, leaving the workforce to get on with trying to achieve objectives with very little help or control from the top. This style can be good for a small, highly motivated team of workers who will enjoy having independence and control over their work. But for workers who need guidance, it'd be a bit of a disaster.

Delegation allows Employees to Make Decisions

Delegation is where an employee is given the authority to make decisions without having to ask their manager first. You need to learn the effects that delegation can have on a business.

ADVANTAGES...
- Motivates employees
- Saves the manager time
- Speeds up decision making

DISADVANTAGES...
- There is more chance of mistakes
- Managers need some way of checking on the work that's been done
- Too much responsibility might be delegated to staff who shouldn't have that amount of authority

I'm delegating responsibility for learning this page to you...

So management styles can be put into four main categories — they range between having complete control, and letting the workforce do as they like. Make sure you can describe each style and the effect it might have on the motivation of a workforce. Then have a think about how much delegation each style involves.

Warm-Up and Worked Exam Questions

Warm-up Questions

1) What is the difference between a skill and an attribute?
2) Under the Health and Safety at Work Act 1974 who has responsibility for safety in the workplace?
3) Describe each of the following motivational theories:
   a) Mayo's Human Relations,   b) Taylor's Scientific Management, c) Maslow's Hierarchy.
4) In the context of salaries, what do the letters PRP stand for?
5) What is the Japanese word that describes the motivational idea of "continuous improvement"?
6) Name the style of management which describes a manager who makes all the decisions on his own.

Worked Exam Question

There's a lot to learn in this section — loads of theories and definitions. You have to make sure you can apply them all to the real world, though, because that's what you'll have to do in the exam.

1   Gee Whizz is a computer retailer with branches nationwide. Each shop has a manager and a number of sales assistants. Shop managers are paid a salary of £18,000. Sales assistants are paid a weekly wage based upon a time-rate system of £5.20 per hour.

a)   State one difference between a salary and a wage.

A salary is fixed monthly, but a wage can change depending upon how much work is done in the month. ✓ [1 mark]

(1 mark)

b)   Calculate how much a full-time member of the sales staff would earn in one week if they worked 37 hours. Show your working. ✓ [1 mark]

37 hours x £5.20 per hour = £192.40 ✓ [1 mark]

You get 1 mark for your working and 1 mark for the answer — don't forget your units.   *(2 marks)*

c)   Gee Whizz must make deductions from the pay of all staff. Give one example of a deduction that must be made.

Income tax ✓ [1 mark]   You could also have had "National Insurance". Those are the only two that are compulsory, so you wouldn't have got the mark for e.g. "pensions".

(1 mark)

d)   The managers of Gee Whizz are considering changing the way that sales staff are paid. They want to introduce a performance-related pay system. Give two advantages and two disadvantages for the business of doing this.

Be careful! The question asks for advantages and disadvantages for the business, not the employee.

Advantages: i) Sales staff will be motivated to sell more. ✓ [1 mark]
ii) Profits may increase. Disadvantages: i) The company will not know its wage costs in advance, making cash-flow forecasts difficult. ✓ [1 mark] ✓ [1 mark]
ii) Customers may be pressured into buying something they don't want, creating a poor reputation. ✓ [1 mark]

(4 marks)

Exam Questions

1   Kitchen Dreamz designs and fits kitchens, and employs teams of fitters to install them. Each team has a supervisor, who is given a deadline for each job but can decide how to organise their team. The firm wants to employ a new manager to manage the supervisors.

a)   According to McGregor's Theory X and Theory Y, which type of person should Kitchen Dreamz look to employ?

....

(1 mark)

b)   List two laws that Kitchen Dreamz must consider when recruiting the new manager.

....

....

(2 marks)

2   Heath Insurance Services is a medium-sized business that employs several office staff. The manager is concerned about staff motivation, as many complain about being bored. Using Herzberg, explain two ways in which staff motivation could be improved.

....

....

....

(2 marks)

3   Kar Parts makes and supplies electronic parts to major car manufacturers. Whenever a new employee starts work they are given an induction on health and safety.

a)   Explain why it is important for Kar Parts to make sure that all staff are aware of health and safety issues in the factory.

....

....

....

(2 marks)

b)   The manager of the factory has recently discovered that one worker has been ignoring the health and safety rules. What implications might this have for the business if this worker caused an accident?

....

....

....

....

(4 marks)

Recruitment — Job Analysis

Firms need to <u>recruit</u> new employees when they <u>expand</u> or existing employees <u>leave</u>. The decision to recruit new people is usually made by the <u>personnel department</u>. The <u>recruitment process</u> is about appointing the <u>best</u> person to do the job. There are <u>two</u> main parts — the first part is deciding <u>what</u> the right person <u>will be like</u>.

The *Job Description* Describes What the Job Is

1) The job description is a <u>written description</u> of what the job consists of. It includes the <u>formal title</u> of the job, the main <u>purpose</u> of the job, the <u>main duties</u> and any <u>occasional duties</u>.

2) It will also include details of who the job holder is <u>responsible to</u> and whether they are <u>responsible for</u> managing other staff. It may include some <u>performance targets</u>.

3) Without a job description it would be impossible to write the <u>person specification</u>.

> **Count Dracula Vampires Ltd. — Job Description**
> Job Title: Junior Vampire.
> Reports to: Senior Vampire.
> Responsible for: Any vampires on work experience from the local school.
> Main purpose of job: To climb through people's windows at night and generally act in a scary way.
> Duties and Responsibilities:
> — to work between the hours of dusk and dawn biting the necks of people whilst they sleep;
> — to wear a large black cape and laugh in a scary way;
> — to meet neck biting targets set by the Senior Vampire.

The *Person Specification* Describes the Ideal Person

> **Junior Vampire — Person Specification**
> Essential: 5 GCSEs including Business Studies, NVQ Vampiring Level 3.
> Desirable: Two years vampiring experience.
> Skills: Ability to climb through windows, bite necks, turn into a bat and fly off. Good communication skills.
> Personal qualities: Scary face, large incisor teeth, must not like daylight, must enjoy meeting new people.

1) The person specification lists the <u>qualifications</u>, <u>experience</u>, <u>skills</u> and <u>personal qualities</u> of the ideal candidate.

2) They are sometimes divided into <u>essential</u> criteria, which the right candidate <u>must</u> have, and <u>desirable</u> criteria — which the right candidate <u>should</u> have.

The *Job Advertisement* Gets People to Apply

Before they advertise a job, a firm might try to fill the vacancy with someone <u>personally recommended</u> by an existing worker. This can be <u>cheaper</u> and <u>less hassle</u> than advertising.

1) The purpose of a job advert is to get <u>as many suitable people</u> as possible to apply for the job. The firm should decide <u>what</u> it should contain, <u>where</u> it will be put and for <u>how long</u>.

2) A firm might decide to advertise <u>internally</u>. Adverts are usually put up on noticeboards or sent round to staff. <u>Advantages</u> of recruiting internally are that it is much <u>cheaper</u> and the post can be filled <u>more quickly</u>. Also the candidates will already <u>know a lot</u> about the firm and its objectives. On the <u>downside</u>, there will be <u>no 'new blood' and ideas</u>, and the promotion will leave another <u>vacancy</u> to fill.

3) If the job is advertised <u>externally</u>, the firm has to decide <u>where</u> to advertise. Locations include <u>local and national press</u>, <u>job centres</u>, <u>trade journals</u> and <u>employment agencies</u>. Only specialist and senior jobs get advertised in the national press — because it's very <u>expensive</u>.

4) The advert should <u>describe the job</u> and the <u>skills</u> required. It will often indicate what the <u>pay</u> is, and what training and other benefits are offered. And it must explain <u>how</u> the person should apply for the job.

My ideal person would look a lot like Johnny Depp...

But sadly looks don't come into it. Apparently qualifications, experience, skills and personal qualities are much more important. The role of personnel staff is to analyse the job, then draw up a job description and person specification. Then it's a case of finding the closest match.

Recruitment — the Selection Process

The second part of recruitment is the selection process. This involves reading all the applications and shortlisting the best candidates. Interviews and other methods help pick the best applicant.

Written Applications Help the Firm Make a Shortlist

The written application enables the firm to decide which candidates meet the person specification — and which don't. There are three kinds of written application.

> 1) In a letter of application the candidates write about themselves at length — it gives the firm an idea of the applicant's personality as well as their written communication skills.
>
> 2) A curriculum vitae (CV) is a summary of a person's personal details, skills, qualifications and interests. It is written in a standard format to give the firm the basic facts.
>
> 3) An application form is designed by the firm and completed by the applicant. It gives the firm the information that it wants — and nothing else.

Shortlisted candidates will have their references taken up. These are statements about the character of the candidate written by someone who knows them — often their line manager. They are usually confidential — the candidate will not see what is written about them.

An Interview is the Traditional Selection Method...

1) Shortlisted candidates are then invited for interview. Interviews are sometimes done by only one person, but for more senior jobs it's usual to have a panel interview, where the candidate is interviewed by two or more people.

2) Interviewers should ask the same questions to all candidates so that the process is fair. They should not ask questions that are irrelevant to the job or unfairly discriminate.

3) Interviews can help a firm assess how confident a candidate is, what the candidate's social and verbal skills are like, and whether they'll be compatible with the firm's other workers.

4) But some people think that interviews are not a good way to select — people don't behave naturally in a formal interview. And the skills needed to be good at interview are often different from the skills needed to do the job.

...but Tests are Increasingly Being Used

Because of the problems with interviews, lots of firms also use tests to help them decide.

- Skills tests or in-tray exercises test whether the candidate has the ability to do the job.
- Aptitude tests find out whether the candidate has the potential to learn how to do the job.
- Personality tests such as handwriting analysis tell the firm whether the candidate has the right personal qualities.
- Group tests find out whether the candidate can work as part of a team — and whether they have good leadership and decision making skills.

Recruitment is so important that some firms hire recruitment consultants to do it for them.

Interviews — scary but important...

Phew, a bit of a scary page. But don't let it worry you — there won't be any interviews in the exam. There might be questions on recruitment though. Make sure you learn what happens at each stage of the process. It's important for firms to get it right, because employing the wrong person for the job can be a serious problem.

Staff Training

Training is the main way that a firm invests in its <u>human resources</u> — a fancy term for its workers. A <u>well trained</u> workforce will usually be <u>more productive</u> because they're better at their jobs. They might also be <u>better motivated</u> because they enjoy feeling that they're <u>good</u> at what they're doing. You need to <u>learn</u> the training methods below.

Induction Training is for New Staff

1) Induction training <u>introduces</u> the new employee to their workplace. It usually happens on the <u>first day</u> of the new job.

2) It includes introducing them to their <u>fellow workers</u> and advising them of <u>company rules</u> — including <u>health and safety</u> rules. They should be given a <u>tour</u> of the site so they don't get lost. It may also include initial training on how to do their new job.

3) It should help to make the new employee feel <u>welcome</u> and meet Maslow's <u>need to belong</u>.

On-the-Job Training is Learning by Doing

1) This is the <u>most common</u> form of training. The person learns to do their job better by being <u>shown how to do it</u> — and then <u>practising</u>. It is also sometimes called <u>internal training</u>.

2) It is <u>cost-effective</u> for the employer because the person <u>continues to work</u> while learning.

3) A problem is that it is often <u>taught by a colleague</u> — so <u>bad working practices</u> can be passed on.

Off-the-Job Training can be Internal or External

1) This happens when the person learns <u>away</u> from their <u>workplace</u>. Sometimes it is still done <u>internally</u>, if the firm has a separate training division. It is called <u>external training</u> if it happens <u>outside</u> the business — for example at college.

2) It's more expensive than on-the-job training and sometimes <u>not as practical</u> — but it is often of a <u>higher quality</u> because it will be taught by better-qualified people.

3) It is best used when <u>introducing new skills</u> or training people for <u>promotion</u>.

Governments Encourage Training

The government wants the workforce to be highly trained. This will raise <u>productivity</u> and so increase the country's <u>national income</u>.

1) The government-funded <u>Learning and Skills Council</u> (LSC) provides training for firms.

2) Firms which invest in staff development can gain <u>Investors in People</u> status. This signals that they are good employers — making it <u>easier to recruit</u> staff.

3) A <u>National Vocational Qualification</u> (NVQ) is given to anyone who has a minimum skill level to perform their job. NVQ Level 3 is equivalent to GCE Advanced Level. The government wants over <u>half the workforce</u> to be qualified at this level.

Training leads to higher productivity...

<u>Three</u> different types of training — each with its uses. Examiners love to test how you can <u>improve the productivity</u> of staff. Now you can suggest <u>training them</u> — just make sure you've learned everything here first. Try a <u>mini-essay</u> comparing on-the-job and off-the-job training.

Trade Units

Trade unions seek to protect the <u>interests</u> of their <u>members</u>. Anyone who is in <u>employment</u> can belong to a trade union. Members pay a <u>subscription</u>. Trade unions are good for their members, but <u>employers</u> often <u>don't like them</u> — they give workers too much <u>power</u>.

Trade Unions Provide **Collective Bargaining**

1) Instead of each worker talking to managers individually, the trade union negotiates <u>on behalf of</u> all its members — the members will usually obtain a <u>better deal</u> this way.

2) The trade union will help its members to obtain higher <u>pay</u>, better <u>working conditions</u>, shorter working <u>hours</u> and legal help in disputes with employers.

3) They give their members <u>social</u> facilities, <u>training</u> and general <u>legal advice</u>. They can also <u>negotiate discounts</u> on behalf of their members for products such as car insurance.

4) Some employers like collective bargaining as it makes it <u>easier</u> to deal with the workforce.

There are **Four Main Types** of Trade Union

<u>Example</u>: Card Setting Machine Tenters Society (CSMTS).

 1) CRAFT UNIONS are the oldest — they represent workers who have a <u>particular trade or skill</u>. Membership may be spread across thousands of different firms.

<u>Example</u>: Rail, Maritime and Transport (RMT).

 2) INDUSTRIAL UNIONS represent workers who work in the <u>same industry</u> regardless of their job in that industry.

<u>Example</u>: Transport and General Workers' Union (TGWU).

 3) GENERAL UNIONS look after the interests of unskilled and semi-skilled workers in <u>any job</u> from <u>any industry</u>.

<u>Example</u>: National Union of Teachers (NUT).

 4) WHITE COLLAR UNIONS represent <u>office workers</u> and <u>professionals</u>.

Trade Unions are **Hierarchical** Organisations

1) The union representative in the workplace is called a <u>shop steward</u>.
2) Either the shop steward or the <u>regional officers</u> will negotiate with the employer.
3) If it is an important issue the <u>national officials</u> will become involved.
4) The trade union's <u>president</u> is a link to the national <u>Trades Union Congress (TUC)</u> — this umbrella organisation is a major <u>pressure group</u> which tries to influence the government's <u>employment policy</u>.

Trade Union Membership is in **Decline**

Trade union membership is <u>down</u> from over 12 million in the 1970s to under 7 million today.
There are <u>three main reasons</u> why.

1) <u>Laws</u> passed in the 1980s have <u>reduced</u> the <u>power</u> of unions.
2) <u>Fewer</u> people work in <u>manufacturing</u>, the sector with the highest union <u>membership rate</u>.
3) A <u>European Works Council Directive</u> is currently been implemented. This requires that firms with at least 50 employees have regular <u>works council meetings</u>, where discussions between management and employee representatives take place. These regular opportunities for discussion with employers mean that employees are less likely to need trade union assistance.

Employers' Interests are **Represented** Too

1) <u>Employers' associations</u> are the employer equivalent of trade unions — they represent the <u>interests of companies</u>.
2) These organisations <u>put pressure on the government</u> to carry out policies which are in the interests of their members. They also <u>negotiate with trade unions</u> on issues such as minimum pay and working conditions.
3) The <u>major</u> employers' association is the <u>Confederation of British Industry (CBI)</u>. This is a <u>national</u> organisation which represents the interests of employers from all areas of business. Other employer organisations include <u>trade associations</u>. These represent the interests of all the firms <u>within an industry</u>.

In the red corner we have the TUC and in the blue corner — the CBI...

Make sure you know the <u>benefits</u> to a worker of belonging to a trade union — plus the <u>four types</u> of union and <u>who</u> they represent. And remember, it's not all about employees — <u>employers</u> have their associations as well.

Industrial Disputes

When employers and unions <u>can't agree</u>, an <u>industrial dispute</u> takes place. Make sure you know how these are <u>resolved</u> and why laws passed in the <u>1980s</u> have made it <u>harder for unions</u> to win them.

Industrial Disputes Include *More Than* just *Strikes*

1 A STRIKE is when a group of workers <u>withdraw their labour</u>. The strike will cost the firm in <u>lost output</u> and <u>disruption</u> to orders. Striking workers <u>do not get paid</u> by their employer.

2 <u>WORK-TO-RULE</u> is where workers do <u>exactly</u> what their <u>job description</u> says — and nothing more. Sometimes rules are very detailed — for example on health and safety issues. A work-to-rule will result in <u>less output</u>.

3 <u>GO SLOW</u> is when workers deliberately do their job as slowly as possible — again <u>productivity</u> will suffer.

4 <u>OVERTIME BAN</u> is when workers <u>refuse</u> to work <u>longer</u> than their <u>standard working week</u>. Some employers rely on overtime to get important orders finished on time.

- Strikes can be <u>official</u> — with the support of the trade union — or <u>unofficial</u>.
- Striking workers will <u>picket</u> the workplace — they stand outside the workplace and try to persuade other workers to join them.

ACAS can Help to End Industrial Disputes

The <u>Advisory, Conciliation and Arbitration Service (ACAS)</u> is an independent organisation that aims to prevent and end industrial disputes.

1) It provides <u>advice</u> and information to firms, trade unions and individual employees.

2) It provides <u>conciliation</u> — <u>talking to both sides</u> in an industrial dispute so that it can find an agreement to end the dispute.

3) It <u>arbitrates</u> between the two sides — ACAS <u>listens to both sides</u> and gives what it thinks is a fair settlement. Both sides <u>agree in advance</u> to accept ACAS's verdict.

1980s Trade Union Laws *Made Life Harder* for Unions

The <u>Thatcher government</u> passed lots of <u>anti-union laws</u> in the 1980s. You only need to remember one or two as long as you know the <u>general effect</u> — a <u>weakening</u> of trade union power.

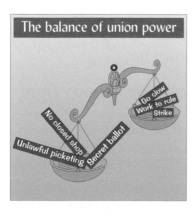

The balance of union power

1) The <u>1980 Employment Act</u> made it <u>harder</u> for unions to use <u>picketing</u> to enforce a strike.

2) The <u>1982 Employment Act</u> made <u>closed shops</u> — compulsory union membership at some workplaces — <u>illegal</u>.

3) The <u>1984 Trade Union Act</u> made it <u>compulsory</u> to hold a <u>secret ballot</u> to vote on strike action.

4) The <u>1988 Employment Act</u> gave individual union members the right to <u>ignore</u> the result of the ballot and <u>refuse</u> to strike.

5) However, the labour government in 1999 passed the <u>Employment Relations Act</u>. This has <u>increased union power</u> — for example by forcing some employers to negotiate with unions.

It's best not to Go Slow in the exam or you won't finish it...

So <u>employees</u> are represented by a union and <u>employers</u> by an association. When the two sides <u>can't agree</u>, an <u>industrial dispute</u> takes place. This is <u>bad news</u> for the employer who wants it stopped. This is where <u>ACAS</u> comes in and hopefully <u>sorts it all out</u>. Got that? If not, read over the last two pages again.

Warm-Up and Worked Exam Questions

Warm-up Questions

1) What is the purpose of a job advertisement?
2) What is the difference between a job description and a person specification?
3) State three kinds of written application for a job.
4) What is induction training used for?
5) What is the main purpose of a trade union?
6) Describe the role of ACAS.

Worked Exam Questions

You know the drill by now. Work through these examples, then try the questions on page 63.

1   When Securepath Stores Ltd was taken over by Buy-Right Supermarkets plc all ex-Securepath employees were invited to apply for jobs in the refurbished stores. Jobs were also advertised in the local press and at the nearest job centre.

a)   State the advantages for Buy-Right of recruiting old Securepath employees.

✓ [1 mark]
Recruiting would be cheaper and training could be done more

✓ [1 mark]
quickly by recruiting experienced local workers who need new jobs.

(2 marks)

b)   What information should be in the local press advertisement?

✓ [1 mark]   ✓ [1 mark]
Adverts should describe the jobs available and skills required.

✓ [1 mark]
Also essential is how and where to apply for the jobs. Rates of pay,

✓ [1 mark]
training and other benefits offered can be included.

(4 marks)

2   Pestkill plc uses various training methods for its workforce of pest control operatives. New employees are sent on training courses covering health and safety and use of equipment. Also they accompany existing operatives to customer sites.

a)   Distinguish between on-the-job training and off-the-job training at Pestkill plc.

✓ [1 mark]
On-the-job: learning to do the work by being shown how, e.g.,

✓ [1 mark]
Make sure you apply your answer to Pestkill plc.
accompanying existing operatives. Off-the-job: learning away from

✓ [1 mark]   ✓ [1 mark]
the workplace, e.g., attending courses on health and safety.

(4 marks)

b)   Describe a problem associated with each type of training.

On-the-job training is often taught by a colleague, so bad habits can

✓ [1 mark]
be passed on. Off-the-job training can be high quality but sometimes

✓ [1 mark]
not as practical as hands-on experience. It's usually more expensive as well.

(2 marks)

Exam Questions

1   When welder Joe O'Brien started work with a train manufacturer, the shop steward urged him to join the union. He said the union was "stronger through collective bargaining".

   a)   Tell Joe what "collective bargaining" is and explain its advantages to union members.

     ....

     ....

     ....

     (3 marks)

   b)   Which two types of union could Joe join?

     ....

     ....

     (2 marks)

2   When a job comes up in his department, Harry Hunch shortlists the applicants then interviews them. Toni Test, the new Human Resources Manager, tests all applicants then selects candidates using their test results.

   a)   What are the advantages of interviewing over other methods of recruitment?

     ....

     ....

     ....

     (3 marks)

   b)   Why might Toni prefer testing to interviewing?

     ....

     ....

     (2 marks)

   c)   List four types of test Toni might recommend.

     ....

     ....

     ....

     (2 marks)

   d)   Explain why it is vital to get the right sort of person for a job.

     ....

     ....

     (1 mark)

Revision Summary for Section Four

There's a real mix of easy and hard stuff in this section. Lots of facts and common sense — but some quite tricky theory too. It's especially important to make sure you learn the main motivation theories and how they help explain the various ways of managing people — but you need to make sure you've mastered all of it. So have a go at these questions — and keep going over the section till you're sure you can answer all of them.

1) Give five reasons why someone might choose to work.

2) What's the difference between a skill and an attribute?

3) What must all employees be given within one month of starting work?

   a) a contract;   b) a pay rise;   c) the sack.

4) What did the Equal Pay Acts of 1970 and 1983 say?

5) Starting at the bottom, list the five human needs on Maslow's hierarchy — and say what firms can do to help meet each one.

6) Name one of Herzberg's hygiene factors, and one of his motivating factors.

7) If you believe that workers can be trusted to take responsibility, what type of manager are you?

   a) Theory x;   b) Theory y

8) What do you call the pay method when workers are paid by the hour?

9) Vlad works 40 hours this week and his wages are £320. How much is that per hour?

10) Explain one problem with the piece rate pay method.

11) What is an advantage of paying staff a salary?

12) Explain the three kinds of performance-related pay.

13) Explain the difference between job rotation, job enlargement and job enrichment.

14) Give one advantage and one disadvantage of each.

15) Name four types of management style.

16) Give one advantage and one disadvantage of delegation.

17) List four things that should be included on a job description.

18) Explain the difference between a job description and a person specification.

19) What are three things you might be asked to send in a written application for a job?

20) Name three types of test a firm might use to help them decide who to employ.

21) What's the advantage of having a well trained workforce?

22) What should happen during induction training?

23) Explain the difference between on-the-job and off-the-job training.

24) Give one advantage and one disadvantage of on-the-job training.

25) Explain three ways the government encourages training.

26) Explain the advantages of belonging to a trade union.

27) List the four main types of trade union.

28) What is the name of the trade union representative in the workplace?

   a) the shop steward;   b) the regional officer;   c) Brian.

29) Explain three reasons why trade union membership is in decline.

30) Name the major employers' association.

31) Describe four methods of industrial action.

32) Explain three services that ACAS provides.

33) Describe the effects of two 1980s trade union laws.

87 '6

Business Costs

This page describes three different ways of looking at business costs.
You need to know what goes in each <u>category</u>.

Costs can be *Direct* and *Indirect*...

1) DIRECT COSTS are expenses that can be attributed to making a <u>particular product</u>.
   Examples include costs of factory <u>labour</u>, <u>raw materials</u> and operating <u>machinery</u>.

2) INDIRECT COSTS are the general <u>overheads</u> of running the business.
   Examples include management <u>salaries</u>, <u>telephone bills</u> and <u>office rent</u>.

direct costs
+ indirect costs
= total costs

3) Firms that make more than one product will want each one to earn enough <u>sales revenue</u>
   to <u>cover</u> its direct costs and make a <u>contribution</u> to indirect costs. If all the products
   together make enough contribution then the business will make a <u>profit</u>.

...or *Fixed* and *Variable*...

1) FIXED COSTS are costs which <u>do not vary</u> with output. They're <u>mostly indirect</u> costs — management
   salaries, telephone bills and office rent. They <u>have to be paid</u> even if the firm produces <u>nothing</u>.

2) VARIABLE COSTS are costs that will <u>increase</u> as the firm <u>expands output</u>.
   They're <u>mostly direct</u> costs — factory labour, raw materials and machinery.

3) Some costs are <u>semi-variable</u> — they only vary a little because they have
   a large <u>fixed element</u>. A good example is <u>workers' wages</u> — most people
   receive a <u>basic salary</u> and only part of their pay is linked to output.

variable costs
+ fixed costs
= total costs

4) Fixed costs are only fixed over a <u>short period</u> of time — if a firm is expanding,
   it will take on more managers and bigger offices so its fixed costs will increase.

5) Firms can work out their <u>break-even</u> level of output if they know fixed and variable costs.

Break-even is explained on the next page.

...or *Average* and *Marginal*...

1) AVERAGE COST is how much <u>each product</u> cost to make. You find it
   by dividing <u>total cost</u> by <u>output</u> — the number of products made.
   To make a profit the firm must charge a <u>higher price</u> than this.

average cost
= total cost
÷ output

2) MARGINAL COST tells the firm how much it will cost to make <u>one more product</u>. In other words it's the cost of
   <u>increasing output</u> by <u>one unit</u>. This helps the firm to decide what price it needs to charge for any <u>new orders</u>.

At an output of 40,000 tennis balls, the <u>total cost</u> is £100,000
The <u>average cost</u> = £100,000 ÷ 40,000 = <u>£2.50 per ball</u>.
The selling price should be <u>more than</u> £2.50 per ball.

Increase the output to 40,001 tennis balls and the total cost is £100,002.
The <u>marginal cost</u> of the 40,001st tennis ball = £100,002 − £100,000 = £2.
So any <u>additional orders</u> should sell for more than £2 per ball.

Average costs usually <u>fall</u> as the firm gets <u>bigger</u> because of <u>economies of scale</u>.

See page 88 for more on economies of scale.

If you don't learn this page it might cost you...

You'll not get far in this section without knowing about <u>costs</u>. Sad, but true. Make sure
you can classify costs as <u>direct</u> or <u>indirect</u> and <u>fixed</u> or <u>variable</u>. And don't forget those
calculations for <u>average</u> and <u>marginal</u> costs — they might come in handy in the exam.

Break-Even Analysis

The <u>break-even point</u> is the level of output where the firm will just <u>cover its costs</u>. Sell more and it will make a <u>profit</u>, sell less and it will make a loss. You need to know how to <u>draw and calculate</u> the break-even point.

A *Break-even Chart* Shows How Much You Need to Sell

1) To draw a break-even chart you need to know: the <u>fixed costs</u>, the <u>variable costs</u> per unit and the <u>selling price</u>. Output is drawn on the horizontal axis and the cost and revenue data on the vertical axis.

2) The <u>break-even</u> level of output is where the lines for <u>total revenue</u> and <u>total costs</u> cross. The <u>margin of safety</u> is the <u>gap</u> between the current level of output and the break-even point.

Output	Fixed cost	Variable cost	Total cost	Total revenue	Profit
0	2000	0	2000	0	-2000
200	2000	400	2400	800	-1600
400	2000	800	2800	1600	-1200
600	2000	1200	3200	2400	-800
800	2000	1600	3600	3200	-400
1000	2000	2000	4000	4000	0
1200	2000	2400	4400	4800	400
1400	2000	2800	4800	5600	800
1600	2000	3200	5200	6400	1200
1800	2000	3600	5600	7200	1600
2000	2000	4000	6000	8000	2000

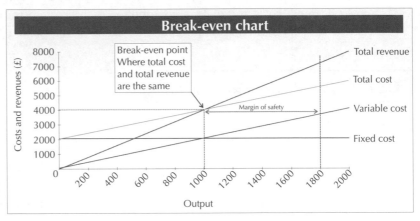

3) Here, the fixed costs are <u>£2000</u>, and the variable cost per unit is <u>£2</u>. The selling price is <u>£4</u>. The firm breaks even if it makes and sells <u>1000 units</u>. If the current output is 1800 then the margin of safety is <u>800 units</u>.

You can *Calculate* the Break-even Point

The break-even chart looks pretty, but you <u>don't need</u> to draw it — you can <u>work out</u> the break-even point like this:

1) First find what's called the <u>contribution per unit</u>. This is the selling price <u>minus</u> the variable cost. So here it's £4 – £2 = <u>£2</u>.

2) Now <u>divide</u> the <u>total fixed costs</u> by the contribution per unit. Fixed costs are £2000 so this calculation is £2000 ÷ £2 = <u>1000</u>. And hey presto, that's the <u>right answer</u>.

BREAK-EVEN OUTPUT = FIXED COST ÷ CONTRIBUTION PER UNIT

Break-even Analysis has its *Limitations*

This analysis is great in theory — but it has <u>problems</u> when you use it in the <u>real world</u>.

1) It assumes that the firm can sell <u>any quantity</u> of the product at the <u>current price</u>. In practice the firm may need to <u>reduce prices</u> to sell at high levels of output.

2) It assumes fixed costs <u>never change</u> — but as <u>output increases</u> the firm may need <u>more machines</u>, bigger offices and so on.

3) Finally it assumes that <u>all</u> products are <u>sold</u>. This doesn't always happen.

Break-even analysis tells you how much you need to sell...

You'll need to know how to <u>draw</u> and <u>read</u> a break-even chart. And make sure you can do the <u>calculations</u>. But beware — a sneaky question on the <u>limitations</u> of break-even analysis might pop up so make sure you know what they are.

Internal Sources of Finance

It's pretty obvious that all private sector firms need to raise finance. You need to know the reasons why, how they can do it and what each method is best used for. First up, internal sources — these are from inside the business.

Firms **Need Finance** for Five Reasons

1) New firms need start-up capital to buy the assets needed to run the business.

2) New firms also need to finance their poor initial cash flow — they'll need to pay their suppliers before they receive money from their customers.

3) All firms need enough cash to meet the day-to-day running of the business — that's called working capital.

4) Sometimes customers delay payment — finance is needed to cover this liquidity shortfall.

5) Firms may need finance to fund expansion — they may be moving to larger premises.

There are Five Sources of **Internal Finance**

Internal finance is a quick and easy way to solve short-term financial problems for most firms. It saves borrowing and having to pay back interest. But there are problems too...

① Retained Profits

These are profits that the owners have decided to plough back into the business after they've paid themselves a dividend.

BUT: new and small firms tend only to make small profits. And PLCs are under pressure from shareholders to give large dividends, reducing the amount of profit they can retain.

② Credit Control

Firms should be good at chasing up people who owe them money. Credit control is about chasing firms who don't pay their invoices on time.

BUT: most firms find it an uphill struggle to get their customers to cough up on time.

An invoice is just another name for a bill. For a credit sale, the invoice is often sent in advance to inform the customer that their goods are being sent. The invoice should show what goods have been supplied, how much money is owed, and when the payment is due.

③ Fixed Assets

Firms can raise cash by selling fixed assets, such as machinery or buildings, that are no longer productive.

BUT: there's a limit to how many assets you can sell. Sell too many and you can't go on trading. Plus it's not much use for new and small firms, who have few assets.

④ Run Down Stocks

Stocks are products that a firm has spent money making, but which have not yet been sold. Firms can improve liquidity by running down their stock levels — selling things from stocks before they spend more money making new things.

BUT: this is dangerous as firms need stocks to cope with unexpected increases in demand.

⑤ Re-invest Savings

Firms may have used retained profit from previous years to build up bank savings or buy stocks and shares. They can use these to get liquidity.

BUT: only big and successful firms have these kinds of cash reserves.

Internal Finance — good for the short term...

Lots to learn here — make sure you can write down every source of internal finance and remember one problem with each. I reckon the only option is to learn, cover the page and start scribbling. Then you'll be ready for...

External Sources of Finance

External sources of finance come from <u>outside</u> the business. It's generally a bit more of a <u>hassle</u> for firms to arrange than internal finance. The <u>length of time</u> you want it for <u>affects</u> the <u>method</u> of finance you choose.

Short-term External Finance is For **Less Than a Year**

1) The owners of a business might use <u>personal savings</u>, especially in providing <u>start-up capital</u> for their business. This is often the case with <u>sole proprietors</u> and <u>small</u> businesses. An <u>advantage</u> of this for the business is that it saves borrowing and having to pay back the interest.

2) <u>Friends and family</u> might be willing to put money into a <u>sole proprietor's business</u>. The main <u>problems</u> with this are that they might want to <u>have some say</u> in how the business is run, or <u>withdraw</u> their money if they need it themselves.

3) An <u>overdraft</u> lets the firm take <u>more money</u> out of its bank account than it currently has deposited in it. <u>Interest charges</u> are <u>high</u> — but only while you're overdrawn.

4) Firms can pay their bills as <u>late as possible</u> — holding onto money that they <u>owe</u> to their <u>creditors</u>. The downside is that this could <u>annoy</u> the firms they're doing business with.

5) It could get a <u>debt factoring agency</u> to take over its credit control. The agency will pay the firm a <u>percentage</u> of what it's owed — say 90% — then <u>take over</u> collecting the debt. The <u>firm</u> gets some money <u>immediately</u> — the agency hopes to <u>make a profit</u> by collecting a <u>higher percentage</u> of the money than it gave the firm.

Medium-term External Finance is For **One to Five Years**

1) Taking out a <u>bank loan</u> is quick and easy but will mean <u>repaying interest</u>. The bank may require <u>collateral</u> — assets the bank can <u>repossess</u> if the loan is <u>not repaid</u>.

2) Firms can <u>lease</u> their fixed assets instead of buying them. Less <u>initial finance</u> is needed to obtain the asset but over time it works out <u>more expensive</u> than buying it.

3) <u>Hire purchase</u> (HP) is similar to leasing except the firm will <u>eventually own</u> the asset — it buys the asset in <u>instalments</u>. The trouble is that <u>interest</u> payments can be <u>very high</u>.

4) Official bodies such as the <u>European Union</u>, the <u>government</u> and <u>local authorities</u> can provide <u>grants</u> and <u>loans</u> for firms. The <u>good thing</u> about grants is that they don't usually have to be repaid and owners keep full control over their business. However, the process of applying for grants can be <u>long and complicated</u>.

Long-term External Finance is For **Over Five Years**

1) A <u>mortgage</u> is a long-term loan used to finance buying <u>property</u>. The property is used as <u>collateral</u>. Interest payments are <u>relatively low</u> compared to other types of borrowing.

2) A limited company can <u>issue more shares</u>. The money raised does not have to be repaid to shareholders — but more shares means <u>less control</u> by the <u>existing owners</u>.

3) Limited companies can issue <u>debentures</u> to the public. These are <u>long-term loans</u> which the firm commits itself to <u>repay with interest</u> — for up to <u>25 years</u> or so.

Four Factors Affect the **Choice of Finance**

1) The golden rule is to match the <u>type of finance</u> to the <u>length of time</u> it is needed for. It'd be daft to take out a mortgage because a customer is a week late paying an invoice.

2) Obviously the <u>amount</u> of money needed is an important factor — you're unlikely to be able to borrow a million pounds from your gran (unless you're very lucky).

3) Think about how much the finance <u>costs</u> — some sources are more expensive than others. <u>Loans</u> are a <u>cheaper</u> way to buy assets than <u>leasing</u>.

4) The <u>size</u> and <u>type</u> of company may restrict you — only <u>limited companies</u> have access to most forms of <u>long-term finance</u>.

The source of finance depends on what the money's for...

...lots more sources of finance — aarrgh there are so many to choose from. But <u>don't panic</u> — you just need to think about it logically. Remember, a lot depends on whether the firm wants the money in the <u>long term</u> or the <u>short term</u>.

Warm-Up and Worked Exam Questions

Warm-up Questions

1) Give three examples of indirect costs in business.
2) Complete the following formula: **"variable costs + fixed costs = ..."**
3) Give the formula used to calculate average cost.
4) Why is the break-even point important to a firm?
5) Give four factors that affect the type of finance a company chooses.
6) What is meant by working capital?

Worked Exam Questions

The types of finance available to businesses are a popular topic with examiners.
Have a look at the worked exam questions below.

1   Bird Homes Ltd is a small business selling luxury bird boxes to gardeners.
Each box is sold for £25. Fixed costs are £15,000 and variable costs are £15 per box.

   a) How many bird boxes must the company sell to break even? ✔ [1 mark]

   Unit contribution = selling price – variable costs: £25 – £15 = £10

   Break-even point = fixed costs ÷ unit contribution:

   £15,000 ÷ £10 = 1500 bird boxes ✔ [1 mark]

   It's always a good idea to state the formulae — that'll earn
   you marks even if you get some of the working wrong.   *(2 marks)*

   b) With reference to Bird Homes Ltd, explain how break-even analysis is limited in the real world.

   " With reference to Bird Homes Ltd" is the most important thing to notice here.

   Break-even analysis assumes that Bird Homes Ltd can sell any ✔ [1 mark]
   quantity of the bird boxes at £25 each, which is unlikely in the real
   world. As output rises, more machinery and larger premises might
   ✔ [1 mark] *be needed, so fixed costs can change.* ✔ [1 mark] *Finally, break-even analysis*
   assumes that all bird boxes are sold, which might not happen. ✔ [1 mark]

   (4 marks)

2) Keynote Music plc, suppliers of musical instruments, has short-term financial problems. The finance director decides on a method of internal financing, but admits that the amount of money the company can access will depend upon the goodwill of the shareholders. Which method of internal financing do you think the finance director has chosen? Explain your answer. ✔ [1 mark]

   The finance director has probably opted for retained profit. If
   shareholders put pressure on Keynote to increase its dividends, the
   amount of profit Keynote can retain would be reduced. ✔ [1 mark]

   (2 marks)

Exam Questions

1   Joe Morris, a sole trader, sells 50,000 trays of bedding plants in a year.
His total costs are £100,000 for the year.

    a)   Calculate the average cost of each tray, and suggest a sensible selling price for one of Joe's trays of bedding plants.

....

....

....

(2 marks)

    b)   The following year, Joe's total costs are £110,000, but the average cost of each tray stays the same. How many trays does Joe make in that year?

....

....

(1 mark)

    c)   Joe wants to expand his greenhouse capacity. He owns the land, but the materials, heating, and watering facilities will cost £50,000. Explain two methods of external finance Joe could use for this project, and outline the risk each carries.

....

....

....

....

....

(4 marks)

2   Becky and her sister Gemma plan to start a small travel agency, organising holidays for disabled clients. Explain to them why they will need finance to set up the business.

....

....

....

....

....

....

....

(5 marks)

Budgeting

A budget is a plan for the firm's <u>income and spending</u> — it's based upon the firm's <u>predictions</u> for the future. It can help the firm to know whether it is likely to make a <u>profit</u> or a <u>loss</u>.

The Budget is Based Upon **Predictions**

1) People take a <u>lot of time</u> doing budgets and working out the figures carefully. But it's important to remember it's all basically <u>guesswork</u>.

2) If Yummo Chocolates have a <u>target</u> to increase sales by 10% next year, that target could be based on the fact that sales have risen 10% each year for the past four years. But there is <u>no obvious reason</u> to assume past trends will carry on into the future — the firm just has to use its <u>best guess</u> or seek the opinion of experts.

Budgets have **Three Main Uses**

1) Budgets can be used to give people <u>targets</u> to work towards. For example Yummo Chocolates can give its sales force <u>extra commission</u> if they exceed the 10% sales increase. However, if the targets are <u>unrealistic</u> and <u>imposed</u> by management they can be <u>demotivating</u>.

2) They can help the business make detailed <u>plans</u> for the future — including <u>contingency plans</u> for if things happen unexpectedly. They can also help the business <u>allocate resources</u> to different departments and projects more <u>efficiently</u>.

3) They can help the business <u>monitor</u> its performance by <u>comparing</u> actual figures with the plans in the budget. This is called <u>variance analysis</u>. Items that are <u>better</u> than planned are called <u>favourable variances</u>, and items that are <u>worse</u> are called <u>unfavourable variances</u>.

Actual value
– forecast value
= variance

Yummo Chocolates Ltd — Budget for October 2004			
	Forecast(£)	Actual(£)	Variance(£)	
Sales revenue(£)	15,000	14,600	–400	Unfavourable
Raw Materials(£)	3,000	3,200	200	Unfavourable
Wages(£)	5,000	4,900	–100	Favourable
Telephone(£)	200	160	–40	Favourable
Petrol(£)	360	390	30	Unfavourable
Electricity(£)	120	160	40	Unfavourable

- <u>Revenue</u> variances are favourable if the actual value is <u>bigger</u> than budgeted — they've <u>earned more</u>.
- <u>Cost</u> variances are favourable if the actual value is <u>less</u> than budgeted — they've <u>spent less</u>.

4) This is part of a <u>monthly budget</u> for Yummo Chocolates — with the <u>actual figures</u> and the variance also shown.

5) The company managers would look at that budget and decide they need to find out why the company's sales are <u>below budget</u> this month — and why it's spending <u>more</u> on raw materials, petrol and electricity.

Favourable variances — better than you'd expect...

Budgets are useful in everyday life. A revision plan is a kind of budget — you set yourself targets for how much revision to do each day. Businesses use them to keep an eye on <u>what they're spending</u>. You need to know how to interpret one. Make sure you can <u>calculate variances</u> and know when a variance is <u>favourable</u> or <u>unfavourable</u>.

Cash Flow

One of the most important parts of any budget is the <u>cash flow forecast</u>. More profitable businesses go <u>bankrupt</u> because of <u>poor cash flow</u> than for any other reason. You've gotta learn all about it.

Cash Flow is **More Than Just Profits**

1) <u>Cash flow</u> is the flow of all money <u>into and out</u> of the business. When a firm <u>sells its products</u>, money <u>flows in</u>. When it buys materials or pays wages, money <u>flows out</u>. It's a bit like water flowing into a bath through the tap and out through the plughole.

2) Cash flow's important because if there's <u>not enough</u> money flowing in, you don't have enough to <u>pay your bills</u>.

3) One thing you should remember — the cost of <u>buying fixed assets</u> is a <u>negative cash flow</u> payment, but it's <u>not included</u> when you're calculating the company's <u>profit</u>.

Poor Cash Flow Means You've Got **Big Problems**

1) Poor cash flow means there is <u>not enough cash</u> in the business to meet its <u>day-to-day expenses</u> — there is a lack of <u>working capital</u>.

2) Staff may not get <u>paid on time</u> — this will cause <u>resentment</u> and <u>poor motivation</u>.

3) Some suppliers offer discounts for <u>prompt payment</u> of invoices — the business will <u>not be able</u> to take advantage of these.

4) <u>Creditors</u> may not get paid on time — they may insist on <u>stricter terms</u> in future.

5) Some creditors <u>may not wait</u> for payment — they might take <u>legal action</u> to <u>recover the debt</u>. If the business does not have the money it may be declared <u>bankrupt</u> and forced to <u>cease trading</u>.

Cash Flow **Forecasts** Help Firms to **Anticipate Problems**

1) A cash flow forecast is a good way of <u>predicting</u> when the firm might face a <u>liquidity problem</u>. It lists all the <u>inflows</u> and <u>outflows</u> of cash that appear in the <u>budget</u>.

2) The firm will see when an <u>overdraft</u> or other short-term finance might be needed.

3) The forecast needs to be <u>monitored</u> — to monitor the impact of <u>unexpected cash flows</u>.

Cash Flow Forecast — Footy Fanzines Ltd.						
	April	May	June	July	August	Sept
Total receipts (cash inflow)	15,000	12,000	5,000	5,000	16,000	16,000
Total spending (cash outflow)	12,000	12,000	10,000	10,000	12,000	12,000
Bank balance at start of month	1,000	4,000	4,000	-1,000	-6,000	-2,000
Bank balance at end of month	4,000	4,000	-1,000	-6,000	-2,000	2000

4) Here's an example of a budget <u>cash flow forecast</u> for a firm publishing football magazines. In <u>summer</u>, when the football season's over, more money flows <u>out</u> than <u>in</u>.

5) The firm can see it will need an <u>overdraft</u> to get it through from June to September.

6) It's useful to know this <u>in advance</u> because it means the firm can <u>plan</u> — it won't suddenly have to <u>panic</u> in June when it starts to <u>run out of money</u>.

Don't worry about exams — just go with the flow...
Cash flow is quite easy — once you've understood how the <u>figures</u> are worked out. There's nothing to trip you up really. Just make sure you know <u>why</u> cash flow is so important, and how firms can use forecasts to <u>plan</u> ahead.

The Trading, Profit and Loss Account

Warning — this page contains maths. But don't worry, it's not too bad. The trading, profit and loss account records the difference between the firm's income and the cost of running the business over a period of one year. It contains three sections.

❶ The Trading Account

1) This section is coloured yellow in the example. It records the profit or loss made as result of making the firm's products.

2) Turnover records the value of all products sold during the year. Cost of sales records how much it cost to make the products that were sold during the year — including all the direct costs.

3) There has to be an adjustment for stock. Say at the start of the year Yummo Chocolates had 200 tons of cocoa in stock, then during the year they bought in 2000 tons, and at the end of the year they had 150 tons left that means they used and sold 2050 tons of cocoa — this figure is used to work out the cost of sales.

4) Gross profit is the difference between the income from selling the chocolate and the cost of making it.

```
Trading, Profit and Loss Account
      Yummo Chocolates Ltd.
   Year ending 31st March 2005
                              £000
Turnover............................. 180
Cost of sales:
    Opening stock......... 3
    Purchases.............. 15
                          18
Minus closing stock......... 5
Cost of sales = ...................  13
Gross profit =.....................  167

Minus expenses
    Wages and salaries.. 93
    Rent and rates........ 10
    Office expenses...... 28
    Advertising............. 5
    Depreciation........... 8
    Other expenses....... 3
Expenses = .........................  147
Operating profit = ...............  20

Interest payable ...................  2
Profit before tax (Net profit)...  18

Taxation .............................  3
Dividends ...........................  9
Retained profit ....................  6
```

❷ The Profit and Loss Account

1) This section is coloured orange — it records all the indirect costs of running the business. It does not include the costs of buying assets such as machinery — only the cost of using them.

2) All assets wear out with use — eventually they need replacing. Firms usually set aside money each year so that there will be money to buy a replacement when it is needed. This is treated as a business expense — it is called depreciation.

3) The money left after paying all the costs of running the business is called operating profit.

4) Finally any interest paid or received is included. What is left is true profit — net profit.

There are two methods of calculating depreciation.
1) Straight line method. This is the easy way. If a machine costs £5000 and will wear out after about 5 years, the depreciation is simply £1000 each year.
2) Reducing balance method. This depreciates the machinery by a percentage of its value each year — say, depreciate a £5000 machine by 25% each year.
Year 1 = £5000 × 25% = £1250.
The value is now £5000 – £1250 = £3750.
Year 2 = £3750 × 25% = £938, etc.

❸ The Appropriation Account

1) Coloured red on the example. This is only included for limited company accounts.

2) It records where the profit has gone — to the government as tax, to shareholders as dividends, or kept in the business as retained profit.

Learn this page — you might profit in the exam...
This isn't too bad — just add up your sales, take off direct costs, take off indirect costs, and there you have your net profit. Depreciation can be tricky to get your head around. Practise a few calculations until you've got it sussed.

Warm-Up and Worked Exam Questions

Warm-up Questions

1) A firm budgeted for sales of £35,000, but actual sales were £40,000. Is this variance in revenue favourable or unfavourable?

2) "A cash flow forecast shows how much profit a firm is making." Is this statement true or false?

3) What does an appropriation account show?

4) What is depreciation?

5) A firm buys a new van for £35,000. It expects to scrap it after five years. How much depreciation should be charged each year if the firm uses the straight-line method?

6) Which costs are included in the trading account — direct or indirect?

Worked Exam Question

Budgeting is crucial for all businesses, and it's really important for your Business Studies GCSE. Have a look at this worked exam question.

1 Amuse Yourself Ltd is an amusement arcade in a busy seaside town. It has drawn up the following cash flow forecast.

Cash Flow Forecast for Amuse Yourself Ltd (£000's)

	Jan	Feb	Mar	Apr	May	Jun
Revenue						
Sales	10	15	15	20	18	22
Total Revenue	10	15	15	20	E	22
Payments						
Rent	2	2	2	2	2	2
Wages	12	12	13	13	13	F
Other Payments	7	2	3	1	2	2
Total Payments	21	B	18	16	17	18
Net Cash Flow	A	−1	−3	4	1	4
Balance (start of month)	10	−1	−2	D	−1	0
Balance (end of month)	−1	−2	C	−1	0	4

a) Calculate the amounts of money represented by the letters A to F.

$A = £10k - £21k = -£11,000.$ ✔ [1 mark] $B = £2k + £12k + £2k = £16,000.$ ✔ [1 mark]

$C = -£2k - £3k = -£5000.$ ✔ [1 mark] $D = C = -£5000.$ ✔ [1 mark] $E = £18,000.$ ✔ [1 mark]

$F = £18k - £2k - £2k = £14,000.$ ✔ [1 mark]

There are 6 marks available here — take care with your maths and you should get them all.

(6 marks)

b) Explain what the company could do to improve its cash flow.

The company could try either to increase the money coming in from sales, perhaps by better advertising, ✔ [1 mark] or decrease outgoings, perhaps by decreasing wages or making one worker redundant. ✔ [1 mark]

(2 marks)

Exam Questions

1   See-Saw manufactures playground equipment. Use the information given in the trading, profit and loss account to answer the questions below:

Trading, Profit & Loss Account for See-Saw
Year ending 31st March, 2005

		£000's	£000's
Sales	Revenue		120
	Cost of Sales:		
	Opening Stock	50	
	Purchases	35	
		85	
	Closing stock	35	
	Total Cost of Sales		50
GROSS PROFIT			**A**
Expenses	Rent	6	
	Wages	40	
	Advertising	5	
	Other Expenses	8	
	Total Expenses		**B**
NET PROFIT			11

a)   Calculate the amounts of money represented by A and B.

....

....

(2 marks)

b)   Explain the difference between gross profit and net profit.

....

....

....

(3 marks)

c)   The directors of See-Saw are considering expanding the factory. They have applied for a bank loan to finance the expansion. Why might the bank manager wish to see the company's trading, profit and loss account before granting See-Saw a loan?

....

....

....

....

....

....

(4 marks)

The Balance Sheet — Net Assets

The balance sheet can be quite tricky to master — but the basic idea is pretty simple. It records where the business got its money from, and what it has done with it. The two balance out exactly — hence the name. The example below shows what Yummo Chocolates has done with the money it's got.

The balance sheet is calculated at a particular date — usually the last day of the financial year.

Fixed Assets will Last for More Than One Year

1) The business has used some money to buy fixed assets — premises, machinery, vehicles.

2) This figure is what they're worth now — they'll have depreciated since they were bought, but that's all taken care of in the profit and loss account.

Current Assets Last for a Few Months

1) These are listed in increasing order of liquidity.

2) Stock is the least liquid. It includes raw materials and finished products that the firm has spent its money on but which have not yet been sold.

3) Debtors are people who owe the business money. So this figure is the value of products sold — usually on credit — that have not yet been paid for by the customers. What's happening here is that the firm is lending its money to customers so they can buy its products.

4) Cash is the most liquid. This is money the firm hasn't spent on anything yet — it's just kept it as cash.

BALANCE SHEET			
Yummo Chocolates Ltd., 31st March 2005			
	£000	£000	£000
Fixed Assets			
Premises			80
Machinery			40
Vehicles			30
			150
Current Assets			
Stock at 31 March 2004	5		
Debtors	12		
Cash	3		
	20		
Current Liabilities			
Creditors 14			
Unpaid Corporation Tax 1			
		15	
Net Current Assets (Working Capital)			5
Net Assets...			155
Financed by			
Shareholders Funds			
Share Capital			80
Retained Profit and Reserves			50
Long-term Liabilities			
Bank Loan			20
Debentures			5
Capital Employed			155

Current Liabilities are Bills the Firm has to Pay Soon

1) These are any payments the firm will have to make within one year of the date on the balance sheet. Creditors are the opposite of debtors — people who the business owes money to. So this figure is money the firm owes to its suppliers. Also included is any unpaid corporation tax — payable to the government out of the previous year's profits — as well as any unpaid dividends to shareholders.

2) This is money which doesn't really belong to the firm, because they're going to have to pay it to someone else pretty soon. So you take this away from the current assets figure.

Subtract Current Liabilities to get Net Assets

1) Net current assets is what you get when you subtract those current liabilities from the current assets. It's also called working capital — we covered it on the cash flow page (p72).

2) Add the net current assets to the fixed assets and you get the net assets, or net worth, of the business. This is everything the firm's spent its cash on — it's what the firm is worth.

Balance sheets — it's easier than spinning plates...

I told you this was tricky. Now, there's a bit more on the next page — but it's definitely worth making sure you understand everything so far. Make sure you know what all the headings mean and what goes under each.

The Balance Sheet — Capital Employed

Now for the second part of the balance sheet — where did all the money come from to create the net worth of the business? It came from shareholders originally buying the shares, profit that the firm has retained over the years, and money loaned to it by other people.

Shareholders' Funds came from the Firm's Owners

1 SHARE CAPITAL is the money put into the business when shares were originally issued. This might have been years and years ago for long-established companies.

This is not the same as what the shares are currently worth. Most shares traded on the stock exchange are second-hand — the person selling them gets the cash, not the firm.

Firms can raise new capital by issuing new shares. The usual way is to have a rights issue. This is where existing shareholders are offered new shares at a reduced price.

2 RETAINED PROFIT AND RESERVES means all the profit that the firm has made over the years that it has decided to retain instead of paying in dividends. Firms retain profit to finance future investment or to protect the firm against future problems.

This comes under "shareholders funds" because profits are really the shareholders' money — they've just decided to leave it in the firm rather than taking it out as dividends.

Long-Term Liabilities is Money Owed to Others

1) Firms don't just get money from their shareholders — they borrow it from other people as well. Included here are any debts that will take more than one year to repay — bank loans and debentures. They were covered in the stuff on external sources of finance (p68).

2) Debts payable in less than a year come under current liabilities instead — see the last page. It's all money the company owes, but it's conventional to split it up like that.

Capital Employed is the Total Put Into the Business

1) Capital employed is what you get when you add shareholders' funds and total liabilities. This is equal to net assets because it shows where the money to fund them came from.

2) If you're confused, think about it this way — all the money the business has got (from shareholders and borrowing from other people) is accounted for by capital employed. And everything it's done with the money it got (buy premises, keep it as cash, etc.) is listed under net assets. They have to be the same — because money doesn't just vanish.

All Companies have to Produce a Set of Annual Accounts

1) All limited companies are required by the Companies Act (1985) to produce a profit and loss account and a balance sheet account every year. These accounts must be audited by an independent accountant to ensure that they are accurate.

2) The government uses these accounts to check how much tax it needs. Banks use them to check whether any loans will get repaid. And potential investors are interested too — PLCs must provide their annual report free of charge to anyone who wants a copy.

Make sure you know what goes under each heading...

This section of the balance sheet shows you where the firm's money has come from. Again make sure you know what goes under each heading, and can explain why the whole thing is called a balance sheet.

Analysis of Accounts — Ratios

This is <u>very tricky</u>. You've got to learn <u>lots of formulae</u>, what they mean, what they are used for and what the size of the number says about the business. There are <u>two</u> main types of ratio — profitability and liquidity.

Profitability Ratios — How Much **Profit** is Made

These three ratios show <u>how much profit</u> the firm makes compared with its <u>size</u>.
The <u>higher</u> the number the <u>greater</u> the profit made.

1 <u>GROSS PROFIT MARGIN</u> shows how much profit the firm earns above the <u>cost</u> of <u>making the product</u>. Gross profit margin = <u>gross profit ÷ sales</u>.

> If gross profit is <u>£5,000</u> and sales (turnover) is <u>£20,000</u>, gross profit margin is <u>25%</u>.

2 <u>NET PROFIT MARGIN</u> shows how much profit is left after <u>all</u> the firm's <u>costs</u> have been paid. It shows how much of every £1 spent by customers is turned into profit. Net profit margin = <u>net profit ÷ sales</u>.

> If net profit is <u>£2,000</u> and sales (turnover) is <u>£20,000</u>, net profit margin is <u>10%</u>.

3 <u>RETURN ON CAPITAL EMPLOYED (ROCE)</u> shows how much profit is made as a <u>proportion</u> of the <u>capital</u> that has been invested in the business. A <u>high</u> ROCE is good for investors. ROCE = <u>net profit ÷ capital employed</u>.

> If net profit is <u>£2,000</u> and capital employed is <u>£100,000</u>, ROCE is <u>2%</u>.

> In <u>all</u> these cases, you do the <u>division sum</u> then <u>multiply by 100</u> to get the <u>percentage</u> figure. For instance: 5,000 ÷ 20,000 is <u>0.25</u>, which becomes <u>25%</u>.

Liquidity Ratios — How Much **Money** the Firm Has

1 <u>CURRENT RATIO</u> — also called the <u>working capital ratio</u>. It shows what proportion of the firm's <u>current liabilities</u> will be met by its <u>current assets</u>. In other words, it shows whether the firm has <u>enough money</u> coming into the business to pay its <u>current debts</u>.

> Current ratio = <u>current assets ÷ current liabilities</u>.

Ideally the figure should be <u>around 1.5</u> — the firm can easily pay its debts. If the result is <u>below 1</u>, the firm <u>owes</u> more than it has. That needn't be a problem if there's <u>more money</u> coming in <u>soon</u>. But the <u>more below 1</u> the figure is, the <u>less likely</u> it is the firm will be able to <u>pay its bills</u>. If the figure is <u>above 2</u> the firm has <u>too much money</u> — it should <u>invest more</u> in the business.

2 <u>ACID TEST RATIO</u> — also called the <u>liquid capital ratio</u>. The current asset that takes the <u>longest time</u> to be turned into money is stock — it is <u>illiquid</u>. So to be safe the firm should check that it has enough money coming in to pay its bills <u>ignoring stock</u>.

> Acid test ratio = <u>(current assets – stock) ÷ current liabilities</u>.

The result will be <u>lower</u> than the <u>current ratio</u>, so the rules are slightly different — <u>much above 1</u> and you've got <u>too much</u> cash lying about, <u>much below 1</u> and you might be in trouble because you haven't got enough <u>liquid</u> assets to pay the bills.

These little ratios tell you lots about a business...

Unfortunately there's <u>only one way</u> to deal with these ratios — learn, cover and copy. Keep on trying until you get <u>every single one</u>. Oh, and don't forget to write down what each one <u>means</u>. It's not easy, or fun — but it <u>works</u>.

Using Ratios

There's no point knowing the <u>formulae</u> if you don't know how to <u>use</u> them and what the <u>answers</u> mean. Just one more page on ratios then <u>that's it</u> for this section.

Ratios Need to be **Used With Care**

1) If you look at the ratios for <u>one year</u>, compare them with ratios from <u>other years</u> — this will help you spot any <u>trends</u>.

2) If you compare the ratios of two <u>different businesses</u>, make sure that the ratios have been worked out in the <u>same way</u>.

Ratios can **Differ Widely** Between Businesses

Different businesses will have <u>different ratios</u> for all sorts of reasons — the <u>most common reason</u> is that they are in <u>different markets</u>.

Trading, Profit and Loss Account for Clevercloggs Websites Plc — Year ending 31 March 2005

	£000	£000
Turnover		120
Minus cost of sales		
Opening stock	1	
Purchases	8	
	9	
Minus closing stock	2	
Gross profit		7
		113
Minus expenses		
Wages and salaries	32	
Rent and rates	8	
Office expenses	8	
Advertising	30	
Depreciation	2	
Other expenses	5	
		85
Operating profit		28
Interest payable		1
Profit before taxation (net profit)		27
Taxation		4
Dividends		14
Retained profit		9

Balance Sheet for Clevercloggs Plc — 31 March 2005

	£000	£000	£000
Fixed Assets			
Premises			30
Machinery			40
Vehicles			18
			88
Current Assets			
Stock at 31 March 2004		2	
Debtors		6	
Cash		12	
		20	
Current Liabilities			
Creditors		8	
Unpaid Corporation Tax		2	
		10	
Net Current Assets (Working Capital)			10
Net Assets			98
Financed by			
Shareholders Funds			
Share Capital			16
Retained Profit and Reserves			73
Long-term Liabilities			
Bank Loan			9
Debentures			0
Capital Employed			98

Trading, Profit and Loss Account for Naturo Pong Plc — Year ending 31 March 2005

	£m	£m
Turnover		780
Minus cost of sales		
Opening stock	89	
Purchases	420	
	509	
Minus closing stock	75	
		434
Gross profit		346
Minus expenses		
Wages and salaries	93	
Rent and rates	75	
Office expenses	35	
Advertising	5	
Depreciation	35	
Other expenses	68	
		311
Operating profit		35
Interest payable		20
Profit before taxation (net profit)		15
Taxation		2
Dividends		9
Retained profit		4

Balance Sheet for Naturo Pong Plc — 31 March 2005

	£m	£m	£m
Fixed Assets			
Premises			550
Machinery			250
Vehicles			6
			806
Current Assets			
Stock at 31 March 2004		75	
Debtors		45	
Cash		12	
		132	
Current Liabilities			
Creditors		62	
Unpaid Corporation Tax		10	
		72	
Net Current Assets (Working Capital)			60
Net Assets			866
Financed by			
Shareholders Funds			
Share Capital			560
Retained Profit and Reserves			126
Long-term Liabilities			
Bank Loan			140
Debentures			40
Capital Employed			866

Ratios for Clevercloggs Plc.
Gross Profit Margin = 94.17%
Net Profit Margin = 22.5%
Return on Capital Employed = 27.55%
Acid Test = 1.8

Ratios for Naturo Pong Plc.
Gross Profit Margin = 44.36%
Net Profit Margin = 1.92%
Return on Capital Employed = 1.73%
Acid Test = 0.79

- Clevercloggs is an <u>internet</u> firm so it <u>doesn't make anything</u>. Its main expenses are its computers and an office. As a result both its <u>gross profit margin</u> and <u>ROCE</u> are <u>very high</u>.
- Its <u>acid test</u> is <u>too high</u> — it should <u>invest</u> some of its <u>unused cash</u>.

- Naturo Pong is a <u>capital-intensive manufacturer</u>. It sells into a <u>competitive</u> market where <u>low prices</u> help firms sell their product. Its <u>high gross profit margin</u> but <u>low net profit margin</u> reflect the <u>high fixed costs</u> of a chemicals manufacturer.
- Its <u>net profit margin</u> and <u>ROCE</u> are very low — that should be <u>extremely worrying</u> for the company's managers.
- Its <u>acid test</u> is also a worry — the firm doesn't have enough <u>liquid assets</u> to pay off its current liabilities.

Warning — handle ratios with care...

Against all odds we've reached the end of the finance section. But before you start celebrating, check that you <u>understand</u> where the <u>answers</u> to the above ratios come from. It's just a matter of <u>sifting</u> through the figures and slotting the relevant ones neatly into your formulae. <u>Even more importantly</u>, make sure you know <u>why</u> the two businesses have such <u>different ratios</u> — you'll need to be able to <u>interpret</u> differences in the exam.

80

Warm-Up and Worked Exam Questions

Warm-up Questions

1) Give another word, which is used in accounts, that means "sales".
2) How is the gross profit margin different from the net profit margin?
3) What type of asset is "stock" — a current asset or a fixed asset?
4) Under what heading on a balance sheet would an accountant enter a loan that must be repaid in two years' time?
5) Name the two main types of ratio used to analyse a firm's accounts.
6) What type of ratio is Return on Capital Employed (ROCE)?

Worked Exam Question

Here's a worked exam question on balance sheets and ratios.

1 Mohammed Razwan is the proprietor of a general retail store. Below are items from his balance sheet at the end of his financial year (31st December).

Balance Sheet Item	Amount (£000's)
Total fixed assets	25
Cash	2
Stock (31st December)	10
Wages owing	1

a) Which of the above balance sheet items are current assets?

Cash and stock ✔ [1 mark] You have to give both answers to get the mark.

(1 mark)

b) Which of these current assets is the most liquid?

Cash ✔ [1 mark]

(1 mark)

c) Calculate the net current assets (working capital) of the company.

Current assets – Current liabilities

= (Cash + Stock) – Wages ✔ [1 mark] *= £2k + £10k – £1k= £11 000* ✔ [1 mark]

Again — show the formula and as much working as possible. It may earn you marks even if you get the final answer wrong.

(2 marks)

d) Calculate the net assets of the company.

Total fixed assets + Net current assets ✔ [1 mark]

= £25k + £11k = £36 000 ✔ [1 mark]

or (Total fixed assets + Current assets) – Current liabilities = (£25k + £2k + £10k) – £1k = £36k ✔ [1 mark] ✔ [1 mark]

(2 marks)

e) What is the value of capital employed?

This is the same as net assets, which is £36 000. ✔ [1 mark]

(1 mark)

SECTION FIVE — FINANCE

Exam Questions

1   a)   Explain how "current ratio" is calculated.

....

....

(1 mark)

b)   A firm has a current ratio that is below 1.

i)   Why should the owner of the firm be concerned?

....

....

(2 marks)

ii)   What advice would you give him or her?

....

....

(2 marks)

2)   Two fashion retailers, Now plc and Tops and Bottoms plc, are in competition in the same market. Summaries of their accounts are shown below.

NOW PLC		TOPS AND BOTTOMS PLC	
Turnover	£500 000	Turnover	£750 000
Cost of Sales	£200 000	Cost of Sales	£400 000
Expenses	£100 000	Expenses	£100 000
Capital Employed	£1 000 000	Capital Employed	£1 000 000

a)   Calculate the net profit margin for Now plc as a percentage.

....

....

(2 marks)

b)   The net profit for Tops and Bottoms plc is £250 000. Calculate the return on capital employed (ROCE) for this company.

....

....

(2 marks)

c)   The ROCE for Now plc is 20%. Which do you think is the better company to invest money in? Give a reason for your answer.

....

....

(2 marks)

Revision Summary for Section Five

It's that time again, I'm afraid — time to check you've learned all the stuff in this section. I know it's a pain but believe me it's worth it. Finance is really important in Business Studies and you can almost guarantee it'll come up somehow or other in your exam. So no slacking — get your nose to the grindstone and check you can answer these questions.

1) What does marginal cost mean?

2) What two things are equal at the break-even level of output?

3) Calculate the break-even level of output given the following information:

   variable costs = £3 per unit, selling price = £6 per unit, and fixed costs = £6000.

4) Explain three limitations of break-even analysis.

5) Give two reasons why firms need finance.

6) List four internal sources of finance. And four external sources of finance.

7) Why might new and small firms not be able to find much finance from internal sources?

8) I want to use external finance to build a new marshmallow factory. Where should I get the money from?

   a) my aunt Flo;   b) paying my bills a bit later;   c) a bank loan;   d) a mortgage.

9) What are the three main uses of a budget?

10) If you spend less than you budgeted for, is that a favourable or unfavourable variance?

11) Why might a firm offer a discount for quick payment of its invoices?

12) Dave's Dodgy Motors Ltd. is suffering from poor cash flow. Explain three problems that might result.

13) In a trading, profit and loss account, how do you calculate the cost of sales figure?

14) Jim's Gym buys a new treadmill for £3000. Jim's accountant decides to depreciate it using the straight-line method, and assumes it will last for six years before it needs replacing. What allowance for depreciation will be in the accounts each year?

15) Put these in order, most liquid first: debtors, stock, cash.

16) What do you get if you deduct current liabilities from current assets?

17) What are the two ways a firm gets funds from its shareholders?

18) What do you get if you divide net profit by capital employed?

   a) gross profit margin;   b) net profit margin;   c) return on capital employed.

19) What do you get if you take away stock from current assets, and divide by current liabilities?

   a) current ratio;   b) acid test ratio.

20) Look at the information on the right, and work out these ratios:

   a) current ratio;   b) acid test ratio;

sales (turnover) = £80,000
cost of sales = £25,000
current assets = £20,000
closing stock = £5,000
current liabilities = £18,000
debtors = £8,000
creditors = £3,750
net profit after tax = £7,000

3. 2000. 14. £500.
20. a) 1.11, b) 0.83.

Starting a New Business

Over 300,000 new firms are set up in Britain every year. You need to know why people start up in business and what it takes to be successful.

People Start Businesses for **Six Main Reasons**

1) Some people enjoy the independence that comes from being their own boss.

2) It can be irritating to see someone else earn profits from your work — if your business succeeds, you keep them all so you might earn more.

3) Some new firms are set up because the owner has a new idea or product — but can't persuade anyone else to adopt it.

4) It may be easier for the owner to set up in business than find someone else to employ them.

5) People who are made redundant by their employer often use some of their redundancy money to set up their own business — it's better than being unemployed.

6) There can be disagreements amongst directors and managers about how to run their firm. People may leave and set up their own business so they can run it the way they want.

Being Your Own Boss has its **Problems**

The big advantage of starting your own business is that you get to order everyone else around — and decide what to do with all the profits. But there are problems:

1) The business may take time to produce a profit — the owner's income may be small and vary from week to week.

2) There is no-one else to take the blame if anything goes wrong — the owner must be prepared to take responsibility.

3) Owners of new firms generally work very long hours — for example, completing the firm's accounts in the evening.

4) As the business grows the owner needs to learn to delegate responsibility to subordinates — not easy if the owner has built the firm up single-handed.

Business Owners are a **Special Breed**

Not everyone has got the kind of personality that it takes to be a successful entrepreneur. Some people really are happier with the easier life of being someone else's employee.

Personal Characteristics of a Good Business person

1) You must be hardworking and prepared to work long hours.

2) You must be resourceful and independent.

3) You must be willing to take risks with your own capital.

4) You must be self-motivated and have a desire to succeed.

Only some people like enterprise...

A nice, easy page to start this section — but you still need to make sure it's learned. Starting your own business sounds like a great idea, but it has its downside too — make sure you know all the problems. Then scribble a mini-essay on why people start businesses and what type of people make good entrepreneurs.

The Business Plan

It's vital that the business has a <u>clear idea</u> of what it is going to do — that's what <u>business plans</u> are for. You need to know <u>why</u> businesses have them and <u>what</u> they should contain.

The Plan is for the **Owner** and **Financial Backers**

1) It is important that the owner <u>thinks carefully</u> what the business is going to do and what <u>resources</u> are needed. This will help calculate how much <u>start-up capital</u> is needed.

2) It is unlikely that the owner will have enough money to start the business — <u>financial backers</u> such as banks or venture capitalists will need to be <u>convinced</u> that the new business is a <u>sound investment</u>.

3) The hope is that if the business is a <u>bad idea</u>, either the owner or the financial backer will realise this at the <u>planning stage</u> — before they've wasted lots of <u>time and money</u> on a business that was never going to work.

The Plan should have **Seven Sections**

Lots of these things are covered in <u>greater detail</u> elsewhere in the book — <u>check the index</u> if you're not sure.

There is no single <u>correct way</u> to write a business plan — but most good 'uns will include all of this stuff.

1) <u>PERSONAL DETAILS</u> of the owner and other <u>important personnel</u> — like their <u>CVs</u>. Financial backers will want to know who they are trusting with their money.

2) <u>MISSION STATEMENT</u> — a fancy way of describing the <u>broad aims</u> of the company. They usually use long words to say something <u>general and obvious</u>.

   "To combine fresh bread and tasty fillings in popular combinations and so become market leader amongst sandwich shops in Bigglesworth."

3) <u>OBJECTIVES</u> — these are more concrete and <u>specific</u> aims.

   "To average 160 sandwich sales each weekday lunchtime over the next four years."

4) <u>PRODUCT DESCRIPTION</u> — including details of the <u>market</u> and <u>competitors</u>. It should explain how the firm will achieve <u>product differentiation</u> — also called its <u>unique selling point (USP)</u>. It should describe its <u>marketing strategy</u> using the <u>4 Ps</u> (page 19). All statements should be supported by <u>field or desk research</u>.

5) <u>PRODUCTION DETAILS</u> — how the firm will make its product or provide its service. It should list all the <u>equipment</u> needed and where it will be <u>located</u>.

6) <u>STAFFING REQUIREMENTS</u> — what <u>personnel</u> will be needed — <u>how many</u> people, their <u>job</u> descriptions and the expected <u>wage bill</u>.

7) <u>FINANCE</u> — it should explain how much <u>money</u> is needed to <u>start up</u> the business. There should be a <u>cash flow</u> forecast and a projected <u>profit and loss account</u> and <u>balance sheet</u>. There should also be <u>ratios</u> to show any backer the <u>likely return</u> on their investment.

Business plan — the business in a nutshell...

Business plans will all be <u>different</u>, but they should all say what the business is about, its aims and how it plans to achieve them. Make sure you've learned the <u>reasons</u> for producing a business plan. Then cover the page and scribble down the <u>seven</u> things a business plan should contain. I reckon the only way to deal with this stuff is to <u>practise</u> — try writing a business plan for a new home-delivery pizza firm.

Starting a Business — Help and Support

Starting a new business isn't easy — even if you've done GCSE Business Studies. You need to know what help is available and why so many organisations are keen to help out.

The Government Gives A Lot of Help

1) The government has a lot to gain by encouraging new businesses. Many people start businesses as an alternative to unemployment. This reduces the amount of state benefits the government has to pay out.

2) The government will also receive taxation revenue when the firm makes a profit. And successful businesses create employment for many people — helping both themselves and the government still further.

3) The government funds Business Link, which operates in each region. It provides guidance on how to produce a business plan and advice on staff training. It also offers financial support.

4) Other government bodies providing help include the Department of Trade and Industry (DTI) — it provides advice and leaflets, most of which are available on its website.

5) New firms can also apply to have bank loans underwritten by the government. This means the government will pay them back if the business fails — making it easier for the new firm to borrow money.

Private Firms also Offer Support

1) Some firms in the private sector aim to make a profit by providing help to new businesses. The most obvious example are banks. They publish guides on how to produce a business plan and have business advisors who will talk to potential entrepreneurs.

2) Banks do this for two main reasons. Firstly, to get the firm to open an account with them and not with one of their competitors. And secondly, to reduce the chances of the new business going bankrupt owing the bank lots of money.

3) Some firms exist to provide management services to other businesses — they charge for their help but sometimes provide free advice to new firms. This is because they hope the new firm will pay for their services once it is established.

A Few Charities Offer Advice and Money

1) Some charities help people start new businesses. These charities are usually started by people who believe that it is good for society to have lots of new firms starting up.

2) The most well known example is the Prince's Youth Trust. The Prince of Wales set it up when he realised there were limited employment opportunities for young people living in inner-city areas. The charity gives advice, grants and low-interest loans to young entrepreneurs.

Chambers of Commerce give Help to Local Firms

1) Chambers of Commerce are groups of business people in a city or town who work together to look after the interests of local businesses.

2) These groups provide information and support for small companies and act as an important link between local businesses and local and central government.

So you're starting a business — I think you need help...

With all that help around it's a wonder so many businesses fail. Still, your job's a lot easier — learn this page, cover it up and scribble down a list of who wants to help and why.

Growth of Firms — Internal Expansion

Once a firm's established, it might start to fancy itself for a spot of world domination. There are <u>two</u> ways a firm can grow — <u>internally</u>, by expanding their own activities, and <u>externally</u>. You need to know the reasons <u>why</u> firms grow, and <u>how</u> they can go about it.

Firms Grow for *Five Main Reasons*

1) <u>ECONOMIES OF SCALE</u> — Larger firms can produce at <u>lower average cost</u> than smaller firms. They can pass on these <u>economies of scale</u> to consumers as <u>lower prices</u>. This will help them increase their <u>sales</u>, their <u>market share</u> and their <u>profits</u>.

2) <u>DIVERSIFICATION</u> — Larger firms can afford to produce <u>more products</u> than smaller firms. They can sell into <u>different markets</u> and so <u>reduce the risks</u> that a decline in sales of one product will harm the business. That means there's less threat to their <u>profits</u>.

3) <u>FINANCIAL SUPPORT</u> — Larger firms are <u>less likely</u> to go <u>bankrupt</u> than smaller firms. That's mainly because they can <u>borrow money</u> more easily from banks so they will find it easier to survive <u>cash flow</u> problems. Larger firms can also receive more financial support from the <u>government</u> than smaller firms because they employ lots of people.

4) <u>PERSONAL VANITY</u> — Some owners also enjoy the <u>power</u> and <u>status</u> that comes from owning a large business.

5) <u>DOMINATION OF THE MARKET</u> — The <u>larger</u> the <u>market share</u> a firm has, the more it can <u>control</u> the price of its products. It will face <u>less threats</u> from competitors and may even be able to <u>eliminate</u> rivals by charging prices that they can't compete with.

> Growth is a <u>key objective</u> for many firms. Larger firms can use economies of scale to help them <u>achieve other objectives</u> — like an <u>increase in sales</u> or <u>market share</u>. This in turn enables them to achieve their most important objectives of <u>profit and survival</u>.

There are *Three Main Methods* of *Internal Expansion*

Internal expansion is also called <u>organic growth</u>.

1) The firm can <u>produce more</u> of its <u>current products</u> to sell in its <u>existing markets</u>. For example Glugg Soft Drinks Ltd. could try to increase its market share in the UK fizzy cabbage juice market from 1% to 20%.

2) The firm can sell its <u>current product</u> into <u>new markets</u>. Glugg Soft Drinks could try to export its fizzy cabbage juice to the USA.

3) The firm could launch a <u>new product</u>. This could be a similar product to existing ones, like fizzy turnip juice — this is called <u>line extension</u>, because you're extending your line of products. Or it could be a completely new product, like sports cars — this is called <u>diversification</u>.

Internal Expansion has its *Benefits* and *Problems*

1) Internal growth is <u>good</u> in that it is relatively <u>inexpensive</u> to achieve. Also, with the exception of diversifying into a completely new product, the firm expands by doing more of what it is <u>already good at</u> — making its existing products. That means it's less likely to go horribly wrong.

2) The <u>problem</u> is that it can take a long time to achieve growth. Some owners are <u>not prepared to wait</u> that long — that's why they go for external growth.

Large firms have lots of advantages over small firms...

So growth is a <u>key step</u> on the road to bigger sales, increased market share, huge profits and ultimately world domination. Splendid. You need to know all the <u>reasons for growth</u> as well as the <u>three types</u> of <u>internal expansion</u>. And don't forget to memorise the <u>benefits</u> and <u>problems</u> too.

Growth of Firms — Takeovers and Mergers

These are the two ways a firm can achieve <u>external expansion</u> — also called <u>integration</u>. A <u>merger</u> is when two firms <u>agree</u> to join together, a <u>takeover</u> is when one firm <u>buys</u> another. Sometimes that firm <u>agrees</u> to be taken over, sometimes it <u>doesn't</u> want to be.

There are **Four Types** of Integration

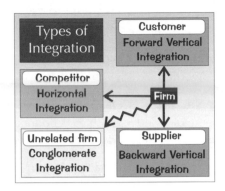

❶ Horizontal Integration...

... is when two <u>competitors</u> join together — they make the same product at the <u>same stage</u> of the <u>production chain</u>. For example, Glugg Soft Drinks Ltd takes over another company which makes fizzy sodas.

- Horizontal integration creates a firm with more <u>economies of scale</u> and a <u>bigger market share</u>. It will be more able to <u>compete</u> than before.

❷ Forward Vertical Integration...

... is when a firm takes over a <u>customer</u>. For example, Glugg Soft Drinks Ltd takes over a drinks wholesaling firm.

- Forward vertical integration gives the firm greater <u>access to customers</u>. Owning its own retail outlets will make it <u>easier to sell</u> its products.

❸ Backward Vertical Integration...

... is when a firm joins with a <u>supplier</u>. For example, Glugg Soft Drinks Ltd takes over a cabbage farm.

- Backward vertical integration gives the firm greater <u>control</u> over its <u>supplies</u> — it helps <u>guarantee</u> a supply of raw materials. It may also be able to obtain <u>cheaper</u> and <u>better quality</u> raw materials.

❹ Lateral / Conglomerate Integration...

... is when two firms with <u>nothing in common</u> join together. For example, Glugg Soft Drinks Ltd takes over a clotheswear firm.

- Lateral integration means the firm will expand by <u>diversifying</u> into new markets. This <u>reduces the risks</u> that come from relying on just a few products.

Mergers and Takeovers have their **Problems**

1) <u>Less than half</u> of all takeovers and mergers are <u>successful</u>. It is very hard to make <u>two different businesses</u> work as one. <u>Management styles</u> often differ between firms — the employees of one firm may be used to one company culture and not be <u>motivated</u> by the style used in the other.

2) Takeovers can create <u>bad feeling</u>. Often a firm <u>agrees</u> to be taken over, but sometimes the takeover bid is <u>hostile</u> and unpopular. And mergers usually lead to cost-cutting by making lots of people <u>redundant</u>, so they lead to tension and uncertainty among workers.

News just in — Lex Luthor involved in hostile takeover bid...

Loads of new stuff to learn here — but nothing too tricky. Just make sure you know the <u>four types of integration</u> — learn, cover up and copy out the diagram. Then scribble down a mini-essay on the pros and cons of each type. Remember, the <u>type</u> of integration a firm chooses will depend on its <u>objectives</u>.

Effects of Expansion — Economies of Scale

Give the examiner a nice surprise — make sure you know everything there is to know about the <u>reductions</u> in <u>average cost</u> that come from producing on a <u>large scale</u>.

There are Six Main **Internal** Economies of Scale

1) <u>PURCHASING ECONOMIES</u> happen when a <u>large firm</u> buys its supplies <u>in bulk</u> and so gets them at a <u>cheaper unit price</u> than a small firm.

2) <u>MARKETING ECONOMIES</u> arise because the cost of an <u>advertising campaign</u> is pretty much a <u>fixed cost</u>. A larger firm will need to spend <u>less per unit</u> advertising its products than a smaller firm.

3) <u>MANAGERIAL ECONOMIES</u> are where a large firm can afford to employ <u>specialist managers</u> who have expert knowledge, such as <u>accountants</u> and <u>lawyers</u>. This <u>managerial division of labour</u> means that management costs do not double every time the firm doubles in size.

4) <u>FINANCIAL ECONOMIES</u> result from <u>banks</u> being prepared to <u>lend more money</u> to larger firms at <u>lower interest rates</u> than smaller firms. This is because the banks know that larger firms are more likely to <u>pay them back</u> than smaller firms.

5) <u>TECHNICAL ECONOMIES</u> occur because a large firm can afford to operate <u>more advanced machinery</u> than smaller firms. Also, the <u>law of increased dimensions</u> means that, for example, a factory that's ten times as <u>big</u> will be <u>less than</u> ten times as <u>expensive</u>.

6) <u>RISK-BEARING ECONOMIES</u> are where the firm can afford to sell a <u>range of products</u> into many <u>different markets</u>. A decline in sales of one product will not significantly harm the firm's cash flow.

There are Four Main **External** Economies of Scale

These happen when a number of <u>large firms</u> locate <u>near to each other</u>.

1) When this happens <u>suppliers</u> will choose to locate <u>near their customers</u>. This reduces delivery times, transport costs and the need for the producers to hold large stocks of raw materials.

2) There will be a <u>local workforce</u> who already have the <u>skills needed</u> — they got them working for other firms in the area. This reduces firms' <u>training costs</u>.

3) Firms will receive support from the <u>local council</u> and <u>national government</u> — for example, motorways may be built which make distribution easier.

4) The area will build up a <u>good reputation</u> for particular products. This will <u>benefit</u> firms in the area and <u>encourage</u> other firms to locate there.

*Diseconomies of Scale — the **Disadvantages** of Expansion*

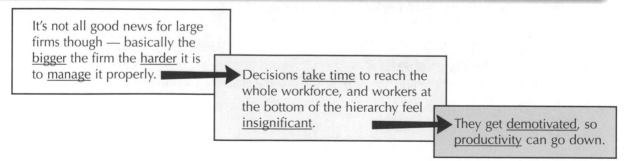

It's not all good news for large firms though — basically the <u>bigger</u> the firm the <u>harder</u> it is to <u>manage</u> it properly.

Decisions <u>take time</u> to reach the whole workforce, and workers at the bottom of the hierarchy feel <u>insignificant</u>.

They get <u>demotivated</u>, so <u>productivity</u> can go down.

Learn the six benefits of large scale production...

When someone talks about economies of scale, they just mean the <u>advantages</u> that a <u>large</u> firm has over a <u>small</u> one. Make sure you memorise them all and know which are <u>internal</u> and which are <u>external</u>. Read over the <u>last three pages</u> and think about the <u>effects</u> that the expansion of a company can have on its <u>stakeholders</u> — its suppliers, customers and competitors. Scribble down as many as you can.

Effects of Expansion — Communication

Good <u>communication</u> is important for all firms — but it is a particular problem in <u>large ones</u>. You need to know <u>how</u> to communicate, what the <u>different methods</u> are and the <u>effects</u> of <u>poor</u> communication.

Communication is a **Two-way** Process

1) It is not enough to just deliver a message — <u>effective communication</u> requires <u>feedback</u> confirming that the message has been <u>understood</u>.

2) <u>One-way</u> communication, which means there is <u>no feedback</u>, runs the <u>risk</u> that the message will be <u>misunderstood</u> by the receiver.

The Choice of **Medium** Should Reflect the **Message**

There are <u>three main methods</u> — written, verbal and visual.

1 <u>WRITTEN</u> methods include <u>letters</u>, <u>e-mails</u>, <u>faxes</u> (mainly to people <u>outside</u> the firm), and messages on <u>notice boards</u>, <u>memos</u> and <u>reports</u> (mainly to people <u>inside</u> the firm).

Written methods are good if a <u>permanent</u> <u>record</u> of the message is needed. The reader can study <u>complex</u> information again and again. Copies can be seen by <u>many people</u>.		But <u>feedback</u> can be <u>difficult</u> to obtain. And if you don't understand what someone has written, it can be <u>hard to check</u> it with them.

2 <u>VERBAL</u> methods include <u>telephone calls</u>, one-to-one <u>conversations</u>, group <u>meetings</u> in person or using <u>video-conferencing</u>.

Verbal methods are good in that information can be given <u>quickly</u>. <u>Body language</u> and <u>tone of voice</u> can <u>reinforce</u> the message and feedback can be <u>easily</u> obtained.		But there is no <u>permanent</u> <u>record</u> of the message and sometimes people <u>forget</u> what they have been told.

3 <u>VISUAL</u> methods include <u>films</u>, <u>posters</u>, <u>diagrams</u> and <u>charts</u>. Watching <u>body language</u> is a very powerful way of obtaining <u>non-verbal information</u> from people.

Visual methods are good in that complicated information can be <u>summarised</u> so the message is received quickly. Pictures can also communicate <u>feelings and emotions</u> better than words.		But people will <u>interpret</u> images in <u>different ways</u>. Some people find complicated diagrams <u>hard</u> <u>to understand</u>.

Poor Communication is **Bad for Business**

1) Poor <u>internal</u> communication can result in <u>poor decisions</u> being made and <u>low morale</u> if people feel that they are <u>not being listened to</u>.

2) Poor <u>external</u> communications can result in customers and suppliers <u>losing confidence</u> in the company — this can result in <u>fewer orders</u>.

So if I write a few e-mails does that count as revision...

I hope this page has <u>communicated</u> a lot of information to you. Give yourself <u>feedback</u> on your understanding by scribbling down everything you know about the <u>main communication methods</u>. The <u>key</u> thing when choosing a method of communication is to think about <u>what</u> it is you want to say and <u>who</u> you want to say it to.

Warm-Up and Worked Exam Questions

Warm-up Questions

1) List three advantages and three disadvantages of being your own boss.
2) What details should be included in a business plan?
3) Give three ways in which the government can help people to set up their own business.
4) Many businesses want to grow bigger. What are the two main processes for growth?
5) State any three of the six means of achieving internal economies of scale.
6) What are the three main methods of communication?

Worked Exam Questions

Take a look at these worked examples, then try the exam-style questions on page 91.

1   Jane Laker set up a fashion shop several years ago, and her business has been very successful. Jane has long thought about expanding her business but is unsure of what to do — she does not want to share control of her business with anyone else.

a) What is another name given to "internal" expansion?

Organic growth ✓ [1 mark]

(1 mark)

b) List and briefly explain three methods she could use to make her business grow internally.

She could try to sell more of her existing products to gain a larger ✓ [1 mark]
share of the market. She could buy a second shop somewhere else ✓ [1 mark] ✓ [1 mark]
and sell into a new market. She could introduce new lines to ✓ [1 mark] ✓ [1 mark]
increase the size of her market or replace lines that do not sell. ✓ [1 mark]

You have to say <u>why</u> each method helps her expand.

(6 marks)

2   Peter has recently been made redundant and has just over £8000 in his bank account. Several of his old workmates have started their own businesses. Peter seeks your advice and wants to know what makes so many people go into business for themselves.

There are several reasons for wanting to start up a business:
perhaps you want to be independent and be your own boss; ✓ [1 mark]
you might have a great idea for a product that you want to sell; ✓ [1 mark]
you can retain all the profit for yourself, or choose where you invest it; ✓ [1 mark]
you get to make your own decisions and run things the way you want; ✓ [1 mark]
if you are unemployed and unable to find suitable work, it can be better
to set up your own business. ✓ [1 mark]

There are five marks available, so try and make <u>five different points</u>.

(5 marks)

Exam Questions

1   Harry Blake runs a market garden, growing fruit and vegetables. He decides to buy a fruit and vegetable shop in the small town nearby.

   a)   How would you describe this type of growth?

   ....

   (1 mark)

   b)   Explain to Harry two advantages of this move and two possible disadvantages.

   ....

   ....

   ....

   ....

   (4 marks)

2   Richards TV and Audio is a retail business with five branches in five neighbouring towns. They intend to stop selling video recorders, and so are having a clearance sale next month when all their video recorders will be sold at half price.   They ask your advice on how to communicate this information to potential customers.

   a)   Identify one risk they run if they use poor methods of communication.

   ....

   (1 mark)

   b)   They decide to advertise the sale on local radio and through posters in their shop windows. Give an advantage and a disadvantage of each method.

   ....

   ....

   ....

   ....

   (4 marks)

3   Carol and Malcolm run a small grocery shop. They find they cannot compete against the big supermarket on the edge of town and are thinking of closing down. Briefly explain four economies of scale which the supermarket enjoys.

   ....

   ....

   ....

   ....

   (4 marks)

Communication — Networks and Hierarchies

A <u>formal communication channel</u> is the <u>official</u> way communication takes place in a firm. You need to know how different <u>organisation structures</u> affect how communication takes place.

A *Long Chain of Command* is a Problem...

1) Communication <u>up and down</u> the hierarchy is called <u>vertical communication</u>. Dodgy Computers has six levels in its hierarchy — so its <u>chain of command</u> has six layers.

2) A long chain of command is <u>bad</u> because messages take a <u>long time</u> to travel up and down the hierarchy. People at each end feel <u>isolated</u> from the other end. This can result in <u>poor morale</u>. Messages may not reach the other end and if they do they might get <u>distorted</u> along the way — rather like a game of <u>Chinese whispers</u>.

3) Some firms have tried to <u>solve the problem</u> of a long chain of command by <u>de-layering</u> — removing tiers of management, usually in the middle.

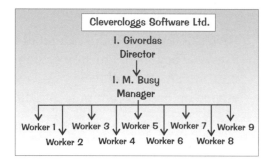

...and so is a *Wide Span of Control*

1) Communication along the <u>same level</u> in the hierarchy is called <u>horizontal</u> or <u>lateral communication</u>. The manager of Clevercloggs Software has a <u>span of control</u> of nine workers.

2) Horizontal communication can cause problems if one person has to give messages to lots of others — it can <u>take time</u> and people may feel they lack <u>personal contact</u>.

3) Firms must find <u>balance</u> between a <u>small</u> chain of command and a narrow <u>span of control</u>.

The Right *Communication Network* can Help...

1) Horizontal and vertical communication takes place along a <u>chain network</u>. Two alternatives are the <u>wheel network</u> and the <u>connected network</u>.

2) The <u>wheel</u> has a <u>key person</u> at the <u>centre</u> who communicates directly with all other parts. It is good for <u>solving problems</u> but bad in that <u>different parts</u> of the network cannot speak to each other.

3) The <u>connected network</u> is good for <u>exchanging ideas</u> between different groups in the firm. However, it is bad for taking <u>decisions</u> because there is no-one in <u>overall control</u>.

...as can Good *Informal* Communication Channels

1) Also called the <u>grapevine</u>. Messages get passed by <u>word of mouth</u> between colleagues throughout the firm. Information gets passed <u>quickly</u>.

2) But so do <u>rumours and disinformation</u>. Some people will not receive the <u>correct messages</u> and the managers are <u>not in control</u> of the information being shared.

I heard it through the informal communication channel...

A page about Chinese whispers and gossip — whatever next? Make sure you understand how this page <u>relates</u> to the idea of <u>diseconomies of scale</u>. Copy out all <u>four diagrams</u> and the <u>benefits</u> and <u>problems</u> that go with each.

Multinational Firms

Some people call them <u>multinational enterprises</u> (MNEs), others call them <u>transnational corporations</u> (TNCs). Either way, they're firms who have operations in <u>more than one country</u>, and you need to know about them.

Firms **Become Multinational** for Many Reasons

1) By producing in various countries they can <u>keep transport</u> costs to a minimum.
2) They can increase knowledge of <u>local market conditions</u>.
3) They can avoid <u>trade barriers</u> by producing <u>inside a country</u>.
4) They can reduce risks from <u>foreign exchange</u> fluctuations.
5) They can gain access to <u>raw materials</u> or <u>cheap labour</u>.
6) By employing <u>expert accountants</u> and shuffling money <u>between countries</u>, big companies can avoid paying tax.
7) They can win <u>subsidies</u> from governments and force workers to accept <u>lower wages</u> by <u>threatening to relocate</u> production in another country.

MNEs Can Benefit the **Host Country...**

1) MNEs are often a source of <u>foreign investment</u> money and <u>create employment</u> for locals.
2) MNEs bring their own methods of working, giving the host country access to <u>foreign technology</u> and working methods — like with Japanese car producers in the UK.
3) The <u>profits</u> of the MNE can be a source of <u>taxation revenue</u> for the host country government — <u>in theory</u> at least (see point 2 below).
4) <u>Export revenue</u> from MNE sales abroad can <u>improve</u> the country's <u>balance of payments</u>.

...But They Cause Plenty of **Problems**

1) The jobs created by the MNE are often <u>unskilled</u>, <u>low paid</u> and in <u>poor working conditions</u>. Many big brand name Western goods are made by <u>child labour</u> in <u>foreign sweatshops</u>.
2) In return for locating in their country the MNEs demand <u>reduced tax</u> and even <u>subsidies</u> from the government — or that the government build them <u>roads</u> and airport links. Often it actually <u>costs governments money</u> to have an MNE locate there.
3) The MNE, benefiting from economies of scale, might drive out <u>local industries</u>.
4) They can exert a <u>strong influence</u> on the government to <u>change laws</u> that do not benefit them — like demanding a reduction in <u>environmental controls</u> or <u>worker protection</u> laws. MNEs are so <u>big</u> nowadays they often have <u>more power</u> than democratic governments.
5) They often cause <u>environmental degradation</u> in poor countries that lasts long after the MNE has left. The company's owners <u>don't live there</u>, so they have no reason to care.
6) Whatever benefits MNEs bring to poor countries, these are <u>much less than</u> the benefits to wealthy MNE <u>shareholders</u> of locating in those poor countries. Many people think there must be a <u>more equitable</u> way of helping poor countries to develop.

Multinationals — Learn the Pros and Cons...
You have to <u>make up your own mind</u> whether MNEs are good or bad — examiners think there's no right or wrong answer, it's <u>how you argue</u> it that counts. Learn everything on this page, then <u>think about it</u> and scribble an answer to the mini-essay question: "Are MNEs <u>good or bad</u>?"

Types of Competition

The basic aim of <u>consumers</u> is to buy as many goods as possible at the <u>cheapest prices</u>. The basic aim of <u>firms</u> is to <u>maximise profits</u> for their shareholders. These aims are <u>not the same</u>.

Consumers want Markets to be *Competitive*

1) A <u>competitive market</u> is one where there is a <u>large number of producers</u> selling to a <u>large number of consumers</u>. Nobody is powerful enough to dictate prices. If a firm charges too much then consumers will go elsewhere — this forces producers to be <u>efficient</u>.

2) If the prices charged by firms are as low as possible then <u>consumers</u> will be able to buy as large a quantity of products as possible. This gives them the highest possible <u>material standard of living</u>.

3) Firms compete by trying to convince the consumer that their product is better than their rivals' — this results in <u>high quality products</u> and good <u>after-sales service</u>.

4) Firms will rush to fill any <u>gap in the market</u> — supplying a previously unmet consumer need. This results in high levels of <u>product innovation</u> and the exploitation of <u>new technologies</u>.

5) However, competition means that sometimes all the firms end up making the <u>same product</u> — the result being fewer different products for the consumer. If each firm makes fewer profits there may be <u>less money</u> available to develop <u>new and better</u> products.

PERFECT COMPETITION...

<u>Perfect competition</u> describes the <u>most competitive</u> type of market. It's an <u>unrealistic model</u> that clever business types need to understand. <u>You</u> just need to know that it describes a market with the <u>following characteristics</u>:

- A <u>large</u> number of <u>producers</u>, none of whom can dictate prices.
- All the rival products are <u>identical</u>.
- <u>All</u> customers <u>know the price</u> of <u>every</u> product.
- Any firm is <u>free</u> to enter or leave the market.
- All firms want to <u>maximise profits</u>.

Producers Want to be a *Monopoly*

1) Being a <u>competitive</u> firm is too much like <u>hard work</u> — firms have to constantly strive to keep ahead of their competitors. They would much prefer to be a <u>monopoly</u>.

2) There are <u>three different definitions</u> of a monopoly. To an economist a monopoly is the <u>only supplier</u> of a product — for example the Royal Mail is the only firm that delivers letters. To the government a monopoly is any firm which has more than a <u>25% market share</u>. To most people a monopoly is any firm that has a <u>dominant position</u> in the market — it can dictate prices to others.

3) A monopoly charges <u>higher prices</u> than a firm in a competitive market because the <u>consumer</u> has <u>less choice</u> about who to buy from. As a result the monopolist earns <u>higher profits</u> for its shareholders.

4) These higher prices mean that <u>consumers</u> end up with a <u>lower standard of living</u> — but the higher profits can be spent on the <u>research and development</u> of new products. A good example is the <u>pharmaceuticals</u> industry.

Oligopoly is somewhere in between

1) Oligopoly exists when a <u>small</u> number of <u>large firms dominate a market</u>. An example is the <u>UK chocolate market</u>.

2) Because there's only a <u>small</u> number of firms in the market, it's possible for them to <u>agree amongst themselves</u> to keep prices at an <u>acceptable level</u>.

3) Firms should be able to charge <u>higher prices</u> than in a <u>more competitive</u> market as customers won't have any <u>cheaper alternatives</u>.

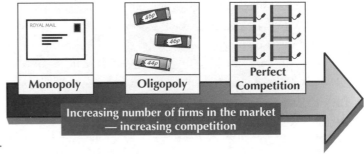

Two opoly words to learn on the way to perfection...

So you can put markets on a <u>scale of competition</u> — with <u>monopoly</u> at one end and <u>perfect competition</u> at the other. Lots of markets lie somewhere between oligopoly and perfect competition, but there are plenty of monopolies out there too. Make sure you understand the <u>benefits</u> and <u>problems</u> of each type of competition.

The Survival of Small Firms

I've spent a lot of time telling you the benefits to a firm of being <u>big</u>. But the <u>vast majority</u> of firms are small. You need to know why this is and what the <u>benefits of being small</u> are.

Firms **Stay Small** for Five Reasons

1) The firm may stay small because the <u>owner</u> feels under less pressure that way.

2) The owner may not have <u>profit maximisation</u> as a main objective — for example they may prefer to close the business for periods and go on <u>holiday</u>.

3) The firm may be limited by the <u>size of the market</u> — for example, the firm may only supply a small rural area.

4) The industry may not have the <u>potential</u> for <u>economies of scale</u> — so the <u>optimum size</u> of the firm is <u>small</u>. This is true of customer services such as <u>hairdressers</u>.

5) The firm might simply not have the <u>financial or human resources</u> to bring about growth.

Small Firms **Have Their Advantages** over Big Firms

1) They can get to know their customers individually and offer a more <u>personal service</u>.

2) As a result they can be <u>more responsive</u> to <u>individual customer needs</u> — for example stocking particular products or taking special orders.

3) The firm can be set up in order to exploit a <u>gap in the market</u> — small firms are more able to supply <u>niche products</u> than larger firms.

4) Small firms have <u>lower fixed costs</u> than large firms — that means they can be <u>more flexible</u> about the <u>prices</u> they charge.

Small Firms have a **Mixed Impact** on the Economy

SMALL FIRMS — ADVANTAGES TO THE ECONOMY

- Because of their low fixed costs small firms tend to be more <u>labour intensive</u> than larger firms. This helps to <u>reduce unemployment</u>.

- Small firms help the economy to exploit <u>new technologies</u> and gaps in the market. They force <u>larger rivals</u> to remain <u>competitive</u>.

SMALL FIRMS — DISADVANTAGES TO THE ECONOMY

- Small firms do not gain from <u>economies of scale</u> — to remain competitive they need to keep their costs down in other ways.

- As a result small firms are more likely to employ people on <u>part-time</u> or <u>temporary</u> contracts, and often pay relatively <u>low wages</u>.

- <u>Employment conditions</u> such as holiday entitlement, canteen meals and the working environment may not be very good either.

They don't make diamonds as big as boulders...

I know I've been going on about the benefits of economies of scale for what seems like years now — and with good reason too. But small firms shouldn't despair. Far from it. There are <u>plenty of good reasons</u> for staying small. You need to <u>know them all</u> and the <u>impact</u> small firms have on the economy.

Business Failure

It's no use running from the truth. The sad fact is that a lot of firms go bust sooner or later. You need to know why this is and what happens to them and their owners when they do.

Businesses Close Because of *Poor Cash Flow*

Most businesses fail because they become insolvent — in other words, they don't have enough working capital (that's cash to you and me) to pay their short-term liabilities. There are three main reasons for this.

1) POOR SALES due to a recession in the economy. There's a lack of demand from consumers for the firm's products, so the firm has less money coming in and it cannot pay its creditors.

2) OVERTRADING — the firm takes on too many orders — as a result it buys in too many raw materials and hires too many staff. Something goes wrong with the orders and the firm doesn't get the money from its customers quickly enough to pay its debts.

3) POOR BUSINESS DECISIONS — for example it decides to bring out new products or expand into new markets but they do not bring in as much money as forecast.

In each case the same thing happens — one or more of the firm's creditors do not get paid and they decide to take legal action to get their money back. What happens next depends on whether the firm has limited or unlimited liability.

Sole Traders and Partnerships can be *Declared Bankrupt*

1) The creditor will sue the firm in court to try to get its money back. If the firm does not have the money to pay them then the court can appoint an Official Receiver to run the business — the business is in receivership.

2) The Official Receiver has full legal rights over all the owner's property. Their first concern is to find the funds needed to pay the firm's debts.

3) If the Official Receiver believes the firm can still be profitable it will be run as a going concern. If not then the owner's assets will be sold to pay the firm's debts, the firm will close and the owner will be declared bankrupt.

Ltds and PLCs face *Liquidation*

1) Things are similar for these firms except that the Official Receiver's main job is to find a use for the assets of the business, not of the owner.

2) If they think the business is a going concern they will try to find a buyer for the business. If not, they will sell off the assets one by one until they have liquidated enough assets to pay off all the debts. To liquidate something means to turn it into cash — that is, sell it.

3) If there are not enough assets to pay everyone then some creditors may not get paid.

Official Receivers are called in to sort out money problems...

Make sure you remember why firms fail and what happens to them when they do. Scribble down a mini-essay telling the whole sad story. Remember, bankruptcy is to do with the owner and liquidation is to do with the firm.

Warm-Up and Worked Exam Questions

Warm-up Questions

1) Give one advantage and one disadvantage of a connected network for communication within a company.
2) What is good and bad about "the grapevine" as a means of communication within a company?
3) What do the letters MNE stand for?
4) What is meant by a competitive market?
5) When does an oligopoly exist?
6) Explain the term "overtrading".

Worked Exam Questions

There are a lot of compromises to make in business. Make sure you understand them, then look at these questions.

1 Sole trader Taj Shah owns four newsagents shops in the same city. He does not want to expand further.

a) Assess possible reasons why Taj wants to remain small?

By staying small, Taj may feel in control and under less pressure. [1 mark]

He may lack the financial or human resources to expand. His local [1 mark]

market may be saturated, so only external expansion is possible. [1 mark]

The business may be at the optimum size for economies of scale. [1 mark]

(4 marks)

Bigger isn't necessarily better — it depends which industry you're in.

b) What advantages might Taj have over big firms in the same market?

Taj knows his customers so can offer a more personal service. He [1 mark]

can exploit gaps in the market by providing specialist magazines to

order. Taj has lower fixed costs, so is more flexible over prices. [1 mark] [1 mark]

(3 marks)

2 Julie Price has booked a holiday with TravelWell Ltd, a small travel agency operating over the Internet. Three weeks before her holiday, she gets an email saying that TravelWell has gone into receivership.

a) Briefly explain to Julie what it means for a company to "go into receivership".

The company cannot pay its debts, so it or its assets will be sold. [1 mark]

(1 mark)

b) If Julie's holiday is cancelled, explain how she might get some of her money back.

If a buyer is found for TravelWell Ltd they will probably honour the

debt. If not, she must apply to the Official Receiver. Alternatively [1 mark] [1 mark]

Julie might get a refund from her travel insurance company. [1 mark]

(3 marks)

98

1   In a speech, the Chancellor of the Exchequer said, "Britain needs small businesses."

a)   Explain how small firms can benefit the economy.

....

....

....

(3 marks)

b)   Jack Benefit has worked for a small firm for five years. Explain why he might be better off working for a bigger organisation.

....

....

(3 marks)

2   Yattoo plc, a major car manufacturer, has plants scattered throughout the world. It has a hierarchical organisational structure with authority centred at their home base. A recent management report criticised their communications network.

a)   Outline Yattoo's possible communication problems.

....

....

....

(4 marks)

b)   Recommend ways in which Yattoo might resolve these problems.

....

....

(2 marks)

3   Global Communications plc has set up plants in the Far East to manufacture telecommunications equipment.

a)   Explain how a country in the Far East could benefit from Global's presence.

....

....

....

(4 marks)

b)   Summarise the problems Global might cause the host country.

....

....

....

(4 marks)

Revision Summary for Section Six

Well, there you are, the whole story of a firm from birth to death. Probably an easier section than Section Five but it still needs learning. And the way to make sure you've learned it is to check you know the answers to these questions. Note down any questions you find tricky and then go over the stuff again until you can do them easily. I know it's a pain but trust me, it's the only way...

1) Give four reasons why people start their own businesses.
2) Explain two problems of running your own business.
3) Describe what should be in a business plan.
4) Give two reasons why the government helps new businesses.
5) Why do banks give help to new firms?
6) Explain three reasons why firms choose to expand.
7) What's the difference between internal and external expansion?
8) If a firm making statues of David Beckham starts making statues of Posh Spice as well, what is this an example of?

   a) diversification; b) line extension.
9) Smellsbad Rhubarb Chutney Ltd., a well known rhubarb chutney manufacturer, merges with the following firms. Which type of integration is each an example of?

   a) Quality Rhubarb Chutneys Manufacturers Ltd.
   b) Exotic Chutney Shops Ltd.
   c) Megalarge Knickers Producers Ltd.
   d) Rhubarb Farms Ltd.
10) Explain the difference between internal and external economies of scale.
11) Give four examples of internal and two examples of external economies of scale.
12) What is meant by diseconomies of scale? Give an example.
13) What are three main ways of communicating? Explain one advantage and one disadvantage of each method.
14) What problems can result from poor business communication?
15) Explain the difference between chain, wheel and connected communication networks. Give one advantage and one disadvantage of each.
16) What is the posh term for the office grapevine?
17) Explain three advantages of operating as an MNE.
18) Give two benefits and two problems for a country of hosting an MNE.
19) Explain three benefits to consumers of a competitive market.
20) Explain two problems to consumers of a monopoly market.
21) Explain what oligopoly means.
22) Explain three reasons why some firms stay small.
23) Give three advantages of small firms over larger firms.
24) Explain three reasons why firms close down.
25) What is the difference between bankruptcy and liquidation?

SECTION SIX — GROWTH OF FIRMS

The Business Cycle

This section is about factors that take place <u>outside the firm</u> which influence what the firm does. They are known as <u>external influences</u>. One of the biggest influences is the <u>economy</u>.

The Size of the Economy is Measured by GDP

1) <u>Gross Domestic Product (GDP)</u> is a measure of the <u>total output</u> of the economy. It is usually measured over <u>one year</u>. It is calculated by adding together the total amount produced by all the firms in the UK.

2) In order to produce their output firms have to <u>pay</u> suppliers and workers — and the profits the firm makes are paid to the owners. That means GDP is <u>also</u> a measure of the <u>total income</u> generated by the UK economy. In 2004 the UK's GDP was <u>£1,782 billion</u>.

Economic Growth is an Increase in GDP

1) Economic growth is defined as the <u>annual percentage change</u> in GDP. An <u>increase</u> in GDP means that, on average, people's <u>material living standards</u> are rising.

2) This <u>doesn't</u> mean that their <u>quality of life</u> is necessarily better — an increase in GDP often also means an increase in <u>pollution</u>. And it <u>doesn't</u> mean <u>everyone's</u> living standards increase <u>equally</u> — some groups of society may benefit a lot while others <u>lose out</u>. Economic growth <u>isn't always</u> a good thing for everyone — though people often <u>assume</u> it is.

3) The United Kingdom's GDP is a <u>lot higher</u> than it used to be — it's about half as much again what it was twenty years ago.

4) But growth rates in the last twenty years <u>varied</u> a lot. In the late 1980s the economy grew by <u>more than 4%</u> a year. But in the early 1980s and early 1990s there were periods of <u>negative growth</u> — when GDP was actually <u>getting smaller</u>.

Changes in Economic Growth result in the Business Cycle

1) Economic growth seems to move in a <u>regular pattern</u>. It grows, declines, and grows again. This regular pattern is called the <u>business cycle</u> — also known as the trade cycle or economic cycle.

2) Periods of <u>high</u> growth are called <u>booms</u>. GDP is <u>increasing a lot</u>, consumer demand is strong and firms will have healthy sales and make <u>big profits</u>.

3) Times of <u>negative</u> growth are called <u>recessions</u>. During a recession GDP is <u>falling</u> — consumer demand is weak and firms will <u>struggle</u> to sell their products. Some firms will <u>make losses</u> and have to <u>close down</u>.

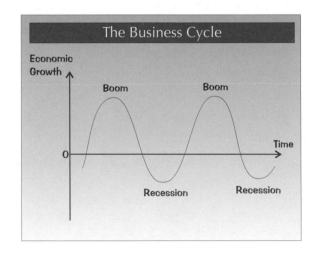

Economic growth cycles between boom and recession...

<u>GDP</u> is used to measure economic growth — which will be <u>positive</u> if GDP increases, and <u>negative</u> if it decreases. Make sure you understand the link between what happened to UK growth in the 1980s and 1990s and the stages of the business cycle. Now you're getting into it, you'll be glad to know there's more about this on the next page.

Unemployment and Inflation

People are <u>unemployed</u> when they want a job but can't find one. Unemployment usually <u>rises</u> in a <u>recession</u> and <u>falls</u> in a <u>boom</u>. <u>Inflation</u> is a general increase in the level of prices — it usually <u>rises</u> in a <u>boom</u> and <u>falls</u> in a <u>recession</u>. You need to know the <u>effects</u> that unemployment and inflation have on <u>businesses</u>.

Unemployment is a **Big Problem**

1) Unemployment means the economy as a whole produces <u>less output</u> than if everyone was employed. So <u>everyone suffers</u> from unemployment — in theory at least.

2) Some <u>firms</u> can actually <u>benefit</u> from unemployment, because they can get away with paying <u>lower wages</u> if there are lots of unemployed people <u>desperate</u> for a job.

3) The <u>problems</u> of unemployment tend to be much worse for the <u>unemployed</u> themselves, and their families, than for <u>anyone else</u>.

PROBLEMS FOR INDIVIDUALS
• Loss of <u>income</u> leads to less <u>spending power</u> and a fall in <u>living standards</u>.
• Loss of <u>status</u>, <u>self-respect</u> and <u>social contact</u> that may come from having a job.
• May find it hard to <u>find another job</u> if their skills are no longer needed by firms.

PROBLEMS FOR FIRMS
• <u>Lack of demand</u> for products from unemployed.
• Unemployed workers may lose skills — firms may need to <u>retrain</u> them.

PROBLEMS FOR THE GOVERNMENT
• Less <u>taxation revenue</u> from the unemployed.
• Need to pay out more <u>welfare payments</u> to the unemployed — Jobseeker's Allowance, etc.

4) Unemployment was very high in the <u>early and mid-1980s</u> in the UK — over <u>three million</u> people. By the <u>late 1990s</u> it was back <u>under two million</u>. In March 2005, there were about 800,000 people claiming jobless benefits.

Inflation Causes **Problems for Firms**

1) Inflation means that firms have to constantly <u>change their prices</u> — this means <u>reprinting</u> price lists and packaging and <u>telling their customers</u>. This is an added business cost.

2) Inflation creates <u>uncertainty</u> — firms <u>don't know</u> how much they will be charging for their products in the future. That means they're <u>less able</u> to <u>judge</u> whether a new investment will be <u>profitable</u> or not. So they end up <u>investing less</u> in new equipment — and over time firms will become <u>less efficient</u> and <u>less competitive</u>.

3) Firms will face <u>demands</u> for <u>pay rises</u>. If the inflation rate is 10% then a worker will need a 10% pay rise just to buy the <u>same quantity</u> of goods.

4) Inflation <u>increases production costs</u>. This doesn't matter if all firms face the same problem. But it's a real problem if the <u>UK's</u> inflation rate is <u>higher</u> than other countries'. This means that over time UK firms become <u>less competitive</u> against firms in other countries and may have to <u>close</u>.

• The <u>UK's inflation rate</u> was very high in the years around <u>1980</u> — <u>over 15%</u> at times.
• It was down to <u>around 5%</u> for most of the <u>1980s</u>, but went up to <u>nearly 10%</u> in the <u>early 1990s</u>.
• In the <u>last few years</u> it's been much lower — <u>below 3%</u> in 2005.
• The government is <u>happy</u> with an inflation rate of about 2.5% — it'd be <u>hard</u> to get it much <u>lower</u>.

Rising inflation means increased business costs...

<u>Unemployment</u> causes lots of problems for <u>individuals</u> — the most important being <u>loss of income</u>. This in turn causes problems for <u>firms</u> and the <u>government</u>. Memorise them all, and the effects of inflation on business.

Government Spending and Taxation

Around 40% of all spending in the economy is done by the government. As a result, it needs to be able to raise money. One of the main methods it uses is to increase taxes. Changes in taxes and the way the government spends the money it raises affect businesses in a big way. You need to know how.

Government Spending Goes *Up* in a *Recession*

1) In a recession, more people become unemployed — so the government has to pay out more in social security to support the unemployed.

2) The effect of this is not only to give them something to live on — it also helps to maintain demand for the economy's businesses.

Social security accounted for about 30% of UK government spending in 2000-2001. Next were health (17%) and education (11%), then about 5% each on defence and law and order.

Public Spending Benefits *Most Firms*

1) Firms benefit from the financial support the government gives to people on low incomes, but some more than others. A firm making food will get more business from the unemployed than one making luxury yachts.

2) Governments spend billions of pounds building new roads, schools and hospitals. This spending is very important to construction firms and civil engineers such as bridge-builders.

3) The defence industry employs hundreds of thousands of people and probably would not exist without government spending on new weapons.

Like Voters, Firms Only Like Tax Cuts

1) The main tax paid by firms is corporation tax — basically it's a tax on the firm's profits. The biggest tax paid by employees is called income tax — the more you earn the more tax you pay.

2) Another tax is national insurance — paid by both the employer and employee. In theory it pays for the Job Seeker's Allowance if the worker becomes unemployed. Firms and households also pay council tax to their local council.

Income tax is the biggest source of government revenue — about 25% in 2000-2001. Next were National Insurance and VAT at about 15% each, then excise duties at 10%. Less than 10% comes from corporation tax — and only about 5% each from council tax and business rates.

3) A tax that everyone pays is value added tax — most purchases have VAT of 17.5% added to the price. Excise duties are similar — here the government places taxes on specific products such as petrol and beer.

4) If the government cuts taxes it has the same effect as an increase in government spending — people's incomes are higher and so they demand more products from businesses. This means firms need to increase output — and they usually take on more workers, which helps to reduce unemployment.

5) But the increase in demand makes it easier for firms to charge higher prices — this can increase inflation.

6) As a result governments sometimes cut taxes in a recession — but they sometimes increase them during a boom.

This page isn't too taxing...

In a recession, the government tends to cut taxes and increase spending, and during a boom they do the opposite. Make sure you know how businesses are affected by government taxation and spending decisions. Then scribble down a mini-essay on why governments might raise taxes.

Government Economic Policy

<u>Two</u> economic policies for you here — <u>fiscal</u> policy and <u>monetary</u> policy. Make sure you understand how <u>businesses</u> are affected by each of them.

Fiscal Policy Involves Taxes and Spending

1) <u>Reducing taxes</u> and <u>increasing government spending</u> have the <u>same</u> effect — greater spending in the economy. The only difference is that when you reduce taxes, the extra spending is done by <u>individuals</u>.

2) Governments will do this if they want to <u>reduce unemployment</u> — the extra spending will <u>increase demand</u> for products which firms will meet by <u>hiring more workers</u>. Firms' profits will increase. This is called an <u>expansionary</u> fiscal policy. A problem is that <u>inflation</u> might increase as a result.

3) If the government wishes to <u>reduce inflation</u> it might <u>increase taxes</u> or <u>reduce spending</u> — a <u>contractionary</u> fiscal policy. There will be <u>less spending</u>, and firms will make less profit. A problem is that <u>unemployment</u> might increase.

Monetary Policy involves Changing Interest Rates

1) When the interest rate is <u>cut</u>, it's <u>cheaper</u> to borrow money and you get <u>less interest</u> when you put money in the bank. So both firms and consumers borrow and <u>spend more</u>, and <u>save less</u>. This increases spending just like a <u>cut in taxes</u>, with the <u>same results</u> — bigger company profits, reduced unemployment but the risk of inflation.

2) <u>Increases</u> in interest rates have the <u>opposite</u> effect — it is better to <u>save</u> than borrow, so both firms and consumers <u>spend less</u>. This <u>helps cut inflation</u> but causes unemployment. It's also <u>bad news</u> for firms which have <u>borrowed a lot</u> to help them invest — they're going to have to <u>pay more back</u> in interest.

3) Governments <u>don't like</u> using <u>fiscal</u> policy to <u>reduce inflation</u> — tax rises and cuts in spending are very <u>unpopular</u> with voters. They prefer to use monetary policy instead. Trouble is, <u>higher interest rates</u> are unpopular with voters as well. So governments give control of interest rates to an <u>unelected central bank</u> in an attempt to <u>avoid the blame</u>.

Economic Policy can be Expansionary or Contractionary...

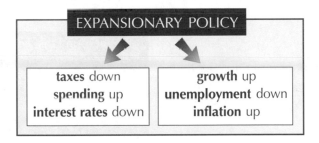

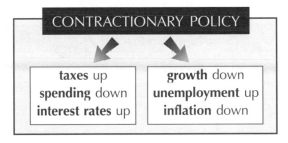

High Interest Rates are bad for Exporters

1) Monetary policy affects the <u>exchange rate</u> between the £ and other currencies. <u>Higher interest rates</u> in the UK result in <u>savers from abroad</u> putting their money in <u>UK banks</u>. To do this they need to <u>buy £s</u>, and this makes the £ <u>more expensive</u>.

2) This makes it <u>more expensive</u> for foreign consumers to buy goods <u>exported</u> from the UK — and <u>cheaper</u> for UK consumers to <u>buy imports</u>. UK manufacturing firms can <u>suffer</u> from this as they become <u>uncompetitive</u>.

Lots to learn about economic policies...

There's some <u>seriously tricky</u> stuff on this page. Try writing a <u>mini-essay</u> saying how fiscal and monetary policies work. Make sure you say how each affects <u>businesses</u> and the <u>economy</u> in general. You'll also need to know which policies are <u>expansionary</u> and which are <u>contractionary</u>. Scribble down a description of each.

Government Policy — Consumer Protection

I told you in Section Four about the government's laws to protect employees. Well, there are also laws restricting how firms sell their products — the aim here is to protect the consumer.

Laws Protect Against *Monopoly Power*

1) Look back at Section Six if you need reminding how monopolies can use their market dominance to increase prices. Governments try to protect consumers against this. In 1998 the Competition Act increased the powers that can be used against monopolies.

2) A government body called the Office of Fair Trading (OFT) can investigate alleged monopolies — it has the power to fine companies up to 10% of their turnover for three years. That would be more than the total profit that most firms make.

3) If it thinks the issue is really serious the OFT asks the Competition Commission to investigate — it has the power to recommend to the government that the monopoly be broken up into smaller companies. This happened a few years back to British Gas, which is now a handful of separate businesses.

4) Industries that have recently been investigated include cars and ice cream.

Laws Protect People when *Buying Goods and Services*

Here are the four main laws about protecting consumers. No shortcuts I'm afraid — you've just got to learn them.

1 Trade Descriptions Act (1968)

This makes it illegal for a retailer to give a false description of something being sold.

2 Consumer Credit Act (1974)

This act protects anyone buying products on credit — such as hire purchase. The customer must be given a copy of the credit agreement, the interest charge should be clearly stated and the customer has 14 days to change their mind and cancel the agreement. The interest charge should be calculated to show the annual percentage rate (APR) — and that is calculated in the same way by all firms so that consumers can compare credit charges.

3 Weights and Measures Act (1979)

It is illegal to sell products that are under the weight or fewer in number than claimed. Some things have to be sold in standard sizes to help people compare prices. The law is enforced by Weights and Measures Inspectors.

> To get round this law, things like matchbox labels state the 'average contents' of the box — so it doesn't matter if they're a bit under.

4 Supply of Goods and Services Act (1982)

and **SALE AND SUPPLY OF GOODS ACT (1994)**. These ensure that goods and services meet three criteria: the product should be fit for its purpose, be of merchantable quality (ie good enough to sell) and match its description. The laws are enforced by Trading Standards Officers.

> For example a pair of size ten non-leather shoes should be size ten and not made of leather (matching the description), should not fall apart when walked in (fit for purpose) and be well made (merchantable quality). If products don't meet this test, consumers are entitled to their money back.

These laws stop firms trying to trick us...

So next time you unpack your shopping to find a wind-up penguin in place of the paper clips you asked for, take it back to the shop. Go on — you have the power. Not the most riveting of pages, I know — but it's in your interest to learn these laws. Memorise and scribble. Keep on doing it 'til you've got 'em all.

Regional Policy

Some areas of the UK have higher unemployment than others. Governments (and the European Union) try to <u>reduce</u> this problem by <u>encouraging firms</u> to create jobs in areas of <u>high unemployment</u>.

There are **Different Types** of **Assisted Area**

An <u>Assisted Area</u> is one where the government wants to encourage firms to locate. These areas usually have an <u>available workforce</u>, <u>competitive wage rates</u> and <u>labour flexibility</u> — in other words, lots of <u>unemployed people</u> who are <u>desperate for jobs</u>.

> **1** <u>DEVELOPMENT AREAS</u> have high levels of <u>structural unemployment</u> due to the <u>decline</u> of their <u>traditional industries</u>. Examples are Merseyside, Tyneside, Glasgow and the former coal-mining areas of South Yorkshire. These areas receive <u>most government support</u>.

> **2** <u>INTERMEDIATE AREAS</u> do not have <u>as many problems</u> as development areas but still qualify for <u>some</u> government support. Examples are parts of Cumbria and Kent.

> A new Europe-wide way of classifying Assisted Areas into three tiers (Tier 1, Tier 2 and Tier 3) is also used — these tiers are pretty similar to Development and Intermediate Areas.
>
> <u>TIER 1</u> areas qualify for the highest level of government and EU support.
> <u>TIER 2</u> areas are still in need of support, but the problems here are not as severe as those in Tier 1.
> In <u>TIER 3</u> areas, small firms (employing up to 250 people) qualify for assistance.

Regional Aid is given in **Three Main Ways**

1 <u>SELECTIVE FINANCE FOR INVESTMENT</u> (SFI) is a scheme that provides grants to support investment projects in Assisted Areas. These projects should create jobs or safeguard existing ones. Any new jobs created must not be at the expense of employment <u>elsewhere</u> in the UK.
SFI replaced <u>REGIONAL SELECTIVE ASSISTANCE</u> (RSA) and <u>REGIONAL ENTERPRISE GRANTS</u>.

2 <u>REGIONAL DEVELOPMENT AGENCIES</u> are organisations set up by the government to promote business efficiency and employment in Assisted Areas. They also encourage firms from <u>outside an area</u> to invest in it. An example is the Welsh Development Agency.

3 <u>GOVERNMENT OFFICES</u> such as the Driver and Vehicle Licensing Agency <u>do not</u> have to be in <u>London</u>. In recent years the government has chosen to locate them in <u>assisted areas</u>. The <u>DVLA</u> is one of the biggest employers in <u>Swansea</u>. Similarly, the main office for <u>National Insurance</u> payments in the UK is in <u>Newcastle</u>.

> There are other schemes to help businesses too — for example, <u>Enterprise Zones</u> (an older scheme, but you might need to know about them) were areas, usually in inner cities, where firms would pay less tax and have fewer regulations to comply with.
>
> <u>English Partnerships</u> also aims to help local economies to grow and improve the quality of towns and cities. Its ultimate aim is to help create communities where people want and can afford to live.

Regional Policy has **Good and Bad Effects** on Businesses

1) Regional policy gives firms <u>financial incentives</u> to make up for the problems of locating in depressed areas.
2) But if the area stops being assisted, it may harm the <u>long-term competitiveness</u> of firms that were tempted to locate where they otherwise wouldn't have done.

Regional aid benefits poorer areas...
Make sure you understand <u>why</u> regional aid is given to <u>some parts</u> of the UK and not others, and learn the <u>different types</u> of support — then scribble down a mini-essay.

SECTION SEVEN — EXTERNAL INFLUENCES

Warm-Up and Worked Exam Questions

Warm-up Questions

1) What do the letters GDP stand for?
2) In a recession, what usually happens to the level of unemployment?
3) What term describes a general increase in the level of prices?
4) Name five major areas of UK government spending.
5) Describe the difference between fiscal and monetary policy.
6) What does OFT stand for?

Worked Exam Questions

There's some tricky economics to get to grips with in this section, and the best way to master it is to practise. So make sure you work through the questions below, then have a go at the ones on the next page.

1 Dave Burns exports antique furniture to the United States. He started his business last year and has a large overdraft at his bank.

   a) Why would a rise in interest rates be bad news for Dave's overdraft?

   He would have to pay more back in interest on his overdraft. ✓ [1 mark]

   (1 mark)

   b) Explain why high interest rates would be bad for Dave's export business.

   High interest rates would affect the exchange rate between the UK ✓ [1 mark] *£ and US dollars. The value of the £ would rise.* ✓ [1 mark] *This means it would be more expensive for Dave's American customers to buy goods exported from the UK.* ✓ [1 mark]

   There are three marks here, so write down three distinct points.

   (3 marks)

2 Allied Electronics Ltd are being forced into making some of their workers redundant due to declining orders for their products. Zak Collins has just received his redundancy notice.

   a) Briefly outline the problems Zak, as an individual, might face.

   Without work Zak's income would fall leading to less spending power and a fall in his living standards. ✓ [1 mark] *Without employment he might lose status, self-respect and social contact.* ✓ [1 mark] *Finding another job may be hard if there are no firms in the area which need his skills.* ✓ [1 mark]

   (3 marks)

   b) If unemployment is widespread throughout the economy, how would this affect government revenue and expenditure?

   The government might collect less taxation revenue as fewer people are earning. ✓ [1 mark] *More welfare payments might need to be paid out to the unemployed, for example Jobseeker's Allowance.* ✓ [1 mark]

   It's always good to put an example if you can.

   (2 marks)

Exam Questions

1. Jodie Stevens set up her hairdressing salon when the economy was booming. Consumer demand was strong, GDP was increasing and Jodie's business thrived.

   a) What is the name given to times of negative growth in GDP?

   ....

   (1 mark)

   b) If the business cycle plunges into negative growth, how might Jodie's business be affected?

   ....

   ....

   ....

   ....

   (4 marks)

2. Shazia Hussain bought a jacket from a leading high street store. She was told by the assistant the garment was washable. However, despite following the washing instructions, the jacket shrank.

   a) Name two consumer protection laws which might help Shazia?

   ....

   ....

   (2 marks)

   b) Explain how these laws might help Shazia to get her money back.

   ....

   ....

   ....

   ....

   (4 marks)

3. Scott and his brother Dean decide to set up their graphic design business in an Enterprise Zone.

   a) What is an Enterprise Zone?

   ....

   (1 mark)

   b) Outline two advantages their firm might gain by locating in an Enterprise Zone.

   ....

   ....

   (2 marks)

Social Influences

Firms have to <u>respond</u> to the changing needs of society — if they ignore what's going on around them they risk <u>losing business</u>. Changes in <u>social trends and opinions</u> can have a <u>big effect</u> on business decisions. Here's how...

Environmental Issues can Affect Business Decisions...

1) People are becoming more and more concerned about our planet and the effects that <u>business activities</u> are having on the <u>environment</u>. Current environmental issues include <u>global warming</u>, <u>acid rain</u>, <u>energy consumption</u>, <u>recycling</u> and <u>waste disposal</u>.

2) As awareness of these issues increases, consumers are changing their <u>buying decisions</u> — more and more people are buying "<u>environmentally friendly</u>" products.

3) In response, many firms are changing their <u>products</u> and <u>packaging</u> to be more <u>environmentally friendly</u>. Businesses are setting themselves <u>targets</u> to reduce <u>pollution</u>, increase their use of renewable energy resources, increase recycling and reduce packaging.

4) Businesses which cause <u>pollution</u> can be <u>forced</u> into cleaning up their act. Firms causing pollution have to <u>report</u> their activities to local environmental inspectors and comply with the latest <u>environmental laws</u>.

5) Taking environmental issues seriously can give firms a <u>competitive advantage</u> — a caring "<u>green image</u>" can attract <u>new customers</u> and <u>increase sales</u>. The main disadvantage is <u>cost</u>. Green production is usually more expensive and the costs of cleaning up pollution can be high.

...As can Social Trends...

1) Changes in the <u>make-up of the population</u> affect the <u>demand</u> for products and services. For example, there are now more retired people and single-parent families.

2) Changes in the <u>working population</u> affect business too. For instance, because more women now go out to work, there's a greater need for childcare.

3) <u>Social awareness</u> of issues like <u>health</u>, <u>fitness</u> and <u>obesity</u> has led to firms changing their <u>marketing messages</u> to emphasise responsibility for health. For example, food labels often indicate the salt, sugar, fat and energy content of the product.

...And so can Ethical Issues

Ethics are the <u>moral principles</u> of right and wrong. People are becoming more and more concerned about ethics in business, so many firms are having to change the way they do things — some even have their own <u>ethical policies</u>.

1) Concern has grown over the use of <u>cheap labour</u> in LEDCs (less economically developed countries), especially <u>child labour</u>. This has prompted some firms to import their raw materials from <u>fair trade sources</u>, which means they pay producers in LEDCs a fair price so they can earn decent wages.

2) Firms might also change their <u>marketing</u> to emphasise this <u>social responsibility</u>. For example, the Co-op advertises all its chocolate as <u>fair trade produced</u>.

3) When <u>promoting</u> products, firms are expected to respect <u>codes of practice</u> — being dishonest or naming other brands in adverts is not on. Certain products, like cigarettes, can't be advertised at all, and TV channels can't show programs containing much strong language or nudity before the 9 o'clock watershed.

4) Firms are also under pressure to carry out <u>product development</u> in an ethical way — this means using non-toxic materials, paying more attention to safety and not using animal testing.

Be environmentally friendly — reuse this book again and again...

Responding to social pressures sounds like a good idea for a business — but it <u>costs money</u>. Whether a business decides to make some ethical change to its policy will usually depend on <u>how much</u> it thinks it will get out of it.

Non-Government Influences on Business

It's not just the government that tries to influence the way that businesses behave. Non-government organisations play an important role in putting pressure on firms as well.

Pressure Groups *Keep Up the Pressure on Business*

A pressure group is any organisation that tries to influence the way that other organisations behave. Some target the government — but many target businesses too.

1) Greenpeace is a well-known example of an environmental pressure group. Its main aim is to publicise the actions of firms that harm the environment.

2) The Consumer Association is another high-profile pressure group. It publishes a monthly magazine that informs consumers about which products offer the best value for money.

3) An example of a single-issue pressure group is Action on Smoking and Health (ASH). They helped persuade the government to pass a law making tobacco advertising illegal.

4) Often the most effective pressure on business comes from informal groups — like the campaigns against Nike for using sweatshop labour, against Shell for its involvement in Nigeria, and against McDonalds for cruelty to animals. The internet is a very important way of spreading information for anti-corporate protestors — through sites like www.corpwatch.org.

> Most pressure groups rely at least partly on the media to publicise their work — and there's been a big growth in recent years in TV and newspaper interest in consumer affairs.

So Do Certain **Non-government Agencies**

These agencies are not part of the government — but they have the power to affect the activities of firms that do not comply with their rules.

1) The Advertising Standards Authority (ASA) regulates all advertising in the UK. Its rules say that all adverts must be legal, decent, honest and truthful.

2) The British Standards Institution (BSI) sets minimum safety standards for many consumer goods. Consumers know that products displaying the BSI 'Kitemark' will be safe.

Firms have to **React** to the Pressure

1) Businesses don't like bad publicity — it can lead to consumers boycotting their products. And this reduces sales and profits. But complying with the demands of pressure groups can increase costs which reduces profits as well.

2) So ideally firms want to do nothing, but persuade people they're doing something. They're becoming better at using the media to influence public opinion — in other words, to convince people they're doing more than they really are about pressure groups' concerns. The big multinationals are especially good at this.

3) The practice of firms pretending to be environmentally friendly is called greenwashing.

SAVE OUR PLANET

SAVE OUR PLANET... SAVE OUR PLANET... SAVE OUR PLANET...
Pressure groups make sure firms can't forget about all those important issues. It'll really impress the examiners if you can give some examples. Make sure you know what these groups do and how businesses are affected by them.

International Trade

You should have got the basic idea by now that businesses exist to buy from other firms, add value through production and then sell on the product to customers — hopefully for a profit.

International trade happens when those suppliers or customers are located in another country. Imports are goods bought from abroad. Exports are goods sold to abroad.

International Trade Happens for **Three Main Reasons**

1) Some products can only be produced in particular places — scotch whisky can only come from Scotland, and guano, a natural fertiliser, only comes from a few places in South America. If people in other countries want these products they have to import them.

2) Some products are far cheaper to produce in some countries than others. The UK could grow all the bananas it wants — but only by building lots of enormous and expensive greenhouses. So it imports them from abroad — they're much cheaper.

3) It may just so happen that a foreign firm produces higher quality products at more competitive prices than a UK producer, so customers choose to buy from abroad.

International Trade Has **Benefits and Problems**

International trade increases the size of the firm's market — it has more customers but also more competitors. This increases choice for consumers, and makes firms more efficient.

① BENEFITS OF INTERNATIONAL TRADE
- Consumers benefit through increased choice and lower prices. This raises living standards.
- Efficient firms benefit as they will increase sales and profits by exporting their products — they also gain economies of scale.
- The economy can specialise in what it is best at. The UK is a world leader in financial services.

② PROBLEMS OF INTERNATIONAL TRADE
- It can be difficult for firms in one country to develop a particular industry when other countries with more experience of that industry are producing cheap exports.
- Overspecialisation can make the economy too dependent on imports and vulnerable if demand for the things it specialises in exporting falls.

But Being a **Successful Exporter** is **Not Easy**

1) The exporter must understand the needs of the local market — the 4 Ps of marketing (see page 19) may need to be different. The exporter has to communicate with local customers — by translating sales brochures and employing people who speak the language.

2) Exporting is risky — there is the foreign exchange risk (see page 111), the risk that the customer will not pay and the risk that the foreign government may put restrictions on trade (see page 112) — closing the market to the exporter.

3) There can be lots of documentation. For example, each country has its own safety standards — though the World Trade Organisation (see page 112) is trying to ease this problem for business by reducing safety standards everywhere.

International trade — countries depend on each other...
Specialisation makes firms interdependent — and the same thing can happen with countries. Make sure you know why international trade happens, then scribble down a mini-essay on the benefits and problems.

Exchange Rates

An exchange rate is simply the price at which one currency can be traded for another. You need to know why exchange rates change, and the effects of this on importers and exporters.

Exchange Rates are Determined by Demand and Supply

A British person or firm might buy another currency, say US dollars, for four main reasons.

1) They are going to the USA for a holiday.
2) They wish to invest in a US bank — perhaps because interest rates are higher.
3) They want to import a product made in the USA and need to pay the US firm in dollars.
4) They think that the value of the dollar will increase in the future and they want to make money by buying the dollar whilst it is cheap and selling it again when it is expensive.

But in order to buy dollars, you need to sell your pounds in exchange. The effect of selling pounds and buying dollars is to make the pound cheaper compared to dollars — in other words the value of the pound has fallen, it has depreciated in value.

If people from the USA want to buy pounds, for example to buy a British export, the value of the pound will increase — it will appreciate in value.

A Strong Pound is Bad for Exporters, Good for Importers

1) In the example on the right the value of the pound is increasing because it can now buy more dollars.

2) British exports now become more expensive abroad — resulting in fewer sales and fewer profits for British firms which export things to America.

3) The strong pound also makes it cheaper to sell American products in the UK. That's bad news for UK firms which compete with goods imported from the US — they have to reduce their prices in order to compete, leading to lower profits.

4) But it's good news for UK firms that use imported raw materials — these are now cheaper so the production costs of these firms are lower.

5) The upshot of all this is that Britain will have fewer exports and more imports. This is bad news for the balance of payments — the difference between a country's income from exports and expenditure on imports.

EXAMPLE:

- If the exchange rate is £1 = $2 then a British cricket ball that costs £5 will have to sell in the USA for $10. And a baseball that cost $6 in the USA can be sold for £3 in the UK.

- If the value of the pound rises so that £1 = $3 the same cricket ball will have to sell for $15. And the same baseball can now be sold in the UK for £2.

A Weak Pound is Good for Exporters, Bad for Importers

Pretty obvious when you think about it. If you try the example in reverse, a depreciation of the pound (in other words, the pound getting weaker or falling in value) makes exports cheaper and imports more expensive — this should improve the balance of payments.

Exchange rates can affect businesses in a big way...

Exchange rates can be confusing — so make sure you fully understand the maths in the examples. Then it's time to learn the page, cover it up and scribble a mini-essay on the effects of exchange rate movements on UK firms.

International Trade Restrictions

Governments sometimes take steps to restrict imports of products — especially if this helps to protect domestic producers. This is becoming more and more rare because of membership of the European Union and the World Trade Organisation.

Governments Restrict Trade for **Four Main Reasons**

1) One of the methods, tariffs, is a way of raising revenue for the government.

2) The government may wish to protect an infant industry — a new domestic industry which doesn't yet have the economies of scale of foreign competitors.

3) The government may wish to protect uncompetitive industries because they are important to the country — perhaps a lot of jobs would be lost if the domestic firms closed down.

4) The government may want to protect its domestic producers from unfair foreign competition. For example some producers may dump unsold products abroad — selling them at prices low enough to drive domestic producers out of business.

There are **Five** Main Methods of **Restricting Imports**

1) QUOTAS   ⟶   are physical limits on the quantity of a product that can be imported — like saying a country will import 10,000 cars and no more.

2) TARIFFS   ⟶   are a tax placed on products when they are imported — the revenue is collected by the government. Tariffs increase the price of imports, making them less competitive.

3) SUBSIDIES   ⟶   to domestic producers might be given by the government — producers can use them to reduce their prices and so make imports less competitive.

4) PRODUCT SAFETY STANDARDS   ⟶   can be used — the government sets standards that are harder to comply with if you are a foreign producer.

5) GOVERNMENT FAVOURITISM   ⟶   the government is a major buyer of things like computers, cars and paperclips. They can buy these from domestic producers — improving their economies of scale.

Import Restrictions have **Good and Bad Effects**

1) In theory, reducing foreign competition helps increase profits for domestic producers and protect domestic jobs. And reducing imports helps to improve the balance of payments.

2) But this tends not to work in practice because other countries retaliate by imposing their own import restrictions. The problems this causes to a country's exporting firms even out any benefits for other domestic firms.

3) A genuine benefit is that safety standards can be maintained — like if a country decides it doesn't want to accept imports of GM food, or potentially BSE-infected beef.

4) Ultimately the big problem is that by restricting efficient foreign competitors, governments protect inefficient domestic producers. As a result those domestic firms have less incentive to become more efficient. And consumers have to pay higher prices — resulting in lower living standards.

Restricting imports — learn the pros and cons...

Dull stuff — still, at least it's not too difficult. Two lists and some good and bad points to learn. Make sure you understand why governments restrict imports, and how domestic producers are affected.

The European Union

Membership of the European Union is one of the most important external influences on British business. You need to know <u>what</u> the EU is, <u>how</u> it is run and how it <u>affects businesses</u>.

The EU currently has **25 Members**

1) The EU was <u>formed in 1958</u>. Its principal aim was to bring the <u>governments</u> and <u>economies</u> of Europe <u>closer together</u> so that no country would have anything to gain by going to war with another member country.

2) The EU is run by a <u>Commission</u> consisting of representatives from the governments of member states. <u>EU Laws</u> are decided by a <u>Council of Ministers</u>. (So if, for example, there is to be a new EU law concerning the environment, the Council will consist of the Environment Ministers from each EU country and it will be known as the 'Environment Council'). Laws then have to be ratified by an <u>elected Parliament</u>.

It Operates a **Single Market**

1) One of the main economic objectives of the EU has been to create a single market. This has largely been <u>in existence since 1992</u>.

2) The single market has <u>free trade</u> between member countries. There are <u>no barriers</u> to trade such as different <u>safety</u> and <u>product-labelling standards</u> — these have all been replaced by a common <u>EU-wide</u> set of rules.

EU members (and dates of joining)	
Belgium	(1958)
France	(1958)
Germany	(1958)
Italy	(1958)
Luxembourg	(1958)
Netherlands	(1958)
Denmark	(1973)
Ireland	(1973)
United Kingdom	(1973)
Greece	(1981)
Portugal	(1986)
Spain	(1986)
Austria	(1995)
Finland	(1995)
Sweden	(1995)
Cyprus	(2004)
Czech Republic	(2004)
Estonia	(2004)
Hungary	(2004)
Latvia	(2004)
Lithuania	(2004)
Malta	(2004)
Poland	(2004)
Slovakia	(2004)
Slovenia	(2004)

3) There is complete <u>freedom of movement</u> of <u>goods</u>, <u>services</u> and, in <u>theory</u>, people. In practice, however, <u>language barriers</u> and the lack of a common set of European <u>qualifications</u> means that the single market for people is <u>not yet a reality</u>.

4) The single market means that it should be <u>as easy</u> to sell English strawberries in France as it is in Wimbledon. Despite that, countries can still <u>sometimes</u> use <u>health standards</u> to protect domestic producers — but this is rare.

This Benefits **Consumers** and **Efficient Producers**

1) Increased competition means <u>lower prices</u> and <u>increased choice</u> for <u>consumers</u>. Consumers also benefit because there is more <u>innovation</u> as producers compete by bringing out new products.

2) <u>Producers</u> have the potential to gain from a bigger market. This can lead to more <u>economies of scale</u> and <u>lower costs</u>.

3) <u>Efficient</u> producers may <u>increase sales</u>, increase economies of scale and become even more competitive. <u>Profitability</u> will increase as a result.

4) More competition is bad news for <u>inefficient</u> producers — they will <u>lose market share</u> and may have to close.

A single market is good for consumers...

Membership of the EU affects us in loads of ways —that's why there's such a big debate over whether Britain should belong to the EU or not. That's not on the syllabus though. You only need to know what the EU means for <u>businesses</u>. Just make sure you know what a <u>single market</u> is and how it affects producers.

The Single Currency and EU Laws

This page completes all the <u>important stuff</u> you need to know about the <u>EU</u>.

A Single Market Needs a *Single Currency*

1) On January 1 <u>1999</u>, eleven of the then fifteen EU countries adopted the <u>euro</u> as their currency (the UK, Greece, Sweden and Denmark didn't join in) — although <u>until 2002</u> each country kept its <u>own notes and coins</u>. Within the EU <u>all prices</u> are set in a <u>common currency</u>. <u>Greece</u> adopted the euro in 2001.

2) The basic effect on businesses is that this should <u>reduce costs</u>. But it should also <u>increase competition</u> — <u>consumers</u> are able to <u>compare prices</u> in different countries and choose the <u>cheapest</u> option more easily than before.

SINGLE CURRENCY— ADVANTAGES...

1) A single currency means <u>lower transaction costs</u> for firms — you have to <u>pay commission</u> every time you <u>change</u> currencies, and that soon <u>mounts up</u>. Reduced transaction costs means <u>lower costs</u> for businesses — and <u>lower prices</u> for consumers.

2) Reduced <u>risks</u> from exchange rates — firms <u>no longer</u> have to <u>worry</u> about exchange rates moving against them. This only happens for trade with countries <u>who have adopted the euro</u> though — trade with other countries will still be affected by exchange rates.

SINGLE CURRENCY— DISADVANTAGES...

1) Conversion is a <u>hassle</u> — businesses have to <u>convert</u> all their prices, tills and cash machines to cope with the new <u>notes and coins</u>, and upgrade <u>computer systems</u> so that <u>accounts</u> can be held in euros.

2) Floating exchange rates <u>help</u> even out <u>regional differences</u> in growth — a country doing badly can <u>depreciate</u> its currency to make its exports more competitive. That <u>isn't possible</u> with a single currency — so some areas may become <u>locked in recession</u>.

EU Laws Have a *Big Influence* on Producers

There are many <u>other ways</u> that the <u>EU influences</u> the behaviour of firms. Here are the <u>main ones</u> you need to know.

1) The <u>European Social Chapter</u> is a set of rules designed to <u>protect the rights</u> of <u>employees</u> in the EU. As a result of the Social Chapter there are <u>equal rights</u> for <u>part-time</u> and full-time employees, improved <u>health and safety</u> rules and a compulsory <u>maximum</u> 48-hour <u>working week</u> for most workers.

2) There is an EU <u>competition policy</u> — all <u>mergers</u> of <u>large firms</u> which sell across the EU market must be <u>approved</u> by the EU and not the member country governments.

3) The EU has tough <u>food labelling</u> laws — for example jam is only jam if it has sugar in it. For years the EU threatened to <u>rename</u> most <u>UK chocolate</u> as "vegelate" — because it doesn't have <u>enough cocoa</u> in it. I reckon Swiss dark chocolate's much nicer anyway...

Vegelate mousse doesn't sound as tasty...

And wasn't there that thing about only being able to sell bananas if they're straight enough? Anyway, the single currency is <u>really important stuff</u> — you need to know it. Learn, cover up, then copy out the <u>advantages</u> and <u>disadvantages</u> of the euro. And make sure you know how EU laws affect producers.

Warm-Up and Worked Exam Questions

Warm-up Questions

1) Why are many firms changing their products and packaging to be more environmentally friendly?
2) According to the ASA, what should all advertising be?
3) What term describes the practice of firms that pretend to be environmentally friendly?
4) What problems can arise from overspecialisation of an economy?
5) What is an exchange rate?
6) Give three examples of European Union laws that influence business.

Worked Exam Questions

You should now be sufficiently warmed up to have a look at these worked exam questions.

1 BioGrow plc produces organic garden fertiliser which is sold in plastic bags.

a) How could BioGrow become more environmentally friendly?

Use environmentally friendly bags (bio-degradable). ✔ [1 mark]

Always try to use the information given to you in the question.   *(1 mark)*

b) The firm is setting itself targets to reduce pollution at its factory.
Suggest three ways the company might achieve this.

The firm could reduce pollution by using renewable energy
resources, ✔ [1 mark] *increasing recycling at the factory and reducing* ✔ [1 mark]
packaging, ✔ [1 mark] *perhaps by selling larger bags of fertilizer.*

(3 marks)

2 Boxit Ltd, a UK company, makes plastic containers which it sells to other companies.
The directors are planning to start exporting to the rest of the European Union.

a) What benefits and problems might Boxit Ltd encounter when it starts trading in
the EU?

Boxit Ltd will hope to see sales and profits rise as the company
moves into a wider market. ✔ [1 mark] *It is generally safer to sell in an*
international market in case domestic sales fall. ✔ [1 mark] *Potential*
problems for Boxit Ltd are differences in language and culture, ✔ [1 mark] *and*
financial difficulties because the UK has not adopted the euro. ✔ [1 mark]

Four marks available, so you'll need to make four points.   *(4 marks)*

b) How would selling to EU members differ from exporting to non-EU states?

The EU is a single market so there are no barriers to trade. ✔ [1 mark]
Non-EU governments can restrict imports, ✔ [1 mark] *especially if they*
want to protect domestic producers.

(2 marks)

Exam Questions

1   Gems4U plc imports fine jewellery from Asia to the UK which it sells through its high street stores.

    a)   How would a rise in gold prices affect the business?

        ....

        ....

        (2 marks)

    b)   Explain what effects a strong pound may have on the company, and on the UK economy at large.

        ....

        ....

        ....

        ....

        (4 marks)

2   UK producer Get-u-fit Ltd has plans to go global with its range of exercise machines. Explain some of the difficulties faced by exporters.

    ....

    ....

    ....

    ....

    ....

    (4 marks)

3   Jo Wong is a designer and manufacturer of skin-care products. Since launching her business on the internet, her sales have rocketed. However, Jo's business does include a limited amount of animal testing, and she is under increasing pressure from animal rights campaigners. Suggest two ways in which Jo could react to this bad publicity, and explain how these two alternatives may affect her business.

    ....

    ....

    ....

    ....

    ....

    (4 marks)

Revision Summary for Section Seven

There's some pretty hard stuff in this section — but then again some of it's pretty easy as well. But if you're going to do well in your exams, you've got to make sure you can handle the tough cookies as well as the pieces of cake. So it's time to get down to the serious business of answering questions. Make sure you can do all these — if one trips you up, go back and learn the stuff again. It's the only way.

1)   What is GDP and how is it measured?

2)   Give one reason why economic growth might be a good thing, and one reason why it might be a bad thing.

3)   Sketch and label a diagram of the business cycle. What happens to firms at each stage?

4)   How does an increase in unemployment affect firms?

5)   Explain four problems of inflation for firms.

6)   How are firms affected by government spending?

7)   Explain how firms might be affected by a decision to reduce income tax.

8)   At what stage of the business cycle might a government use an expansionary policy?

9)   What problems are caused by high interest rates?

10) How might cutting taxes help get the economy out of recession?

11) What does the OFT do?

12) Give three examples of consumer protection laws and state how they work.

13) The government decides it wants to encourage firms to set up in Cumbria. Explain two different types of regional aid it can use.

14) Describe three ethical issues which might affect a business.

15) Why do businesses not like bad publicity?

16) Why does the UK buy goods from other countries?

17) Explain two benefits and two problems of international trade.

18) Who benefits from a strong pound? And who loses out?

19) What's the difference between a tariff and a quota?

20) Britain wishes to protect its pineapple farmers from unfair foreign competition — explain two methods apart from tariffs and quotas it could use.

21) What does WTO stand for?

22) How many countries are in the EU? Name them. Yep, all of them. That's right. Hch, hch, hch.

23) Who benefits from the European single market?

24) Explain two benefits and two problems of the single currency. And what's the currency called?

Deindustrialisation

In recent decades the size of the UK manufacturing sector has declined, and the service sector has increased. This is called deindustrialisation. You need to know why it happens.

Deindustrialisation Happens for **Three Main Reasons**

Over the last half-century British industry has become uncompetitive. As a result the UK has exported fewer manufactured goods and has imported more of them. There are three main theories about why this has happened.

1) Some people blame the restrictive practices of trade unions and argue that British firms have become more competitive since the 1980s' trade union reforms were introduced.

2) Some people think the problem has been a lack of investment in new equipment. They argue that consumers do not save enough, banks do not want to lend to firms and firms face too much pressure from shareholders to pay them high dividends — leaving too little retained profit to be spent on new investment.

3) Some people think that as people get richer they tend to spend a greater proportion of their income on services, such as restaurant meals and insurance. As a result the proportion of people employed in manufacturing will naturally have to fall.

- About three-quarters of UK workers are employed in the service sector.
- Thirty years ago it was only just over half.

Deindustrialisation Affects **Some Areas** Worse than Others

1) Deindustrialisation has led to the decline of some of Britain's traditional manufacturing industries such as shipbuilding, textiles and steel. These industries were concentrated in particular areas — for example textiles in Yorkshire and Lancashire.

2) So these areas have suffered increases in structural unemployment. That means the local people have less money to spend, so other local businesses see a drop in demand — and so they'll have to make people redundant too. This is called the multiplier effect.

3) It's a downward spiral that can devastate an area. That's why governments often try to help these areas using regional policy (see page 105).

But There's Some **Good News** as Well

1) As industrial jobs disappear, lots of new jobs are being created in the service sector.

2) Some of these are in knowledge-based industries such as software, pharmaceuticals and genetics. Others are in businesses such as restaurants, cinemas and call centres where skill and pay levels are generally much lower.

3) People who have been laid off from their jobs in manufacturing often have to retrain to get jobs in the service sector.

Structural unemployment leads to a spiral of doom...

Deindustrialisation means that less and less people are working in traditional manufacturing industries. Make sure you know all the causes, then learn the effects on the local area. These are just common sense really, but they've been given a grand-sounding name — the multiplier effect. There's something to impress the examiners with.

Supply-Side Policies

UK governments since the 1980s have been trying to make British firms more <u>efficient and competitive</u>. They do this using <u>supply-side policies</u> — such as privatisation and deregulation.

Privatisation has Increased Competition...

1) Between 1945 and 1979 many British industries were <u>nationalised</u> — taken into the public sector, to be <u>owned and controlled</u> by the <u>government</u>. Examples include the railways, coal mines and car production.

2) In the 1980s and 1990s almost all of these industries were <u>privatised</u> — they were <u>sold back</u> to private sector shareholders, creating new PLCs and Ltds. Other <u>public sector corporations</u> were <u>sold</u> too — British Telecom, and the companies in the gas and electricity industries.

3) Part of the reason was that it was thought the firms would be <u>better run</u> if the managers were <u>accountable to shareholders</u> instead of to <u>government</u>. Making a <u>profit</u> became the main aim of these firms.

4) Often the companies were split up and <u>competition</u> was introduced. This also was aimed at increasing the <u>efficiency</u> of the firms.

5) In a few cases though the government <u>did not</u> create competition but instead turned a state-owned monopoly into a <u>private sector monopoly</u>. These firms made <u>very large profits</u> — which proved <u>unpopular</u> with voters. In the late 1990s they were forced to pay the government a <u>windfall tax</u> on top of the usual corporation tax.

... And so has Deregulation

1) Deregulation happens whenever the government <u>lifts restrictions</u> that <u>limit competition</u> between firms. As a result firms become <u>more efficient</u> and <u>consumers benefit</u> through better choice, quality and prices.

2) One example is when the government allowed competition in the <u>bus industry</u> — anyone can now operate a bus on a popular bus route. Another example is the <u>domestic energy</u> market — <u>gas</u> firms can now sell <u>electricity</u> and vice versa.

Other Policies Have Made Firms More Competitive

1) The 1980s and 1990s <u>trade union reforms</u> had the aim of making British firms more <u>competitive</u>. As a result of these reforms employers have been able to introduce <u>flexible working practices</u>. These are covered on page 120.

2) In recent years the government has made changes to the <u>education system</u> with the aim of raising the <u>skill levels</u> and <u>productivity</u> of the UK workforce. The <u>National Curriculum</u> was introduced in England and Wales in the 1980s. A new system of vocational, work-related qualifications, including the General National Vocational Qualification (<u>GNVQ</u>) and <u>Modern Apprenticeships</u>, was introduced in the 1990s.

Supply-side policies aim to improve efficiency...

Facts, facts, facts — basically there's a load of facts on this page. For each policy you need to know how it helps make firms more <u>competitive</u>. Try learning the whole page — then draw up a table with two columns headed '<u>Supply-side policy</u>' and <u>Effect on firms</u>'. Then fill it in with all the details.

Flexible Working

Until recently the typical job has been full time on a permanent contract. But this type of job is now in decline. Flexible working is taking over — with big effects on firms and workers.

There's Been a Rise in Part-Time Employment...

1) Working full time usually means around 40 hours a week. Part time is very hard to define — but it usually means between 10-30 hours per week.

2) Some employees choose to work part time so they can spend more time with their families. Some would prefer to have a full-time job. Working part time means less income for the employee.

3) Until recently firms did not have to give their part-time employees the same fringe benefits as full-time workers — this is one reason why part time work increased a lot in the 1990s. But the European Union's Social Chapter now gives equal employment rights to both part-time and full-time workers.

...An Increase in Temporary Contracts...

1) A permanent contract of employment has no end date — the only ways the firm can stop employing the person is by dismissing them or making them redundant.

2) A temporary contract is for a fixed period — for example one year. At the end of the period the firm can decide if it wants to renew the contract.

3) Temporary contracts make it easier for the firm to adjust the number of staff employed without having to pay redundancy money — though the law does now give more protection to temporary workers.

4) The main problem for temporary workers is that they have less job security. This might make it more difficult to get loans or a mortgage.

...And Greater Numbers of Self-Employed People

Someone is self-employed if they run their own business, taking their income out of the profits of the firm. The number of self-employed people is still small but it's increasing — for three main reasons.

> 1) Since the 1980s there's been more of an enterprise culture — people are more willing to take risks and set up on their own.
>
> 2) Some people who were made redundant, particularly in the recessions of the early 1980s and 1990s, chose to put their redundancy money into setting up their own business.
>
> 3) Many firms have made some staff redundant only to re-hire them at a later date as self-employed contract workers.

Most of the benefits and problems of being self-employed were covered on page 83.

Flexible working — nothing to do with yoga instructors...

Three main types of flexible working — part time, temporary contracts and self-employment.
Make sure you learn what each one is, why employers are keen on the first two, and the benefits and problems they cause employees. Learn, cover up the page and scribble down three mini-essays.

Warm-Up and Worked Exam Questions

Warm-up Questions

1) Which sector, service or manufacturing, employs more workers in the UK?
2) Give two examples of traditional manufacturing industries.
3) Give two types of supply-side policy used by UK governments since the 1980s to make British industry more competitive.
4) Explain the aims of the 1980s and 1990s trade union reforms.
5) What employment rights does the European Union's Social Chapter give to part-time employees?

Worked Exam Questions

British industry has changed a lot in the last 50 years or so. Make sure you know how and why.

1   Jim Smith owns a small chain of convenience stores in an area of the UK where the main industry was shipbuilding. In the 1980s, he was worried at the decline of this industry which employed 10,000 skilled people in the area served by his shops.

   a)   What is the name given to the type of unemployment caused by the decline or change of a major industry?

   Structural unemployment ✓ [1 mark]

   (1 mark)

   b)   The diagram below shows the spiral of decline in a shipbuilding area when a shipyard closes. Fill in the missing words/phrases to complete the diagram.

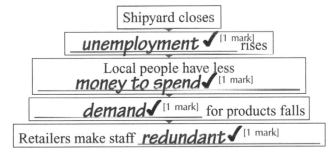

   Shipyard closes
   unemployment ✓ [1 mark] rises
   Local people have less *money to spend* ✓ [1 mark]
   demand ✓ [1 mark] for products falls
   Retailers make staff *redundant* ✓ [1 mark]

   (4 marks)

2   a)   Give two examples of knowledge-based industries.
   Pharmaceuticals ✓ [1 mark] *and software design* ✓ [1 mark]

   (2 marks)

   b)   Give two reasons why the UK has become deindustrialised over the last 30 years.
   There has been underinvestment in manufacturing industry so firms ✓ [1 mark]
   could not produce goods as cheaply as their competitors. ✓ [1 mark]
   As consumers get richer they spend more money on services such ✓ [1 mark]
   as holidays and eating out than on manufactured goods. ✓ [1 mark]

   You could also have mentioned the restrictive practices of trade unions.   *(4 marks)*

Exam Questions

1 The following advertisement was received by a customer of a domestic gas supply company.
"We supply you with your gas. You could save £200 a year if you let us supply your electricity as well."

a) Before the early 1990s it would not have been possible for a gas company to send such an advertisement. What change in the law means they can do this now?

....
(1 mark)

b) In what three ways did the government believe customers of the gas and electricity supply industries would benefit from the change in part a).

....

....

....
(3 marks)

2 A retailer puts this advertisement for staff in his shop window:
"Vacancy for a shop assistant, Saturdays only."

a) What type of employment contract will the person who gets the job receive?

....
(1 mark)

b) Explain the difference between a temporary and a permanent contract of employment.

....

....
(2 marks)

c) Explain why a retailer would want to employ more staff just before Christmas but would not want to give them a permanent contract.

....

....

....

....

....
(5 marks)

New Technology — In the Workplace

Developments in technology have had a major impact on the way businesses are organised — both in <u>making and selling products</u> and in <u>communicating information</u>. You need to know how.

CAD/CAM is Changing the way Goods are Manufactured

1) <u>**CAD**</u> stands for <u>Computer-Aided Design</u>. CAD software enables a designer to create a <u>three-dimensional computer model</u> of the product, <u>rotate</u> it on the screen to see it from all angles and make <u>instant changes</u> to the design.

2) <u>**CAM**</u> stands for <u>Computer-Aided Manufacture</u>. Products such as computers, which need to be manufactured with great <u>accuracy</u>, are suited to this method.

3) The <u>benefits</u> of CAD/CAM are that <u>design and manufacture</u> can be carried out quickly and with great accuracy — both <u>quality</u> and <u>productivity</u> should <u>improve</u>. Also the problems resulting from <u>human error</u> are minimised — robots are more <u>reliable</u>.

> **COMPUTER-INTEGRATED MANUFACTURING (CIM)** is the system by which different stages of the design process are <u>linked together</u> by a <u>central computer system</u>. The different stages are <u>coordinated</u> using a central computer database, which means that <u>everyone</u> involved in making the product knows what's going on. The <u>software</u> held on the central computer <u>automatically updates</u> any changes made and alerts all the related stages. This can save a lot of <u>time</u> and <u>cut out</u> costly <u>mistakes</u>.

EPOS And EFTPOS Make Shopping Easier

1) <u>**EPOS**</u> stands for <u>Electronic Point of Sale</u> — the fancy high-tech tills in supermarkets. When you buy something, the <u>bar code</u> details are scanned into the shop's <u>computer system</u>. This system contains the price of the product in a database — so the price is passed back to the till, which processes and prints the bill and receipt. The computer then reduces the <u>recorded stock</u> of the product, and when stocks fall to the <u>reorder level</u>, an order is <u>automatically</u> sent to the shop's warehouse or supplier.

2) <u>**EFTPOS**</u> stands for <u>Electronic Funds Transfer at the Point of Sale</u> — this is where customers pay for shopping using a <u>debit or credit card</u>. The card is <u>swiped</u> through a <u>magnetic reader</u> which tells the <u>computer</u> which bank account the money will come from. A request for payment is then automatically sent via the telephone network.

Computer Software is Improving Office Productivity...

In the bad old days <u>before computers</u> people had to <u>write</u> everything <u>by hand</u> or on a <u>typewriter</u>. There'd be loads of <u>bits of paper</u> to <u>file</u>. Thankfully these days <u>computer technology</u> makes things much <u>easier</u> and more productive.

1) <u>Writing</u> to customers is now quicker and easier thanks to <u>word processing</u> and <u>desktop publishing</u> software. <u>Templates</u> can be kept of <u>standard letters</u>, and old letters can be retrieved and <u>edited</u> to create updated versions. <u>Mail-merge</u> routines can send <u>personalised letters</u> to selected people in the firm's <u>database</u>.

2) <u>Calculating costs</u>, producing <u>invoices</u>, keeping <u>accounting records</u> and the production of profit and loss and balance sheets can all be done using standard <u>spreadsheet</u> software.

3) <u>Communicating with customers</u> can now be done via <u>e-mail</u> and the <u>internet</u>. Communication <u>within the firm</u> can be done using an <u>intranet</u> — which is like the internet but only available to employees within the firm.

Improvements in Communication are Changing How and Where we Work

Improvements in business communication are changing the way we work in several ways.

1) Advances in technology have led to an increase in <u>teleworking and remote offices</u> — employees work at <u>home or away from the main office</u>, keeping in contact with company headquarters through <u>telephone, computer and fax</u>. This can <u>reduce costs</u> for the employer — they don't have to provide as much office space and facilities for their employees, so have fewer overhead costs. Employees have more <u>freedom</u> to work as they want, but miss out on <u>social contact</u> with fellow workers.

2) More and more firms are conducting business through large <u>call centres</u>, where telephone staff take orders, answer queries and deal with customer complaints.

3) Customers and firms can order products <u>on-line</u>, which can be sent <u>directly to them</u> or to <u>regional</u> distribution centres. This reduces the need for <u>large warehousing facilities</u>.

4) However, advances in technology can lead to less work for people — <u>technological unemployment</u>. For example, the introduction of <u>internet and telephone banking</u> has led to <u>job losses</u> in high street <u>banks</u>.

New Technology — E-Commerce

One of the biggest changes of the last ten years has been the increase in buying and selling on the internet. You need to know how the internet is changing the way that businesses operate.

The Internet Aids *Information* and *Communication*

There are two main aspects to the internet.

> 1) The world wide web (www) joins computers together so any one computer can gain access to information made available on other computers elsewhere in the world.
>
> 2) Electronic mail (e-mail) lets you send messages quickly across the world.

E-Commerce is Buying and Selling *On-line*

1) E-commerce is growing. Firms put details of their products on their website. Customers can browse through the product range, or search through the firm's database using a keyword search to locate the products they want.

2) Products are ordered on-line using a credit or debit card. Encryption software converts the card details into a code that means no one can steal them to make unauthorised purchases. The products are then delivered to the customers.

3) The most popular on-line shopping products include books, music, holidays and groceries.

4) The internet is having a big impact on small firms. With a website small companies producing specialist goods can sell easily to anywhere in the world.

E-Commerce is *Reducing Business Costs*

1) By doing business over the internet firms can reduce some of their fixed costs. This is because the cost of downloading information is paid by the internet user not the provider. So things like sales brochures and product information no longer need to be printed and posted by the firm.

2) Firms which employ lots of people to give out information over the telephone, such as airlines and bus companies, can save money by sacking some of those people and putting the information on-line instead.

Firms use the *Internet* as a Method of *Promotion*

The internet provides a way of getting information across to millions of potential customers. So as well as offering people the chance to buy goods on-line, many firms also use websites to promote their products.

1) Websites give customers information about what the firm does and how it does it. This is a great way of getting important messages across. For example, you can make people aware of the fact that your paints are environmentally friendly, or that you produce more varieties of tea than anyone else.

2) These sites are designed to be attractive and provide easily accessible information. Firms can pay search engines such as Google to advertise their sites and provide links to them.

3) Many firms include 24-hour on-line ordering services on their website. This makes it easier for the customer to buy, and so should increase sales. Sometimes firms, such as airlines, offer discounts if you book on-line. This is another way of attracting more sales.

Brand Image May Become Even More Important

1) One feature of the internet is that it's nearly impossible to tell whether the website belongs to a trustworthy firm — unless you've actually heard of the business. People prefer to buy products from producers they trust to provide a good level of service.

2) As a result some of the most well-known e-commerce firms currently place quality of service above the need to make a short-term profit — they're building up a favourable brand image. But as they get well known this will probably change.

New Technology — E-Commerce

So you know how e-commerce benefits a business, but what about <u>consumers</u>...

Buying On-line has its **Benefits** and its **Problems**

E-COMMERCE — BENEFITS TO CONSUMERS
1) You can shop from home at <u>any</u> time of the day or night.
2) It's easy to look at several sites to <u>compare</u> products and prices offered by different firms.
3) It's often possible to <u>track the progress</u> of your order so you know when it's likely to be delivered.

E-COMMERCE — PROBLEMS FOR CONSUMERS
1) It's often impossible to tell whether a website belongs to a <u>trustworthy</u> firm.
2) There's a chance that <u>credit or debit card details</u> could be used by others illegally.
3) If goods are <u>unsuitable</u>, it can be difficult to exchange them, or get your money back.
4) Once you've bought from a company on-line, you tend to receive lots of <u>direct mail</u> — advertising new products, sales etc.

 Firms take the following measures to try to protect consumers from <u>internet fraud</u>:

- <u>Encryption software</u> codes financial and personal data when it is sent to the seller, so it can't be intercepted and used by anyone else.
- Many firms require you to set up <u>security ID</u>, such as passwords, to access secure sites.
- The <u>Data Protection Act</u> stops firms passing on personal information to other firms unless the customer gives permission.

Businesses are **Under Pressure** to adopt E-Commerce...

There are <u>three</u> main pressures on business for the adoption of e-commerce. Make sure you learn them.

(1) <u>COMPETITION</u> — if a firm is to survive in business it has to keep up with the competition. If one firm in the market starts to sell their goods on-line, then consumers will expect the same service from its competitors.

(2) <u>PROFITABILITY</u> — businesses are always looking for ways to <u>increase their profits</u>. E-commerce allows firms to <u>save money</u> by employing less staff, and by reducing fixed costs. It might also be possible for firms to <u>locate in more remote areas</u> where wages tend to be cheaper. By advertising and selling goods through a website, <u>new markets</u> can open up all over the world, leading to increased sales and profits.

(3) <u>POLITICAL PRESSURES</u> — companies face pressures from the <u>government</u> to become more productive because this creates more <u>wealth</u> for the country. <u>On-line ordering</u> can lead to firms opening <u>remote offices</u> or <u>regional distribution centres</u>. This creates jobs in areas which may suffer from high levels of unemployment.

...But using E-Commerce **Isn't as Easy** as it Sounds

So there are lots of benefits to a firm of selling over the internet, but it's <u>not as straightforward</u> as it sounds. Setting up the facilities to be able to use e-commerce can be <u>expensive</u> and <u>time-consuming</u> for four main reasons:

1) Special <u>equipment</u> has to be bought and installed.
2) Firms may need to employ a <u>specialist web designer</u> to produce their website, who will have to be paid.
3) Staff need to be <u>trained</u> in using the equipment and in how to provide good customer service.
4) Some consumers are <u>reluctant to buy on-line</u> — they might not have access to the internet, or maybe they prefer to visit a shop where they can see what they're getting. As a result, firms might have to spend more on <u>marketing</u> in an attempt to <u>persuade</u> more people to use their on-line services.

In my day we actually had to go to the shops...

There's so much information crammed into these three pages that you might be wondering where to start. I reckon the best thing to do is to <u>cover up</u> page 123, write down the <u>headings</u>, then scribble <u>as much as you can</u> under each. Then write a <u>mini-essay</u> describing the effects of e-commerce on businesses.

Globalisation

A lot of what's been covered in this book helps explain why the <u>trend</u> in business is towards a <u>small number</u> of <u>very large firms</u> competing in a <u>single global market</u>.

Economies of Scale Lead to Integration

1) Industries such as <u>car</u> manufacturing and <u>telecommunications</u> have enormous <u>fixed costs</u> — for instance, it costs billions of pounds to <u>research and develop</u> a new car.

2) <u>Very few</u> firms can <u>afford</u> this — so the trend is for <u>mergers and alliances</u> to create a <u>small number</u> of mega-firms which have the <u>resources</u> to compete worldwide.

More International Trade is creating a Global Market

1) There are fewer and fewer barriers to <u>international trade</u>. As a result the world is increasingly being seen as <u>one big market place</u>.

2) Only the <u>largest</u> firms can afford the costs of <u>marketing</u> on this scale — so again the trend is for <u>fewer</u>, <u>larger firms</u>.

Technology is making Global Communication Possible

1) New information technologies such as <u>satellite TV</u> and the <u>internet</u> mean that it's possible for a single advertising campaign to reach a <u>global audience</u>. As a result consumers are starting to buy the <u>same things</u> all around the world — like <u>fashion</u> goods and <u>soft drinks</u>.

2) Some <u>brand names</u> are changing — firms are increasingly using a <u>single brand name</u> that can be <u>remembered</u> and <u>understood</u> all over the world.

New Markets are Opening Up All Around the World

1) In the last twenty years <u>lots of countries</u> have moved from being <u>command</u> economies to having more <u>market-based</u> economies — in Eastern Europe, Russia, even China.

2) This creates <u>new opportunities</u> for firms to <u>sell</u> into — but also means <u>more competition</u> for existing firms.

3) Western firms lost out in competition with the "<u>tiger economies</u>" in South-East Asia. Now those countries are starting to lose out to places like <u>China</u>, where labour is <u>even cheaper</u>.

GLOBALISATION — GOOD OR BAD?

1) Whether globalisation is a <u>good</u> or <u>bad</u> thing is <u>hotly debated</u>.

2) The arguments are <u>mostly the same</u> as the ones about <u>monopolies</u> and <u>multinationals</u>.

3) Globalisation leads to big global firms which may produce more <u>efficiently</u> and at a <u>lower cost</u>.

4) These firms become tremendously <u>powerful</u> — in some ways as powerful as governments. Unlike most governments, though, they aren't <u>democratically accountable</u>.

5) Some say that the <u>economic growth</u> which globalisation brings will benefit <u>everyone</u>.

6) Others contend it will <u>benefit the rich</u> at the <u>expense</u> of the <u>poor</u> and the <u>environment</u>.

We live in a global world...

Examples of globalisation are <u>all around us</u> — every time you go to the supermarket you face a choice of products from all over the world. Make sure you understand what's <u>causing</u> globalisation, and all the arguments <u>for</u> and <u>against</u> — sounds like it's time for another mini-essay to me...

Warm-Up and Worked Exam Questions

Warm-up Questions

1) Give three benefits of CAD/CAM to manufacturing businesses.
2) What do the initials EFTPOS stand for?
3) List four ways in which computer software improves office productivity.
4) What is the meaning of the term "remote office"?
5) What does the term "encryption" mean?
6) Some Eastern European countries have shifted from command economies to free-market economies. Why might this help some British firms, but hinder others?

Worked Exam Question

Remember that exam questions require you to apply all this knowledge of technology to specific businesses.

1 Chateau Metro is a wine merchant with four retail outlets and one central warehouse. The directors of the company are considering installing EPOS in their retail outlets.

a) What does EPOS stand for?

Electronic Point of Sale ✓ [1 mark]

[1 mark]

b) Discuss the likely benefits to Chateau Metro of installing EPOS.

A benefit of EPOS is that the bottles of wine would not need to be priced individually. ✓ [1 mark] For example, if they decided to put a wine on offer, they would not need to reprice all the individual bottles of wine. ✓ [1 mark] The bottles would each have a bar code, ✓ [1 mark] and then the price would only need to be changed once on the computer system and on the shelf. EPOS would also help the retail outlets to control stock levels. ✓ [1 mark] When stocks of a wine fall below the reorder level, an order ✓ [1 mark] would be automatically placed at the warehouse. ✓ [1 mark]

You could also mention that the warehouse will then have a better idea of how much stock it needs to order from its suppliers.

[6 marks]

Chateau Metro are also considering setting up an on-line ordering facility for customers who want wine delivered directly to their homes. The directors are concerned that this new branch of the business might simply "cannibalise existing demand".

c) What do you think the directors mean by "cannibalise existing demand"?

The new branch of the business might not attract new customers. ✓ [1 mark] Customers who had used their retail outlets might use the on-line service instead. ✓ [1 mark]

[2 marks]

Exam Questions

1   Ramish wants to buy a new monitor for his computer. He sees one in a shop on his local high street for £90, and he sees exactly the same type of monitor on the internet for £82. He decides to buy the monitor from the high street, and says that it is worth paying the extra £8 for peace of mind.

a)   What concerns might Ramish have had about buying over the internet?

....

....

....

....

(4 marks)

b)   What can a business that sells on-line do to ensure that internet transactions are safe?

....

....

(2 marks)

2   a)   What do you understand by the term "globalisation"?

....

....

....

(4 marks)

b)   How has global communication technology influenced the marketing strategies of multinational firms?

....

....

....

(3 marks)

c)   Give two advantages and two disadvantages of globalisation?

....

....

....

....

(4 marks)

Practice Exam

Once you've been through all the questions in this book, you should feel pretty confident about the exam. As final preparation, here is a **practice exam** to really get you set for the real thing. The questions in Sections A and C are based on particular case studies, whereas Section B consists of questions based on brief business scenarios. Your actual exam may consist entirely of case study based questions, or might contain no case study element at all, depending on which syllabus you're following. Either way, all these questions are great practice. If you're doing Foundation then you won't have learnt every bit — but it's still good practice.

CGP Practice Exam Paper
GCSE Business Studies

General Certificate of Secondary Education

GCSE
Business Studies

Centre name					
Centre number					
Candidate number					

Paper 1

Surname	
Other names	
Candidate signature	

Time allowed: 2 hours

Instructions to candidates
- Write your name and other details in the spaces provided above.
- Answer **all** questions in the spaces provided.
- Do all rough work on the paper. Cross through any work you do not want marked.
- If you need additional space, you should continue your answers at the end of the paper, indicating clearly which question you are answering.

Information for candidates
- The marks available are given in brackets at the end of each question or part-question.
- Marks will not be deducted for incorrect answers.
- In calculations show clearly how you work out your answers.
- There are 7 questions in this paper.
- The maximum mark for this paper is 112.

Advice to candidates
- Work steadily through the paper.
- You are advised to spend approximately:
    - 20 minutes on Section A,
    - 50 minutes on Section B,
    - and 50 minutes on Section C.
- You will be assessed on your ability to organise and present information, ideas and arguments clearly and logically, using specialist vocabulary where appropriate. Your use of spelling, punctuation and grammar will also be taken into account.
- If you have time at the end, go back and check your answers.

FOLD THIS PAGE OUT
Read the following information on Dewdrops plc, before answering the questions in Section A.

DATA A

Dewdrops plc

Dewdrops plc manufactures clothing for three major high street retail groups. The business began as a private limited company in 1967. At first, Dewdrops Ltd had one factory where it produced quality clothing for a wide range of specialist outlets. Within two years, the company was making a reasonable level of profits. By 1975, it had opened three new factories, financed by a combination of retained profits and bank loans.

When profits reached a record level in 1986, the company decided to expand further. This expansion included product diversification, opening additional factories and expanding into export markets. To finance this expansion, Dewdrops changed from a private limited to a public limited company.

Dewdrops plc has continued to expand by taking over existing factories and has built a large factory employing 520 workers in Penwerris. As the Mayor of Penwerris said, when opening the new factory:

"When our car factory closed, the future of Penwerris seemed bleak. Unemployment reached 25% and you could see the young folk desperate to leave the area to look for work. We had to attract new companies into the area. Thanks to companies such as Dewdrops, the future of our town and its community seems to be a lot more secure."

DATA B

Dewdrops plc

One of Dewdrops plc's targets was to increase production by investing in new machinery and new ways of working. Dewdrops plc continued to produce its clothes in batches but it also introduced elements of flow production. It set up a production line. Workers became specialised in separate tasks such as cutting, shaping, sewing, pressing and packaging.

In an attempt to improve efficiency, Dewdrops plc reviewed its buying, stock control and storage system. It developed close links with its main suppliers of cloth and other materials so that it operated a form of just-in-time stock control. Dewdrops plc also improved its links with the major high street retailers.

AQA, 2004

SECTION A

Read and use **Data A** to help you answer Questions 1 and 2.

1   Explain the term 'product diversification'.

....

....

....

....

....

....

....

....

(1 marks)

AQA, 2004

Revision Summary for Section Eight

You can run, but you can't hide... yep, it's revision questions time again. But look on the bright side — this is the last lot of them. Then there's just a practice exam to whiz through, and you've finished the book. That's right. Don't all cheer at once. But don't let it slip now — make sure you've learned this section thoroughly and you can answer all these questions in your sleep.

1) Explain what deindustrialisation is.

2) Explain three reasons why deindustrialisation happened.

3) What is the difference between nationalisation and privatisation?

4) Give one reason why firms were privatised in the 1980s.

5) What is the difference between privatisation and deregulation?

6) What is the difference between full-time and part-time employment?

7) Why might some workers like to work part-time?

8) Give one reason why firms might have taken on a lot more part-time workers in the 1990s.

9) Give one advantage to employers and one disadvantage to employees of a temporary contract.

10) When is somebody self-employed?

11) Explain three reasons why the number of self-employed people is increasing.

12) What is the difference between CAD and CAM?

13) Describe what CIM means.

14) What does EPOS stand for?

15) Where is EFTPOS used?

16) List three things that a business can do with spreadsheets.

17) Explain the difference between the internet and an intranet.

18) What is teleworking?

19) Explain how on-line shopping works.

20) Explain two ways the internet is reducing business costs.

21) Give two benefits to a consumer of buying on-line.

22) What does the Data Protection Act stop firms from doing?

23) Why are businesses under pressure to adopt e-commerce?

24) Explain four reasons why globalisation is happening.

SECTION EIGHT — BUSINESS AND CHANGE

2   Explain the reasons why you think Dewdrops changed from being a private limited company to being a public limited company.

Leave blank

....

....

....

....

....

....

....

....

....

....

....

....

....

....

....

(9 marks)

AQA, 2004

Turn over

132

Read and use **Data B** to help you answer Question 3.

3   Describe the advantages **and** disadvantages of adding elements of flow production when making batches of clothes. Explain whether you think Dewdrops plc was right to do this.

Leave blank

(12 marks)

AQA, 2004

SECTION B

4   (a) Jane Sanders and Mihir Abbas have started a partnership called Olympic. It makes sports clothes. The partnership sells these clothes to a number of local shops in the county of Moorshire.

Recommend **two** ways in which Olympic could persuade the owners of sports shops to sell the sports clothes. Give reasons for your recommendations.

One ....

Reason ....

....

....

....

Two ....

Reason ....

....

....

....

....

(8 marks)

(b) Jane and Mihir are thinking about spending £10 000 on advertising the sports clothes to the public.

Recommend whether or not they should spend this money on advertising to the public. In your answer consider the advantage(s) and/or the disadvantage(s) of advertising to the public.

....

....

....

....

....

....

(4 marks)

Turn over

134

(c) State **two** pricing strategies that Olympic may use. Explain fully when it would be appropriate for Olympic to use each of these.

Price Strategy 1 ....

When appropriate to use ....

....

....

Price Strategy 2 ....

When appropriate to use ....

....

....

(6 marks)

(d) Recommend whether or not Olympic should use sponsorship to promote its clothes in Moorshire. Give reasons for your recommendation.

....

....

....

....

....

....

(4 marks)

(Total 22 marks)

OCR, 2003

5   (a)   Each year Olympic imports $30 000 of material from Canada to make clothes.

(i)   In the first year of trading, the value of the pound was £1 = $2. Calculate how much Olympic paid for the imported materials in pounds. Show your working.

....

....

(2 marks)

(ii)   In the second year of trading the value of the pound was £1 = $3. Explain whether or not Olympic would benefit from this change in the exchange rate.

....

....

....

....

....

....

(4 marks)

(b)   In the second year of trading, the U.K. government raised the rate of income tax by 3p in the pound. Explain how this might affect Olympic.

....

....

....

....

....

(3 marks)

Turn over

(c) A summary of the Trading and Profit and Loss Accounts for Olympic for the first two years of trading is shown below.

Olympic — Summary Trading and Profit and Loss Accounts

	Year 1 £	Year 2 £
Sales Revenue	200 000	350 000
Cost of Goods Sold	110 000	180 000
Gross Profit	90 000	170 000
Expenses	40 000	100 000
Net Profit	50 000	70 000

Using the information in the accounts, discuss whether or not Jane and Mihir are likely to be pleased with the performance of the business in Year 2 compared with Year 1.

....

....

....

....

....

....

....

....

....

....

....

....

....

....

....

....

....

....

(12 marks)

FOLD THIS PAGE OUT
*Read the following
information on Fortune Ltd,
before answering
the questions in Section C.*

Context — Fortune Ltd

John Fortune was a sole trader in the haulage and storage business. When his son, Leslie, joined the business in the 1970s, the business purchased its first passenger coach and became a private limited company. The haulage and storage side of the business stopped and it was decided to concentrate on coach hire and developing the coach tour side of the business.

In 1995 Leslie Fortune's sons, Graham and Keith, joined the business and today are joint Managing Directors with their father as Chairman of Fortune Ltd. They employ a Finance Director and a Sales and Marketing Manager.

The coach hire and coach tour business is in a highly competitive market where there are approximately 5 000 similar companies. However, they have some groups of customers who booked with them when the coach tour side of the business was developing and have remained customers ever since.

As Fortune Ltd has expanded, the main services offered are:
- private hire;
- school travel;
- day trips;
- a tour planning service (British and European) for groups, which includes arranging the itinerary, travel, accommodation, insurance and currency.

Fortune Ltd has 32 coaches and has a policy of continually updating its fleet of coaches. It employs a full-time coach-driving instructor to train its own drivers and drivers from other coach companies.

Nearly all Fortune Ltd's drivers are full-time and are paid a guaranteed weekly wage with generous overtime and commission on any tour booked from brochures given out by the drivers. Drivers are trained in basic first aid and defensive driving. When drivers complete their training they get pay rises. Fortune Ltd were 'Coach Operators of the Year' in 1998, in part due to the consistent quality of service offered.

Web sites:
Confederation of Passenger Transport   *www.cpt-uk.org*
Coach Marque   *www.coachmarque.org*
Guild of British Coach Operators   *www.coach-tours.co.uk*

Weekly trade paper   *Coach and Bus Weekly*

Edexcel, 2004

SECTION C

---

6   One of Fortune Ltd's aims is to provide a quality service to its customers. In order to help
     it achieve this aim it has adopted Total Quality Management (TQM).

(a) (i)   What is meant by TQM?

....

....

....

....

(2 marks)

     (ii) Explain **TWO** benefits Fortune Ltd might gain by adopting TQM.

....

....

....

....

....

....

....

....

....

(6 marks)

     Fortune Ltd faces additional costs when trying to maintain and improve the quality of its
     services.

     (iii) Explain **TWO** costs associated with quality control.

....

....

....

....

....

(4 marks)

(d) Olympic has been advised to raise its prices in order to increase total sales revenue. Explain why this strategy might **not** be successful.

....

....

....

....

....

....

(4 marks)
(Total 25 marks)

OCR, 2003

Turn over

As Fortune Ltd has expanded it has benefited from economies of scale. These economies of scale are:

- technical economies;
- managerial economies;
- financial economies;
- trading/marketing economies.

(b)   Select **TWO** of the above and analyse how they might benefit Fortune Ltd.

....

....

....

....

....

....

....

....

....

....

....

(8 marks)
(Total 20 marks)

Edexcel, 2004

7   Fortune Ltd employs a full-time coach-driving instructor, Gus Lester, to train drivers and drivers from other companies.

(a) Explain why Fortune Ltd does this.

....

....

....

....

....

....

....

....

....

....

....

....

....

....

....

....

....

....

....

....

....

....

As Fortune Ltd has expanded it has benefited from economies of scale. These economies of scale are:

- technical economies;
- managerial economies;
- financial economies;
- trading/marketing economies.

(b) Select **TWO** of the above and analyse how they might benefit Fortune Ltd.

....

....

....

....

....

....

....

....

....

....

....

....

(8 marks)
(Total 20 marks)

Edexcel, 2004

7   Fortune Ltd employs a full-time coach-driving instructor, Gus Lester, to train its own drivers and drivers from other companies.

(a)   Explain why Fortune Ltd does this.

....

....

....

....

....

....

....

....

....

....

....

....

....

....

....

....

....

....

....

(8 marks)

In 1998 Fortune Ltd was 'Coach Operator of the Year'. John Fortune said, "... this is mainly down to our loyal and well motivated employees."

(b) Explain how Fortune Ltd might motivate their employees and use Maslow's motivational theory to justify your suggestions.

....

....

....

....

....

....

....

....

....

....

....

....

....

....

....

....

....

....

....

Turn over

142

....

....

....

....

....

....

....

....

....

....

....

....

....

....

....

....

....

....

....

....

(12 marks)

(Total 20 marks)

Edexcel, 2004

END OF QUESTIONS

If you use the following lined page to complete the answer to any question, the question number **must** be clearly shown.

Section One — Business Basics

Page 9 (Warm-Up Questions)

1) Private and public

2) Free-market economy; planned economy; mixed economy

3) Between 2 and 20

4) Private limited company; public limited company

5) A person/firm who has bought the right to trade under the name of another firm.

6) To make a profit in order to survive.

Page 10 (Exam Questions)

1   a) A business based on the name and logo *(1 mark)* of an existing business *(1 mark)*.

   b) Advantages: A successful, established business model is used *(1 mark)*, consequently there is less risk for Anna *(1 mark)*.

   Disadvantages: Anna is obliged to sell only the franchisor's products *(1 mark)*. This means that Anna has limited freedom *(1 mark)*.

   c) E.g. army, police, fire service, NHS hospitals, state schools *(1 mark each, to a maximum of 2 marks)*.

2   a) Public corporation *(1 mark)*

   b) As a public corporation and not a PLC, the BBC is less concerned with making a profit *(1 mark)*, so it can concentrate on making high quality programmes *(1 mark)*. A PLC has to satisfy its shareholders and the companies that advertise on its channel(s) *(1 mark)*, whereas the BBC follows objectives set by the government which are felt to be for the good of the public *(1 mark)*.   BBC programmes are not interrupted by advertisements, which can irritate viewers *(1 mark)*. *(Maximum of 4 marks)*

   c) Because their employers are in competition with one another *(1 mark)*.

Page 16 (Warm-Up Questions)

1) Sole trader

2) Chair of the Board

3) By function; by product; by region

4) Internal: owners (shareholders), employees
   External: customers, suppliers, local community, government

5) Water, food, clothing, shelter, warmth

6) Land, labour, capital, enterprise

Page 17 (Exam Questions)

1   a) Clothing is defined as a human need *(1 mark)*, because it is essential for survival *(1 mark)*. However the purchase of clothing and jewellery with the aim of following fashion is a luxury *(1 mark)* and so is a human want *(1 mark)*. Clothes Seller plc could therefore be said to satisfy both its customers' wants and their needs *(1 mark)*. *(Maximum of 2 marks)*

   b) E.g. increasing production of a different range, researching new products, training employees, etc. *(1 mark for a sensible example)*.

   c) *(1/2 mark for each factor and example:)*
      - Land/Raw Materials: leather, plastic, gems, cotton.
      - Labour: Use of human resources to design, manufacture, deliver, serve customers, offer advice, manage, etc.
      - Capital: Machines for manufacturing clothes, delivery vehicles, cash tills, computers, etc.
      - Enterprise: The people who set up the business.

   d) E.g. it is likely to be organised regionally *(1 mark)*, with each store reporting to a regional or national headquarters *(1 mark)*. *(2 marks for a type of organisation and sensible justification)*

   e) In order to increase productivity, the company may try to cut costs *(1 mark)* by making some of the workforce redundant *(1 mark)*, or by freezing or reducing workers' pay *(1 mark)*. Working conditions may deteriorate *(1 mark)*, which may cause staff morale to fall *(1 mark)*. This means the quality of work may suffer, which may result in lost orders for the company *(1 mark)*. *(Maximum of 4 marks)*

   f) Employees may receive bonuses as a consequence of increased profits, and increasing profitability may make employees feel safer in their jobs *(1 mark for either point)*.

Section Two — Marketing

Page 24 (Warm-Up Questions)

1) The marketing mix is the combination of factors that help a business sell its products, often summarised as the 4 Ps: product, price, place and promotion.

2) A marketing strategy based on meeting the needs of a small market segment, often involving a specialist product and high profit margins.

3) Field (primary) and desk (secondary)

4) Information about feelings and opinions.

5) Random, quota and target sampling

6) The sections show the proportion of different responses within one sample. A 1% share is represented by a 3.6° section of the pie.

7) Strengths, Weaknesses, Opportunities and Threats

Page 25 (Exam Questions)

1   a) Primary research:
      - A questionnaire *(1 mark)* establishing demand for the bar *(1 mark)*.
      - Interviews *(1 mark)* of existing bar owners *(1 mark)*.
      - Focus group *(1 mark)* to establish consumer reaction to / views on the bar *(1 mark)*.
      - Observation *(1 mark)*, for example footfall survey to count the number of people passing a particular place *(1 mark)*.
      (Maximum of 5 marks)

      Secondary research:
      - Study internet sites, books or brochures *(1 mark)* to establish the set-up costs for the bar *(1 mark)*.
      - Market research reports, e.g. MINTEL *(1 mark)*, to establish market conditions and trends, e.g. student leisure *(1 mark)*.
      - Government reports *(1 mark)* to establish how changing attitudes to leisure may affect the bar *(1 mark)*.
      - Study newspapers and magazines *(1 mark)* — local papers may have adverts regarding competitors *(1 mark)* or potential suppliers *(1 mark)*.
      (Maximum of 5 marks — total marks from primary and secondary research must be no more than 8 marks)

   b) Would you go to the sports bar at least once a week?

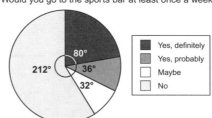

   (Accept answers to within ±1°. Award 1 mark for each segment correctly drawn, plus 1 mark for correct labelling. Or award 2 marks for a pie chart which has segments of approximately the right sizes, plus 1 mark for correct labelling.)

   c) Arguments for "yes" *(1 mark each)*:
      - 22% of respondents said they would definitely go at least once a week.
      - "Definitely" and "Probably" total 32%, nearly a third of the sample.
      - Although it is unlikely that *all* these people would actually go to the bar, these statistics could translate into good demand for the bar.

      Arguments for "no" *(1 mark each)*:
      - 59% of respondents said they would not go at least once a week.
      - "No" and "Maybe" together represent two thirds of respondents.
      - The negative responses far outweigh the positive responses, and this could translate into poor demand for the bar.

      General arguments *(1 mark each)*:
      - It depends on the total market size, i.e. the population of 18-30 year-olds in the area.
      - Bob's results might be biased, and not reflect the population accurately.
      - Would need to examine other factors, e.g. costs, prices, location, competition etc.

      Judgment *(1 mark)*:
      One mark for a conclusion — Yes or No — supported by an explanation.

      (Award 1 mark for each argument up to a maximum of 5 marks, plus 1 mark for a judgement)

d) E.g. by showing national and international sports matches on the television *(1 mark)*; by making staff wear sporting outfits *(1 mark)*; by giving the bar a sport-related name *(1 mark)*; by having sports memorabilia around the bar *(1 mark)*; by forging links with local sports clubs *(1 mark)*. *(1 mark for any sensible point — to a maximum of 3 marks)*

Page 26 (Exam Questions)

1 a) and b)

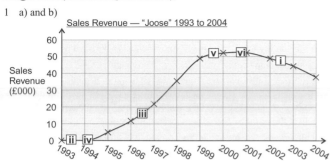

Sales Revenue — "Joose" 1993 to 2004

(For part a), award 1 mark for title, 2 marks for correct scales on x- and y-axes, 1 mark for some but not all points correctly plotted and 2 marks for completely correct plotting, and 1 mark for a line of best fit.

For part b), award 1 mark for each label in the correct position.)

c) Advantages *(1 mark each, maximum of 2 marks)*:
- Management can concentrate on other brands / new products.
- Money spent on "Joose", e.g. advertising budget, can be used for other things.
- Production can be switched to other product lines.
- May be more expensive to withdraw later.

Disadvantages *(1 mark each, maximum of 2 marks)*:
- Loss of sales revenue.
- "Joose" is a cash cow, providing revenue for investment in other products.
- Morale of workforce may be damaged by withdrawal of a major product.
- Loss of market share to competitors.

d) Knowledge of changing business environment *(1 mark each, maximum of 2 marks)*:
- Changes to the market, e.g. size, market shares, trends.
- Changes to competition, e.g. competitor activities, new products.
- Changes to the political environment, e.g. laws, politics, elections.
- Changes to the economy, e.g. government policy on taxation, interest rates, inflation, exchange rates, etc.
- Changes to society, e.g. fashion, population changes.
- Changes to technology, e.g. new production processes, ICT & Internet.

Analysis / Application *(1 mark each, maximum of 6 marks)*:
Supporting argument:
- If "Joose" were meeting the needs of customers, it would still be growing.
- There is no evidence that the management have anticipated the change, or planned for it.
- There is no indication that extension strategies have been tried.

Arguments against:
- All products have a life cycle — "Joose" is following the pattern.
- External influences are beyond the control of the business.
- "Joose" has simply gone out of fashion.

Evaluation *(1 mark each, maximum of 2 marks)*:
- It depends upon the economic cycle — whether the economy was in a period of growth or decline.
- It depends on the market for soft drinks and what has happened to competitor products during the same period.
- We do not know the sales volumes — they may have been selling more drinks at a lower profit margin.
(N.B. if the argument is totally one-sided award a maximum of 5 marks)

e) Reasons why soft drinks are a mass or niche market *(1 mark each, maximum of 3 marks)*:
Mass market:
- Soft drinks are sold to large numbers of people.
- Cost of soft drinks is generally quite low.
- Profit margin fairly low for producer selling to retailer.

Niche market:
- Some soft drinks (e.g. exotic fruit juices) could be considered a niche market.

Page 33 (Warm-up Questions)

1) The law of supply is that as the price of a product increases, the quantity supplied increases and vice versa.

2) Penetration pricing is where a firm charges a low price when the product is new to get people interested in it. The price is increased once the product becomes established. Skimming is the opposite — firms charge a high price to begin with, so that the product is desirable to people with large incomes. The price may be decreased later to help it become a mass-market product.

3) Advertising is any message about a firm or its products that the firm has paid for.

4) Any five from: television, radio, newspapers, magazines, posters, cinema, leaflets, internet sites.

5) Any five from: buy one get one free, discounts, competitions, free gifts, product trials, point of sale advertising, use of credit.

6) Manufacturer — wholesaler — retailer — consumer

Page 34 (Exam Questions)

1 a) This method is common with chocolate manufacturers because: they tend to have a number of products already in the market place *(1 mark)*; the market is dominated by a few manufacturers *(1 mark)*; manufacturers do not want to be drawn into a price war *(1 mark)*; manufacturers prefer to differentiate their products through branding *(1 mark)*, or advertising *(1 mark)*. *(Maximum of 3 marks)*

b) Persuasive advertising is aimed at convincing customers that they want the product by playing on their fears / vulnerabilities *(1 mark)*, or to create desires where none existed before *(1 mark)*.

2 a) "Cost-plus" pricing means setting the price of a product either by adding a percentage mark-up to the cost of the product *(1 mark)*, or by setting a required profit margin *(1 mark)*.

b) Steel components are a specialist product *(1 mark)*, and so mass media, such as TV, radio and national newspapers, would not be cost-effective *(1 mark)*, especially since a newly established business will probably not have a very large budget for advertising *(1 mark)*. Posters and billboards might not be able to give potential customers the necessary information about a specialist product *(1 mark)*. The business should consider advertising in a specialist magazine, which is likely to reach the target market *(1 mark)*. Leaflets and junk mail are good for targeting potential customers *(1 mark)*. Setting up a website is a good idea because it could be found by anyone who enters something like "steel components" into a search engine *(1 mark)*, and the customers could order products on-line *(1 mark)*. However, the website is unlikely to be seen by many surfers of the net *(1 mark)*. The owners of the business should make the most of any contacts they might have in the trade *(1 mark)*, and use personal selling by approaching these potential customers directly *(1 mark)*.
(Maximum of 7 marks for discussion plus 1 mark for an overall judgement on which media to use)

c) Analysis:
Arguments for penetration pricing:
Newly established businesses need to win market share quickly in order to survive *(1 mark)*. This approach enables sales to grow rapidly *(1 mark)*. Once customers have started to use the supplier, they may remain loyal to them in the future *(1 mark)*.
Arguments against penetration pricing:
- A newly established business may not be totally sure of its costs *(1 mark)*.
- Penetration pricing could become "loss leading" *(1 mark)*.
- Penetration pricing could lead to liquidation particularly if competitors respond and a price war occurs *(1 mark)*.
- Cost-plus pricing would be a safer approach, since it would mean the company can cover its costs *(1 mark)*.
Evaluation:
The decision to use penetration pricing would depend upon:
- the relative strength of competitors *(1 mark)*;
- the ability of the firm to sustain lower profit margins *(1 mark)*;
- whether or not the newly established business is a subsidiary of an already established business *(1 mark)*.
(Maximum of 2 marks)

Judgement on whether it would be a sensible strategy *(1 mark)*.
(Award a maximum of 10 marks in total)

THE ANSWERS

Section Three — Production

Page 39 (Warm Up Questions)

1) Primary
2) Tertiary
3) Secondary
4) To make their production more efficient.
5) Interdependence
6) Economies of Concentration

Page 40 (Exam Questions)

1   Advantages of relocating:
- There should be a good supply of labour, which Peter will need for expansion.
- The communication and transport links should be better.
- Peter might benefit from economies of concentration.
- Location of the market — the business will be closer to its customers, and will be accessible to many more people.
- Peter could receive government aid if he locates in an area of high unemployment.

Disadvantages of relocating:
- The cost of new premises in the city may be high.
- Peter will be further away from his source of raw materials, so the cost of transporting materials will be higher.
- Personal factors — Peter may have to leave behind family and friends and a way of life that he enjoys in the country.
(1 mark for each factor, maximum 7 marks + 1 mark for a judgement on whether Peter should relocate)

2   a)   The term interdependent describes businesses which are in the same production chain (which rely on each other) *(1 mark)*.
   b)   Production chains enable firms to specialise in what they do best *(1 mark)*. Concentrating on one area of the production process is a more efficient way to produce goods than if one firms tries to do everything *(1 mark)*.
   c)   As the wool mill didn't produce as much fabric, the local clothing manufacturer may have had less fabric supplied to them *(1 mark)* and therefore made less clothes for James Right's business *(1 mark)*. James Right may have then struggled with supplying his customers *(1 mark)*.

Page 45 (Warm Up Questions)

1) Job production
2) Job and batch production
3) To keep employees interested in the work they are doing so productivity is increased.
4) To reduce the costs of having to hold stocks of raw materials until they are needed.
5) A quality award given to firms by the British Standards Institution.
6) Total Quality Management

Page 46 (Exam Questions)

1   a)   It is the attempt to satisfy customers by making sure that quality standards are agreed and met throughout the organisation *(1 mark)*.
   b)   When raw materials are delivered *(1 mark)*, during work in progress *(1 mark)* and when the goods have been finished *(1 mark)*.
   c)   i)   Quality circles are where groups of workers from different departments meet *(1 mark)* to identify problems and suggest solutions *(1 mark)*.
       ii) Staff can share expertise and ideas to improve quality *(1 mark)*.
       iii) TQM encourages workers to get things right first time, whereas quality control suggests that it doesn't matter too much if mistakes are made because they will be picked up later. Therefore TQM should cut down on waste *(1 mark)*. Quality inspectors employed to carry out quality control need to be paid. These costs could be avoided by using TQM *(1 mark)*. TQM may lead to improvements in overall quality and efficiency *(1 mark)*.

2   a)   They are given more variety and responsibility so are likely to be more interested in their work *(1 mark)*.
   b)   The group production method uses teams of workers who are responsible for making the whole product *(1 mark)*. In cell production, a group of workers is responsible for a number of tasks at a single stage of production *(1 mark)*.

Section Four — People

Page 55 (Warm up Questions)

1   A skill is an ability to do something. An attribute is a personal quality.
2) Employers and employees
3) a)   Mayo thought that workers were motivated by more than just money. If managers want to get the most out of their staff, they should show an interest in them, make sure their employees' goals are the same as the goals of the business and encourage staff to socialise with each other.
   b)   Taylor thought that workers were lazy and only motivated by money. He thought bosses should carry out a "time and motion" study to work out the most efficient way of performing a task. A manager should then be appointed to make sure that workers carry out the tasks in exactly that way.
   c)   Maslow thought that everybody has the same needs, and that they have to be met in the right order — most basic first. These are physical survival (a good enough wage to pay for food, clothes etc.), safety (job security), love and belonging (team work and social contact), self-esteem (praise and encouragement), self-actualisation (reaching personal targets).
4) Performance-Related Pay
5) Kaizen
6) Authoritarian or autocratic

Page 56 (Exam Questions)

1   a)   Kitchen Dreamz should look for a Theory Y manager *(1 mark)*, because the supervisors need to be given responsibility.
   b)   They must take into consideration, for example, the Sex Discrimination Act 1975 *(1 mark)*, and the Race Relations Act, 1976 *(1 mark)*. *They also have to think about the Disability Discrimination Act 1975. There are other recruitment laws as well, but these are the main three.*

2   Heath Insurance Services should improve the motivating factors if the workers are bored. They could do this by offering workers encouragement so that they feel more valued *(1 mark)*. They could also improve their motivating factors by giving workers more responsibility *(1 mark)* since this would encourage them to take on extra work to stop them being bored.

3   a)   They have a legal responsibility under the Health and Safety at Work Act to ensure that the workplace is safe *(1 mark)*. They must also ensure that staff are aware of their responsibilities under the Health and Safety at Work Act *(1 mark)*.
   b)   If this worker caused an accident it may affect the business in a number of ways. First of all the business would be short-staffed, especially if the accident hurt other workers *(1 mark)*, and this may mean they are unable to supply their customers. This could give the business a poor reputation *(1 mark)*. Secondly the business is likely to be fined under the Health and Safety at Work Act *(1 mark)*, which would reduce the profits that the business makes *(1 mark)*.

Page 62 (Warm up Questions)

1) To get as many suitable people to apply as possible.
2) The job description gives details about the job itself, whereas the person specification describes the ideal person for it.
3) Letter of application, CV (Curriculum Vitae) or resumé, application form
4) To introduce new employees to their workplace.
5) To protect the interests of their members in the workplace.
6) To act independently to prevent and end industrial disputes.

Page 63 (Exam Questions)

1   a)   Instead of each worker talking to managers separately, the union negotiates on behalf of all its members together *(1 mark)*. By uniting as one body, unions have the power to disrupt businesses if necessary *(1 mark)*. Union members usually get a better deal this way *(1 mark)*, whether higher pay, better working conditions or shorter working hours.

b) As a welder he could join a craft union *(1 mark)*. Working in the transport industry – he helps build trains – he could join an industrial union *(1 mark)*.

2 a) You can ask the same questions to all the candidates and compare their answers *(1 mark)*. You can assess a candidate's confidence, social and verbal skills *(1 mark)* and whether they will fit in with the other workers in the department *(1 mark)*.

b) Toni might believe candidates don't behave naturally in an interview *(1 mark)*. To be good at an interview doesn't necessarily mean you'll be good at the job *(1 mark)*.

c) Skills or in-tray tests, aptitude tests, group tests, personality tests *(1 mark for each 2 correct answers — no half marks)*

d) If someone doesn't fit in or can't do the job you can end up with disruption in the workplace. As a result you are less efficient and profits may go down *(1 mark)*. *(1 mark for any sensible answer)*

Section Five — Finance
Page 69 (Warm-Up Questions)

1) E.g. managers' salaries, telephone bills, office rent *Other answers are possible here.*

2) Variable costs + fixed costs = total costs

3) Average cost = total cost ÷ output

4) It shows the level of output at which the firm will just cover its costs. If its output rises above this level, the firm will make a profit.

5) The length of time the finance is needed for, the amount of finance needed, the cost of the finance, the size and type of the company.

6) Working capital is the money (cash) required to meet the day-to-day running costs of the business.

Page 70 (Exam Questions)

1 a) Average cost = total cost ÷ output
Therefore, average cost = £100,000 ÷ 50,000 = £2 per tray *(1 mark)*. Accept any selling price between £2.50 and £5 (over £5 would be unrealistic) *(1 mark)*.

b) Output = total cost ÷ average cost
Therefore output = £110,000 ÷ £2 = 55,000 trays *(1 mark)*.

c) Joe could take out a bank loan, which he would have to repay with interest *(1 mark)*. Joe could use his land as collateral, which means that the bank could repossess the land if the loan is not repaid *(1 mark)*. For a longer-term loan, Joe might remortgage the garden centre *(1 mark)*. Interest payments are relatively low but Joe's whole business could be at risk if he fails to keep up the payments *(1 mark)*. *(Maximum of 2 marks for each method — 1 mark for explanation and 1 mark for a risk)*

2) They need start-up capital to buy assets to run the business, e.g. a computer with internet access *(1 mark)*. They are likely to have cash-flow problems initially. For example, they may have to secure bookings with deposits before their clients have paid for their holidays *(1 mark)*. They will need enough cash to meet the day-to-day running of their agency (working capital) *(1 mark)*. Customers may delay payments until the last moment, so some money will be required to cover liquidity shortfalls *(1 mark)*. They will also need finance to promote their business *(1 mark)*.

Page 74 (Warm-Up Questions)

1) Favourable
2) False
3) It shows where the profit of a limited company has gone.
4) The fall in value of an asset due to wear and tear.
5) £7000
6) Direct

Page 75 (Exam Questions)

1 a) A = £120 000 – £50 000 = £70 000 *(1 mark)*
B = £6 000 + £40 000 + £5 000 + £8 000 = £59 000
(or £70 000 – £11 000 = £59 000) *(1 mark)*

b) Gross profit is the difference between sales revenue and the direct costs of making the products *(1 mark)*. Net profit is the difference between sales revenue and the total costs of the business *(1 mark)* — direct costs of making the products plus indirect costs of running the business *(1 mark)*. Net profit is the amount that a firm is actually left with once all costs have been paid *(1 mark)*. *(Maximum of 3 marks)*

c) Since the bank would be risking its money in See-Saw, the bank manager will want to know that it is a sound, profitable business *(1 mark)*. Without evidence that See-Saw is a profitable business, the bank manager may not risk granting See-Saw a loan because if the business 'went under', the bank would lose money *(1 mark)*. The net profit figure for the past year will give the bank manager some idea of how much is a reasonable amount to lend See-Saw *(1 mark)*, and how long it will take the company to repay the loan *(1 mark)*.

Page 80 (Warm-Up Questions)

1) Turnover

2) The gross profit margin is found by dividing gross profit (sales – direct costs) by sales, while the net profit margin is found by dividing net profit (sales – total costs) by sales.

3) A current asset

4) Long-term liabilities

5) Profitability ratios and liquidity ratios

6) Profitability ratio

Page 81 (Exam Questions)

1 a) Current ratio = current assets ÷ current liabilities *(1 mark)*

b) i) The firm does not have enough money to pay its current debts *(1 mark)* and could go bankrupt *(1 mark)*.

ii) The owner should try to get more liquid assets *(1 mark)* by holding less stock or getting debtors to pay quickly *(1 mark)*.

2 a) First find Net Profit: Turnover – Cost of Sales – Expenses
= £500 000 – £200 000 – £100 000 = £200 000
% Net Profit Margin = (Net profit ÷ Turnover) × 100
= (£200 000 ÷ £500 000) × 100 = 40%
(2 marks for correct answer, otherwise 1 mark for finding Net Profit)

b) ROCE = (Net Profit ÷ Capital Employed) × 100
= (£250 000 ÷ £1 000 000) × 100 = 25%
(2 marks for correct answer, otherwise 1 mark for stating correct formula)

c) It would be better to invest in Tops and Bottoms plc *(1 mark)*. The amount of capital employed is the same, but Now plc's ROCE of 20% compared to 25% for Tops and Bottoms shows that it does not use the money as efficiently *(1 mark)*.

Section Six — Growth of Firms
Page 90 (Warm-Up Questions)

1) Advantages include: you get the independence of being your own boss; you can keep all the profits of your hard work; you can run the business exactly how you want to.
Disadvantages include: it may take a while for the business to produce a profit, so in the meantime you do not have a steady income; you are responsible if anything goes wrong; people who own their own businesses generally have to work long hours; if the business grows enough, you might have to employ other people.

2) The personal details of the owner, a mission statement, detailed objectives, a product description, production details, staffing details, finance.

3) The government offers guidance, training and financial support through the Learning and Skills Council. The Department of Trade and Industry provides small-business advice. New firms can apply to get their loans underwritten by the government to give them some security if the business fails.

4) Internal (organic) expansion and external expansion (takeovers and mergers)

5) Any three of: purchasing economies (buy in bulk), marketing economies (lower cost per unit), managerial economies (employ specialist managers), financial economies (banks will be prepared to back you), technical economies (you can use more advanced machinery), risk-bearing economies (you can afford to take risks with different products).

6) Written, visual, verbal

Page 91 (Exam Questions)

1 a) Forward vertical integration *(1 mark)*

   b) Possible advantages include:
       - Direct access to customers.
       - Easier and guaranteed outlet for his products.
       (1 mark each for two advantages, maximum of 2 marks)
       Possible disadvantages include:
       - May create difficulties in managing two businesses.
       - He will have to learn to delegate to others.
       (1 mark each for two disadvantages, maximum of 2 marks)

2 a) Any one of, for example:
       - They may not be able to sell all their stock.
       - Customers might lose confidence in the business and go elsewhere.
       (1 mark for any sensible risk)

   b) Radio advertising, for example:
       Advantage: Covers a wide area quickly.
       (1 mark for any sensible advantage)
       Disadvantages: People forget what they have been told.
                           Radio advertising is quite expensive.
       (1 mark for any sensible disadvantage)
       Poster in the shop window, for example:
       Advantages: Permanent copy which can be studied by many readers.
                           Posters are cheap to produce.
       (1 mark for any sensible advantage)
       Disadvantages: People will have to pass shop to see it.
       (1 mark for any sensible disadvantage)

3   Any four from: buying in bulk; widespread, relatively cheap advertising; specialist staff; easier finance from banks; can stock a wide variety of products — choice *(1 mark for each point — maximum of 4 marks)*.

Page 97 (Warm-Up Questions)

1) A connected network is good for exchange of ideas between different groups in the company but bad for taking decisions as no one is in overall control.

2) It is fast, as messages get passed by word of mouth, but the wrong messages, rumours and disinformation get passed on too. Also, managers are not in control of the information being shared.

3) Multinational enterprise

4) Where a large number of producers sell to a large number of consumers and no one is powerful enough to dictate prices.

5) When a small number of large firms dominate a market, e.g. UK chocolate market.

6) Overtrading is when a firm takes on too many orders, buys raw materials and hires staff to meet these orders. Something goes wrong and the firm doesn't get enough money in from sales to pay its debts.

Page 98 (Exam Questions)

1 a) With lower fixed costs small firms tend to be more labour intensive than larger firms. More small firms means more jobs, which reduces unemployment *(1 mark)*. Small firms can exploit new technology *(1 mark)* and respond to gaps in the market quicker *(1 mark)*. So they force larger rival firms to remain competitive.

   b) Struggling to keep costs down, Jack's employer probably pays lower wages than larger organisations *(1 mark)*. Jack's promotion prospects *(1 mark)* and employment conditions — holiday entitlement, canteen facilities and workplace *(1 mark)* — may be better with a larger company where there are greater opportunities.

2 a) With a hierarchical organisational structure, Yattoo's chain of command is long. Messages take time to travel up and down the different layers of management *(1 mark)*. People at each end can feel isolated from each other *(1 mark)*. Information can get distorted along the way *(1 mark)*. Since authority is located in Yattoo's home country, there may be language and cultural differences *(1 mark)*.

   b) By de-layering *(1 mark)*, that is removing tiers of management, usually in the middle. Also giving each plant in each country autonomy — self-management *(1 mark)*.

3 a) *One mark each for any four sensible points*, for example:
       - Global is a source of foreign investment and creates employment in the host country *(1 mark)*.
       - With its own hi-tech working methods, Global will give the host country access to foreign technology *(1 mark)*.
       - The host country can tax some of Global's profits *(1 mark)*.
       - Export revenue raised by Global's sales abroad can improve the host country's balance of payments *(1 mark)*.

   b) *One mark each for any four sensible points*, for example:
       - Jobs created by Global may be unskilled and low paid *(1 mark)*.
       - Working conditions may be poor *(1 mark)*.
       - Global might demand reduced taxes and even subsidies from the host country's government in order to locate there *(1 mark)*.
       - Global might influence the host country's government to change laws on environmental pollution and employment *(1 mark)*.
       - With fewer environmental controls Global might contaminate the site and then quit without cleaning up *(1 mark)*.

Section Seven — External Influences

Page 106 (Warm up Questions)

1) Gross Domestic Product

2) Unemployment rises

3) Inflation

4) Social Security, health, education, defence, law and order

5) Fiscal Policy involves taxes and government spending whereas Monetary Policy involves changing interest rates.

6) Office of Fair Trading

Page 107 (Exam Questions)

1 a) Recession *(1 mark)*

   b) In a recession consumers may lose their jobs and have less income to spend *(1 mark)*. As consumer demand is weakened, Jodie may have fewer clients or they may want their hair doing less often *(1 mark)*. So Jodie's sales revenue might go down *(1 mark)*. She might cut her prices but if she cannot cover her overheads she will have to close down *(1 mark)*.
       (1 mark each for any four sensible points)

2 a) Trade Descriptions Act (1968) *(1 mark)*
       Supply of Goods and Services (1982) and/or Sale and Supply of Goods Act (1994) *(1 mark)*

   b) The jacket shrank when Shazia followed the washing instructions therefore it is not fit for purpose *(1 mark)*. She is entitled to her money back *(1 mark)*. If the retailer does not refund her money, Shazia can complain at her local Trading Standards Office *(1 mark)*. Shazia was also given a false description by the retailer that the jacket was washable. However, as this was a verbal statement it can be difficult to prove *(1 mark)*.
       (1 mark each for any four sensible points)

3 a) A small development area where new businesses are encouraged to locate by the government using financial incentives *(1 mark)*.

   b) - Scott and Dave will pay less tax on their profits.
       - They will have fewer government regulations to meet, for example, planning permission may be fast-tracked.
       - They may qualify for a grant, for example, to train other workers in graphic design.
       (1 mark each — maximum of 2 marks)

Page 115 (Warm up Questions)

1) Because a "green" image can attract new customers and increase sales, and prevent existing customers moving to other more environmentally friendly firms.

2) Legal, decent, honest and truthful

3) Greenwashing

4) The economy is too dependent on imports and vulnerable if demand for its specialist products falls.

5) The price at which one currency can be traded for another.

6) The European Social Charter, EU competition policy and EU food labelling laws

Page 116 (Exam Questions)

1 a) A rise in gold prices would increase costs of production for jewellery producers *(1 mark)*. These cost increases are likely to be passed on to Gems4U plc. This may mean that Gems4U has to increase its prices in its stores *(1 mark)*.

b) The strong pound should make it cheaper to import foreign products into the UK *(1 mark)*. Gems4U plc imports jewellery so prices in its stores should fall *(1 mark)*, causing an increase in sales and ultimately in profits *(1 mark)*. The UK will have fewer exports and more imports *(1 mark)*, which will have a harmful effect on the balance of payments *(1 mark)*. *(Maximum of 4 marks)*

2 Exporters must understand the needs of each local market *(1 mark)*. Their approach to marketing might need adjusting, and language difficulties overcome *(1 mark)*. Exporting is risky financially as customers might not pay up *(1 mark)*, and foreign governments might place restrictions on trade or close the market to foreign trade *(1 mark)*. There will be a lot of documentation as each country has its own laws and safety guidelines *(1 mark)*. *(Maximum of 4 marks)*

3 Any two of the following:
- Jo could stop animal testing in her business *(1 mark)*. This may prompt concern among her customers that her products are not safe, causing a decline in sales. However, it might also attract new customers *(1 mark for either effect)*.
- Jo could redesign her website and inform customers that animals are treated as humanely as possible *(1 mark)*. This is unlikely to satisfy animal rights campaigners, and may also inform customers who were previously unaware that animal testing is taking place *(1 mark for either effect)*.
- Jo could do nothing in the hope that the animal rights campaigners will lose interest *(1 mark)*. Sales have not been affected by the campaign so far, but sales and profits may fall if the campaign continues to gather momentum *(1 mark)*.

Section Eight — Business and Change
Page 121 (Warm up Questions)

1) The service sector
2) Any two of: shipbuilding, coal mining, steel production, textiles (wool or cotton)
3) Privatisation and deregulation
4) To make British firms more competitive by allowing them to introduce more flexible working practices.
5) The European Union's Social Chapter gives part-time employees the same employment rights as full-time employees.

Page 122 (Exam Questions)

1 a) The gas and electricity industries were deregulated by the government *(1 mark)*.

b) Consumers would have more choice *(1 mark)*. Competition would force companies to lower prices *(1 mark)*. Companies would give better quality services by becoming more efficient *(1 mark)*.

2 a) A part-time contract *(1 mark)*

b) A temporary contract is only valid for a fixed period of time, e.g. six months *(1 mark)*, but a permanent contract has no end date *(1 mark)*.

c) More staff are needed over Christmas in the retail industry than at any other time of year *(1 mark)*. If staff are employed on permanent contracts the only way an employer could get rid of them would be to dismiss them *(1 mark)* or make them redundant *(1 mark)*. If he employed staff for over a year he could be taken to an industrial tribunal *(1 mark)* if he dismissed them or would have to pay redundancy money if employed for over two years *(1 mark)*.
(1 mark each for any five sensible points)

Page 127 (Warm-Up Questions)

1) i) Design and manufacture can be carried out quickly and accurately.
   ii) Quality and productivity improves.
   iii) Problems resulting from human error are minimised.
2) Electronic Funds Transfer at the Point of Sale

3) Any four of the following: less paper to file; templates of standard letters can be used with word processing software; personalised letters can be sent using a mail-merge; accounts can be kept on spreadsheets; communication is made quicker and easier by the internet and intranet.

4) A workplace located away from the main business premises but connected to it electronically.

5) A method of electronically encoding data while it is being transferred via the telephone system.

6) The new free-market economies are potentially new markets for British firms to sell to, which will increase their sales. Other British firms might struggle to compete with the exports from Eastern European countries, where labour costs are generally lower.

Page 128 (Exam Questions)

1 a) Ramish may have been worried that:
   - the company selling on-line was not trustworthy
   - his bank details would be used illegally
   - he would not be able to exchange the monitor if he is not happy with it
   - he would be pestered by direct mail from the company
   - the monitor may get damaged in the post
   (1 mark each, maximum of 4 marks)

b) Companies can use encryption software to prevent personal data being intercepted *(1 mark)*. Companies can make some information available only to people with a security ID *(1 mark)*.

2 a) There are fewer and fewer barriers to international trade *(1 mark)*. This means that the world has become one big market place *(1 mark)*. Increased global communication means that some firms can advertise worldwide *(1 mark)*, but only large firms have the resources to afford this. This means that the global market place tends to be dominated by a small number of super-rich firms *(1 mark)*.

b) Satellite TV and the internet *(1 mark)* means that a single advertising campaign can reach audiences all over the world *(1 mark)*. This allows them to cut advertising costs, since they are not required to buy advertising space in a large number of countries *(1 mark)*. Firms increasingly use one brand name worldwide so that potential customers can recognise the brand wherever they are *(1 mark)*. *(Maximum of 3 marks)*

c) Advantages *(maximum of 2 marks)*:
   - Global firms can produce goods and services at a lower cost because of economies of scale *(1 mark)*.
   - Globalisation causes worldwide economic growth, which benefits everyone *(1 mark)*.
   - World trade means that goods and services are available from different countries and cultures, which results in greater choice for consumers *(1 mark)*.

   Disadvantages *(maximum of 2 marks)*:
   - Some large companies become very powerful, but they are not democratically accountable *(1 mark)*.
   - Poorer countries find it harder to compete in a global market because their infrastructure is not as developed. This means that the gap between rich and poor countries increases *(1 mark)*.
   - The increase in world trade means that many more goods are transported around the world, which increases pollution *(1 mark)*.

150

Exam Paper Answers

Please note: The answers to the past exam questions have not been provided or approved by the examining bodies (AQA, OCR and London Qualifications Ltd - Edexcel). As such, AQA, OCR and London Qualifications Ltd do not accept any responsibility for the accuracy and method of the working in the answers given. CGP has provided suggested solutions — other possible solutions may be equally correct.

Section A

1 *Award a maximum of 4 marks — 1 mark for each statement and 1 mark for any sensible example given to back up a statement (maximum of 1 example per statement).*

Possible statements about 'product diversification' include:
it means producing different types of products *(1 mark)*; new products might be similar to existing products *(1 mark)*; or might be very different *(1 mark)*; it reduces the risk that a decline in one product will harm the business *(1 mark)*; it means moving into other markets *(1 mark)*; it involves changing existing products *(1 mark)*; it widens the existing product range *(1 mark)*; more products should appeal to more customers *(1 mark)* which should lead to increased sales and profits *(1 mark)*.

Possible examples of 'product diversification' include:
"Before you might have sold t-shirts, but now you sell t-shirts and trousers." *(1 mark)*
"As well as making clothes, Dewdrops could start to make shoes as well." *(1 mark)*. **Examples do not have to relate to Dewdrops.**

2 **Possible disadvantages of being a <u>private</u> limited company:**
limited finance to carry out the major further expansion; limited finance to bring in greater expertise if expansion were to continue, especially into export markets; the company was at risk of being taken over if it stayed small; operating as a private limited company restricted chances to become a household name.

Possible advantages of being a <u>public</u> limited company:
selling shares to the public would provide a major source of funding for expansion; they might be able to attract greater management expertise to handle continued expansion; they might benefit from even greater economies of scale e.g. more sources of finance; there might be benefits from a greater exposure of the company name.

Other possible points:
profits were at a record level — Dewdrops could afford to make the change / take the risk.

Level 1:
Straight copying of case study material. *Either* the possible disadvantages of operating as a private limited company *or* the possible advantages of operating as a public limited company are stated. *(1-3 marks — 1 mark for each of 3 undeveloped points)*

Level 2:
Business Studies knowledge is applied to the case study. Relevant points are made about the disadvantages to Dewdrops of operating as a private limited company and/or the advantages of operating as a public limited company, but the response doesn't compare them. *(4-6 marks — 4 marks for discussing only the pros <u>or</u> cons — 6 marks for discussing <u>both</u> the pros and cons)*

Level 3:
Information is selected from the case study and business terms/concepts are applied in analysing the situation of Dewdrops. The disadvantages for Dewdrops of operating as a private limited company are clearly compared to the advantages of operating as a public limited company. *(7-9 marks)*

3 **Possible advantages from adding flow to batch production include:**
faster production process and higher output; economies of scale result in lower unit costs; workers may become more skilled at specific tasks; less time will be lost making changes to machinery.

Possible disadvantages from adding flow to batch production include:
workers may become less motivated; reduced quality; large orders will be needed to meet output, otherwise there will be a surplus of clothes; products may become more standardised when clothing production usually requires variation; the production process might be less flexible; the costs of new machinery could be high.

Level 1:
Straight copying of case study material. Simple pros and cons of flow production are given with no application to clothing or to batch production. *(1-3 marks — 1 mark for each of 3 undeveloped points)*

Level 2:
Business Studies knowledge is applied to the case study. Relevant pros and cons of using flow methods for the production of clothing are given. *(4-6 marks)*

Level 3:
Relevant information is selected from the case study, and business terms/ concepts are used to discuss the pros and cons of flow production as applied to batch production for clothing. There is a conclusion as to whether Dewdrops made the right decision, but the judgement is based on insufficient or incorrect interpretation. *(7-8 marks)*

Level 4:
Relevant information is selected from the case study, and business terms/ concepts are used to discuss the pros and cons of flow production as applied to batch production for clothing. Judgements as to whether Dewdrops was right to combine flow production with batch production are based on and justified by a weighing up of the pros and cons. *(9-12 marks)*

Section B

4 (a) *Award a maximum of 4 marks for each of 2 methods — 1 mark for an appropriate method of promotion or communication and 1 mark for each point of justification of that method, up to a maximum of 3 marks. The justification should explain why the method would persuade shop owners to sell the clothes.*

E.g. Olympic could sell their goods at lower prices than their competitors *(1 mark)*. This in turn would enable shops to sell the clothes at lower prices than their competitors *(1 mark)*, which should lead to increased sales *(1 mark)* and therefore increased profits for the shops *(1 mark)*.

E.g. Olympic could send out leaflets to each shop *(1 mark)*. These would give information about the goods for sale and the prices *(1 mark)*, which would hopefully persuade shop managers to buy the clothes *(1 mark)*. This form of advertising would directly target the potential buyers, so should be cost-effective for Olympic *(1 mark)*.

E.g. Olympic could offer the shops trade credit *(1 mark)*, which would allow them to pay for the goods at a later date when they will have some revenue from selling the goods *(1 mark)*. This would enable the shops to buy a greater amount of stock *(1 mark)*, and would release money for other purposes *(1 mark)*.

E.g. Olympic could use personal selling *(1 mark)* by sending a representative to talk to the manager of each shop *(1 mark)*. This representative could take samples of the clothes to illustrate their high quality *(1 mark)*, and could attempt to convince the managers that they should buy Olympic's clothes *(1 mark)*.

(There are other possible answers)

(b) **Advantages for Olympic of advertising to the public:**
increases awareness of their goods, which should increase sales *(1 mark)*; it might persuade other shops to sell their clothes because if customers are more aware of the goods, the shops will be more confident they can sell them *(1 mark)*; a successful advertising campaign would mean that Olympic would get their money back in increased sales *(1 mark)*.

Disadvantages for Olympic of advertising to the public:
it will increase Olympic's costs, so reducing profits *(1 mark)*; an opportunity cost of advertising would be cutting prices, which could increase sales and profits *(1 mark)*; the shops will advertise to customers so it is not necessary for Olympic to advertise themselves *(1 mark)*.

Effectiveness of advertising to the public:
it might be worth advertising if the correct market is targeted *(1 mark)*, perhaps the local market that Olympic intends to sell to, or a target market indicated by market research *(1 mark)*; the cost of advertising should be recouped by large enough sales *(1 mark)*.

(Award 1 mark for each point up to a maximum of 3 marks + 1 mark for a sensible judgement as to whether Olympic should spend the money)

(c) *Award a maximum of 3 marks for each of 2 pricing strategies — 1 mark for the strategy and 1-2 marks for points of description/explanation of when it would be appropriate to use the strategy.*

E.g. Competitive pricing *(1 mark)* — it would be appropriate to use this strategy when there is little difference in quality between Olympic's products and those of competitors *(1 mark)*, or if they are trying to attract customers from a similar market segment *(1 mark)*. Olympic would need to charge similar/lower prices to competitors for people to buy the products *(1 mark)*. *(Maximum of 3 marks)*

E.g. Penetration pricing *(1 mark)* — it would be appropriate for Olympic to use this strategy if they are introducing a new product onto the market *(1 mark)*. Olympic would charge a low price to get people interested in the product, then increase the price once the product becomes established *(1 mark)*.

E.g. Skimming/Creaming *(1 mark)* — it would be appropriate to use this strategy if Olympic are selling a product which is of a superior quality to other products on the market *(1 mark)*. Charging a high price will help to make the product desirable to people with large incomes *(1 mark)*. Once the product has become established Olympic may lower the price to make it a mass-market product *(1 mark)*. *(Maximum of 3 marks)*

E.g. Cost-plus pricing *(1 mark)* — it would be appropriate to use this strategy if Olympic want to make sure that they make a profit *(1 mark)*. They can decide on a particular percentage mark-up or profit margin as long as it will result in a price that customers are prepared to pay *(1 mark)*.

(d) **For example...**
Olympic should use sponsorship because it would increase awareness of the business *(1 mark)*, which should increase sales *(1 mark)*. Olympic could afford to sponsor a local team, which would increase awareness amongst local people as they would see the logo on the players' shirts *(1 mark)*. This would make sense for Olympic because they only sell their clothes locally *(1 mark)*.

...or...

Olympic should not use sponsorship because it will be expensive *(1 mark)*. An opportunity cost of sponsorship would be cutting prices, which could lead to increased sales and profits *(1 mark)*. Olympic would not be able to afford to sponsor a famous/national team or person *(1 mark)* so the sponsorship would not bring much publicity *(1 mark)*.

(Award 1 mark for any relevant point justifying the recommendation, up to a maximum of 4 marks)

5 (a) (i)   Cost in pounds $= \dfrac{30\,000}{2} = £15\,000$

(2 marks for the correct answer, otherwise 1 mark for some correct working)

(ii) **Possible answer**:
Olympic would benefit from lower production costs *(1 mark)* because the pound buys more dollars *(1 mark)*. For example, they could import the same quantity of material for £10 000 instead of £15 000 **(1 mark)**. This should lead to increased profits *(1 mark)*.

Other possible comments:
Olympic could reduce their prices *(1 mark)*; they could increase production *(1 mark)*; the money saved due to reduced production costs could be used for other purposes such as advertising or investment *(1 mark)*; the change might give Olympic an advantage over competitors who do not import their raw materials from Canada *(1 mark)*.

(Award 1 mark for each point, up to a maximum of 4 marks)

(b) **Possible answer**:
A rise in income tax will reduce people's disposable income so they will have less money to spend *(1 mark)*. This could lead to reduced sales for Olympic *(1 mark)*. Olympic may have to reduce prices to maintain sales *(1 mark)*.
Other possible comments:
reduced demand for products may lead to redundancies *(1 mark)*; Olympic's employees will have more deducted from their pay and may want higher pay as a result *(1 mark)*. This would increase business costs therefore reducing Olympic's profits *(1 mark)*.

(Award 1 mark for each point, up to a maximum of 3 marks)

(c) **Level 1 (1-3 marks)**:
Discusses the positive and/or negative changes in the Profit and Loss Accounts (credit appropriate calculations):
Jane and Mihir will be pleased because both gross and net profits have increased *(1 mark)*, gross profit by £80 000/89% *(1 mark)* and net profit by £20 000/40% *(1 mark)*; they will be pleased because sales revenue has increased *(1 mark)* by £150 000/75% *(1 mark)*; they will not be pleased because expenses have increased *(1 mark)* by £60 000/150% *(1 mark)*.

Level 2 (4-6 marks):
Answer as for Level 1, but with the addition of a discussion of the impact of the rise in expenses. For example — the huge increase in expenses has resulted in the increase in net profit being far less than the increase in gross profit. Jane and Mihir are likely to be worried about this rise in expenses and will want to do something about it.

Level 3 (7-10 marks):
Uses ratio analysis to draw appropriate conclusions.
Year 1:

Gross profit margin $= \dfrac{\text{Gross Profit}}{\text{Sales Revenue}} \times 100$
$= \dfrac{90\,000}{200\,000} \times 100$
$= \textbf{45\%}$

Net profit margin $= \dfrac{\text{Net Profit}}{\text{Sales Revenue}} \times 100$
$= \dfrac{50\,000}{200\,000} \times 100$
$= \textbf{25\%}$

Year 2:

Gross profit margin $= \dfrac{\text{Gross Profit}}{\text{Sales Revenue}} \times 100$
$= \dfrac{170\,000}{350\,000} \times 100$
$= \textbf{48.6\%}$

Net profit margin $= \dfrac{\text{Net Profit}}{\text{Sales Revenue}} \times 100$
$= \dfrac{70\,000}{350\,000} \times 100$
$= \textbf{20\%}$

The answer should discuss the rise in gross profit margin and the fall in net profit margin and the reasons for each — the gross profit margin has increased because sales revenue has risen more than the cost of goods sold. The net profit margin has decreased because of the huge rise in expenses. Judgements should be made on how pleased Jane and Mihir are likely to be with these changes.

(Award a further 1-2 marks for each level for clearly, fluently, and legibly expressed answers, and accurate spelling, punctuation and grammar.)

(d) **Level 1**:
General statement about the circumstances in which an increase in prices might not result in an increase in sales revenue. For example — sales revenue will fall because there will be a decrease in sales *(1-2 marks)*.

Level 2:
The concept of elasticity of demand is applied *or* the answer makes clear why the rise in price might bring about a fall in sales.
Possible comments:
E.g. if demand for the product is price elastic, then a rise in price will have a large effect on demand for the product. Even a small increase in price will result in a large decrease in sales, and sales revenue will decrease.

E.g. sales revenue might not increase if the rise in price results in a lot of people deciding not to buy the product because it is more expensive. If the price increase results in only a small drop in sales, then sales revenue is still likely to increase.

E.g. a rise in price might fail to increase sales revenue if there is competition in the market. Customers will be able to buy a similar product from a cheaper competitor, resulting in decreased sales for Olympic. A large number of competitors would make a fall in sales revenue more likely.

E.g. a rise in the price of the product might not increase sales revenue if Olympic is not established as a desirable brand name. If it is a desirable brand name, then people might be willing to pay a higher price. If not, then a rise in price might persuade customers to switch to other products, resulting in decreased sales and sales revenue.

(3-4 marks)

Section C

6 (a) (i) Total Quality Management is a strategy which aims to establish a culture of quality within a firm *(1 mark)*. It makes improving quality the responsibility of every employee *(1 mark)*.

(ii) **Possible answers**:
The emphasis of TQM is on getting things right first time, which should help to avoid costly errors *(1 mark)*. This should save Fortune Ltd money *(1 mark)*, and help to make them more competitive *(1 mark)*.

Fortune Ltd's employees might meet in 'Quality Circles' to discuss problems and possible solutions *(1 mark)*. This should have the effect of raising quality *(1 mark)* and may lead to greater morale/motivation amongst employees *(1 mark)*.

An important feature of TQM is high quality customer service *(1 mark)*. This should result in customer satisfaction *(1 mark)*, and encourage customers to stay loyal to Fortune Ltd in the future *(1 mark)*.

(Award a maximum of 2 × 3 = 6 marks, award only 1 mark each for undeveloped points)

(iii) **Possible points include**:
Training costs *(1 mark)* — initial and ongoing *(1 mark)*.
Monitoring system costs *(1 mark)*, e.g. salaries of supervisors/quality inspectors *(1 mark)*.
Setting up quality control system(s) *(1 mark)*, maintenance/cleaning *(1 mark)*.
Costs of detecting low quality *(1 mark)*, e.g. if goods have to be scrapped/changes have to be made to procedures/repairs have to be carried out *(1 mark)*.
(Award a maximum of 2 × 2 = 4 marks, award only 1 mark each for undeveloped points)

(b) **General benefits of economies of scale**:
Technical — use of computers/technology/specialised machinery leads to improvements in efficiency.
Managerial — larger firms can afford to employ specialist managers – can offer higher salaries to attract well qualified staff – expertise/experience leads to the firm being better run.
Financial — more sources of finance – easier to raise capital (banks are more likely to lend money to larger firms and interest rates are often lower, because larger firms are more likely to be able to pay the money back).
Trading/marketing — bulk buying of supplies results in lower unit costs – overheads/expenses/advertising costs are spread over more services/products leading to lower unit costs.

Level 1:
General descriptive points about the benefits of economies of scale with no real link to Fortune Ltd. *(1-2 marks)*

Level 2:
Some explanation of the benefits of two economies of scale to Fortune Ltd, *or* detailed explanation of the benefits of one economy of scale to Fortune Ltd. *(3-5 marks)*

Level 3:
Detailed explanation of the benefits of two economies of scale to Fortune Ltd. *(6-8 marks)*

For example — possible analysis of financial economies of scale:
Expansion of the business has led to benefits from financial economies of scale. Changing to a limited company has given the business access to more sources of finance through its shares. As Fortune Ltd has expanded they may have found it easier to borrow money from the bank and negotiate better interest rates because they have more assets to offer as security for a loan. Bank loans may have enabled the business to expand further, e.g. into tour-planning services, or to maintain the quality of the services they provide.

For example — possible analysis of managerial economies of scale:
Expansion of the business may mean that Fortune Ltd can afford to employ specialist managers, such as their Sales and Marketing Manager, to oversee important areas of the business. This should improve the running and efficiency of the business. They might also be able to offer higher salaries to attract well qualified staff with specific expertise/ experience. This is needed if the continued expansion of the business into new areas such as tour planning is to be successful.

7 (a) **Reasons for training include**:
Drivers will be better at what they do and should be better motivated. Drivers will do their jobs more efficiently and safely, leading to greater customer satisfaction and loyalty.
Reasons for employing a full-time internal instructor include:
Internal training – drivers will be trained in Fortune Ltd's systems and procedures, not in anyone else's way of doing things.
On-the-job training – drivers can learn while working – remain productive.
Having a specialist on site continually – easy to provide ongoing training – easy to update training procedures – always someone to give advice.
Training drivers internally is cheaper than sending them away to be trained externally.
Reasons for training other drivers include:
Fortune Ltd will gain extra income from other companies.
Training drivers from other firms may lead to greater prestige within the industry.

Level 1:
General descriptive comments about the benefits of training are given. *(1-2 marks)*

Level 2:
Reasons for training are applied to Fortune Ltd. *(3-5 marks)*

Level 3:
As for level 2, with additional analysis of why Fortune Ltd might employ a coach-driving instructor in this way. *(6-8 marks)*

(b) **Possible points include**:
Maslow's motivational theory:
Maslow's hierarchy of needs — physical survival – safety – love and belonging – self-esteem – self-actualisation.
The three basic needs have to be achieved before the two higher needs can be met. If a person's basic needs are not met, they will not be motivated to achieve anything else. Once the needs at one level have been met, the needs at the next level become important.

Methods of achieving needs:
Physical survival — achieved through pay levels/working conditions.
Safety — achieved through job security/safe working conditions.
Love and belonging — achieved through team work/social contact.
Self-esteem — achieved through recognition/praise/encouragement/ rewards.
Self-actualisation — achieved through opportunities/challenges/targets.

Level 1:
Shows basic knowledge of methods of motivation. *(1-3 marks)*

Level 2:

Discusses ways in which Fortune Ltd can motivate their employees, using Maslow's theory to justify each method. E.g. paying workers a good enough wage to enable them to have a reasonable standard of living will satisfy the first level of Maslow's hierarchy. *(4-6 marks)*

Level 3:

Describes how, according to Maslow, a person's basic needs must be met before they can be motivated to achieve anything else. The answer should discuss ways in which Fortune Ltd can satisfy the basic needs of their employees e.g. by providing good pay/ job security/ good working conditions — safe, warm, comfortable coaches etc. It should go on to discuss the ways in which they can then satisfy the motivational needs at higher levels of Maslow's hierarchy of needs. *(7-9 marks)*

Level 4:

As for Level 3, with the addition of examples of motivation drawn from the case study. E.g. Fortune Ltd satisfies the first level of motivational needs by paying their workers a guaranteed weekly wage, generous overtime and commission on tours booked from brochures given out by drivers. *(10-12 marks)*

Working out your Grade

• *Find your average percentage for the whole exam.*

• *Look it up in this table to see what grade you got. If you're borderline, don't push yourself up a grade — the real examiners won't.*

Average %	78+	67 – 77	57 – 66	47 – 56	40 – 46	30 – 39	23 – 29	17 – 22	under 17
Grade	A*	A	B	C	D	E	F	G	U

Important

• *Obviously these grades are only a guide — and the more practice you do the better...*

Index

A

acid test ratio 78, 79
Action on Smoking and Health (ASH) 109
advertising 19, 29-31, 124, 126
Advertising Standards Authority (ASA) 109
Advisory, Conciliation and Arbitration
      Service (ACAS) 61
annual percentage rate (APR) 104
appropriation account 73
Article of Association 7
assembly line 42
asset 76-78
assisted area 105
average cost 65

B

balance of payments 111, 112
balance sheet 76, 77
bar chart 22
batch production 41, 42
BBC 8
board meeting 11
BOGOF 31
brand image 23
brand loyalty 28
break-even analysis 66
break-even point 43, 66
British Standards Institution (BSI) 44, 109
budgeting 71
bulk-increasing firm 38
bulk-reducing firm 38
business cycle 100

C

capital 15, 77
capital good 36
case studies 3
cash and carry 32
cash flow 14, 72, 96
cell production 42
centralised organisation 12
chain of command 92
Chair of the Board 11
closed question 21
collective bargaining 60
command economy
      (see planned economy)
command words 3
commission 52, 71
Companies Act (1985) 77
Competition Act (1998) 104
Competition Commission 104
competition pricing 28
computer-aided design (CAD) 123
computer-aided manufacture (CAM) 123
computer-integrated manufacturing (CIM)
      123
Confederation of British Industry (CBI) 60
Consumer Association 109
Consumer Credit Act (1974) 104
consumer good 36
contribution per unit 66
co-operative 8
cost-led pricing 28
credit control 67
current ratio 78
curriculum vitae (CV) 58
customer loyalty 23
customer service 32

D

data logging sheet 22
Data Protection Act 125
data response questions 2
decentralised organisation 12
deindustrialisation 118
delegation 11, 54
demand 27
department 12, 13
Department of Trade and Industry (DTI) 85
depreciation 73, 76, 111
desk research 20
destroyer pricing 28
direct cost 65
Disability Discrimination Act (1975) 49
diseconomies of scale 88
distribution channel 32
division of labour 37

E

e-commerce 124, 125
economic policy 103
economies of concentration 38
economies of scale 41, 86, 88, 95,
      112, 113, 126
economy 100, 101
electric point of sale (EPOS) 123
electronic funds transfer at the point of sale
      (EFTPOS) 123
Employment Act (1980) 61
Employment Act (1982) 61
Employment Act (1988) 61
Employment Protection Act (1978) 49
Employment Protection Act (1975) 49
Employment Relations Act 61
Employment Rights Act (1996) 49
encryption 125
enterprise 15
environment 13, 108, 109
Equal Pay Act (1970) 49
Equal Pay Act (1983) 49
equilibrium 27
ethical issues 108
European Social Chapter 114, 120
European Union (EU) 68, 112-114
exchange rate 110, 111
extension strategy 23

F

Factories Act (1961) 49
factors of production 15
field research 20, 21
financial services 36
fiscal policy 103
fixed asset 67, 76
fixed cost 65, 66
flexible working 120
flow production
      (see mass production)
franchise 8
free-market economy 5, 126

G

General National Vocational Qualification
      (GNVQ) 119
globalisation 126
government 8, 14, 20, 38, 59, 61,
      73, 77, 85, 102, 103, 104,
      105, 109, 110, 112, 119, 125

Greenpeace 109
greenwashing 109
Gross Domestic Product (GDP) 100
gross pay 52
gross profit margin 78, 79
group production 42

H

Health and Safety at Work Act of (1974) 49
Herzberg 50
hierarchy 11
hire purchase (HP) 68
human resources (HR) 59

I

incorporated 7
indirect cost 65
inflation 101-103
informative advertising 29
integration 87
interdependence 37
interest rate 103
international trade 110, 112, 113, 126
international trade restrictions 112
internet 124-126
intranet 123

J

job enlargement 53
job enrichment 53
job production 41, 42
job rotation 53
Job Seekers Allowance 102
just-in-case (JIC) 43
just-in-time (JIT) 43

K

kaizen 43, 44, 53
kanban 43

L

labour 15
labour-to-capital ratio 41
land 15
law of demand 27
law of supply 27
leading question 21
lean production 43
Learning and Skills Council (LSC) 59
less economically developed country
      (LEDC) 108
life cycle 23
limited company 7, 12
limited liability 7
liquidity 76, 78
liquidity ratio 78, 79
loss leading 28

M

mail-merge 123
management styles 54, 87
managing director 11
manufacturing 36
marginal cost 65
market 4, 19
market-driven 23
market economy 5
market research 13, 20-22

155

Index

market segment 19, 21
market share 4, 13
marketing 19-23, 27-32, 125, 126
marketing mix 19
Maslow 50, 59
mass market 19
mass-market product 28, 30, 41
mass production 41, 42
Mayo 51
McGregor 50
Memorandum of Association 7
merger 87
MINTEL 20
mission statement 84
mixed economy 5
monetary policy 103
monopoly 94, 104, 119
mortgage 68
motivation theory 50, 51
multinational enterprise (MNE) 93
multiple choice questions 1

N

National Insurance (NI) 52, 102
National Minimum Wage 49
National Vocational Qualification (NVQ) 59
nationalisation 119
needs 15
net profit margin 78, 79
niche market 19

O

occupational immobility 37
Office of Fair Trading (OFT) 104
oligopoly 94
open question 21
open-ended questions 2
operative 11
opportunity cost 15, 30
ownership 6 8, 11

P

partnership 6, 7
penetration pricing 28
percentage mark-up 28
performance related pay (PRP) 52
personal selling 31
persuasive advertising 29
pie chart 22
piece rate 52
planned economy 5
point of sale 32
pollution 14, 108
predatory pricing
        (see destroyer pricing)
pressure group 13, 109
price discrimination 28
price elasticity of demand 27
pricing strategy 28
primary research
        (see field research)
primary sector 36
private limited company 7
private sector 4, 5, 85, 119
privatisation 119
process layout 42
product differentiation 23
product placement 31
product range 23

product-driven 23
production chain 37
production line 42
profit margin 28
profit-sharing 52
profitability ratio 78
promotion 19, 29-31, 124
public corporation 8
public limited company (PLC)
        7, 11, 96, 119
public relations (PR) 31
public sector 4, 5
public sector corporation 119

Q

qualitative data 20
quality assurance 44
quality control 44
quality management 43, 44
quantitative data 20
questionnaire 21, 22
quota 112
quota sampling 21

R

Race Relations Act (1976) 49
random sampling 21
rationalisation 43
raw materials 36, 38, 93
recruitment 57, 58
regional aid 105
remote offices 123
research and development 23
retailer 32
retained profit 67, 73, 77
return on capital employed (ROCE) 13, 78

S

sample 21
secondary research
        (see desk research)
secondary sector 36
self-employed 120
semi-variable cost 65
Sex Discrimination Act (1975) 49
share capital 77
shareholder 7, 11, 13, 14, 73, 77, 119
shares 7
short answer questions 1
single currency 114
single market 113
skimming 28
social trends 108
sole trader 6
sources of finance 67, 68
specialisation 37
specialist consumer 19
specialist product 30
stakeholder 8, 13, 14
start-up capital 67
statistical process control 44
stock control graph 43
stock exchange 77
strike 61
subsidy 112
supplier 14
supply 27
Supply of Goods and Services Act (1982) 104
supply-side policies 119

SWOT 23

T

takeovers and mergers 87
target audience 29
target sampling 21
tariff 112
tax 14, 76, 77, 85, 93, 101-103, 119
Taylor 51
team production 42
teleworking 123
tertiary sector 36
time rate 52
total quality management (TQM) 44
trade barriers 93
Trade Descriptions Act (1968) 104
trade union 60, 61, 119
Trade Union Act (1984) 61
Trades Union Congress (TUC) 60
trading, profit and loss account 73, 76
training 59
turnover 13

U

unemployment 101 - 103, 105, 123
unincorporated 6
unique selling point (USP) 84
unlimited liability 6

V

variable cost 65, 66
variance analysis 71

W

wants 15
Weights and Measures Act (1979) 104
wholesaler 32
working capital 67, 72
working capital ratio
        (see current ratio)
Working Time Directive 49
Workplace Regulations (1992) 49
World Trade Organisation 112

THE INDEX

Make sure you're not missing out on another superb CGP revision book that might just save your life...

...order your **free** catalogue today.

CGP customer service is second to none

We work very hard to despatch all orders the **same day** we receive them, and our success rate is currently 99.9%. We send all orders by **overnight courier** or **First Class** post.
If you ring us today you should get your catalogue or book tomorrow. Irresistible, surely?

- Phone: 0870 750 1252   (Mon-Fri, 8.30am to 5.30pm)
- Fax: 0870 750 1292
- e-mail: orders@cgpbooks.co.uk
- Post: CGP, Kirkby in Furness, Cumbria, LA17 7WZ
- Website: www.cgpbooks.co.uk

...or you can ask at any good bookshop.

BUHS41